M000159957

PERMACRISIS

A Plan to Fix a Fractured World

GORDON BROWN, MOHAMED A. EL-ERIAN AND MICHAEL SPENCE, WITH REID LIDOW

**SIMON &
SCHUSTER**

London · New York · Sydney · Toronto · New Delhi

First published in Great Britain by Simon & Schuster UK Ltd, 2023

Copyright © Gordon Brown, Mohamed A. El-Erian,
Michael Spence and Reid Lidow, 2023

Illustrations © Martin Lubikowski

The right of Gordon Brown, Mohamed A. El-Erian, Michael Spence and
Reid Lidow to be identified as the authors of this work has been asserted
in accordance with the Copyright, Designs and Patents Act, 1988.

1 3 5 7 9 10 8 6 4 2

Simon & Schuster UK Ltd
1st Floor
222 Gray's Inn Road
London WC1X 8HB

www.simonandschuster.co.uk
www.simonandschuster.com.au
www.simonandschuster.co.in

Simon & Schuster Australia, Sydney
Simon & Schuster India, New Delhi

The author and publishers have made all reasonable efforts
to contact copyright-holders for permission, and apologise
for any omissions or errors in the form of credits given.
Corrections may be made to future printings.

Sustainable Development Goals symbols reproduced by kind permission of
the United Nations (www.un.org/sustainabledevelopment). The content of
this publication has not been approved by the United Nations and does not
reflect the views of the United Nations or its officials or Member States.

A CIP catalogue record for this book
is available from the British Library

Hardback ISBN: 978-1-3985-2561-0
Trade Paperback ISBN: 978-1-3985-2562-7
eBook ISBN: 978-1-3985-2563-4

Typeset in Perpetua by M Rules

Printed and Bound in the UK using 100% Renewable
Electricity at CPI Group (UK) Ltd

To our families

CONTENTS

PROLOGUE

This book is not meant to be a substitute for melatonin. Quite the contrary – the state of the world kept us all up at night leading to conversations that led to conclusions that then led to this book.

All of us have known one another since long before the pandemic. During the pandemic, we ratcheted up how often we spoke and huddled on Zoom to talk through the global challenges choking the headlines.

The more we discussed the challenges in place and ahead, the more we found ourselves searching for – and finding – realistic ways governments can make a difference; where international organisations can step up to their historic role of driving collective action; and where, by engaging and bringing together civil society and the private and public sectors, we could deliver breakthroughs.

Our regular talks exploring ever-mounting problems did more than just worry us about the path the global economy was on. It made us realise that there is nothing preordained or inevitable about the gloomy certainty present in economic, financial and social discourse. Informed by our experience, each of us brought different perspectives. Yet we shared a common goal: achievable solutions. So, we put our thoughts on paper, and this book is a product of that thinking.

Mohamed has been at the forefront of economics and finance

for decades and brings considerable private sector experience and know-how to discussions, as well as drawing on his time at the International Monetary Fund. He currently serves as President of Queens' College, Cambridge and is also the chief economic advisor at Allianz, the corporate parent of PIMCO where he was CEO and co-CIO. In addition to being a columnist at *Bloomberg News* and a *Financial Times* contributing editor, Mohamed is a professor of practice at the University of Pennsylvania's Wharton School of Business, Chair of Gramercy Funds Management, and sits on the boards of Barclays, Under Armour and the National Bureau for Economic Research. He previously served as Chair of President Obama's Global Development Council and President of Harvard Management Company.

Michael has done it all, from serving as Dean of the Stanford Graduate School of Business to advising some of the world's leading companies and governments. He is currently a senior fellow at the Hoover Institution and Philip H. Knight Professor Emeritus at Stanford Graduate School of Business. He was the chairman of an independent commission on growth and development focused on growth and poverty reduction in developing countries. In 2001, he was awarded the Nobel Memorial Prize in Economic Sciences for his contributions to the analysis of markets with asymmetric information. He has also received the John Bates Clark Medal of the American Economic Association, awarded to economists under forty. His theories on economic growth and competition have changed how the world conducts business, and he has served on the board of directors of a number of public and private companies.

Gordon brought with him his lifetime of public service. As Chancellor of the Exchequer, a role he held for more than a decade, and then as Prime Minister of the United Kingdom, he oversaw the independence of the Bank of England, the refinancing of public services and anti-poverty programmes, the withdrawal of troops from Iraq and the world's first climate change act. He is credited with preventing a second Great Depression through his leadership at the 2009 London G20 summit where he mobilised global leaders to walk the world back from the financial brink. Today he is fully engaged in international development work serving as the United Nations Special Envoy for Global Education, spearheading efforts to deliver a quality and inclusive education for all of the world's children, and as the World Health Organization's Ambassador for Global Health Finance.

A true meeting of the minds isn't defined by blind agreement of another's view, but rather robust dialogue that challenges assumptions, changes minds and leads views to evolve. Time and again, that's what kept happening. While our personal and professional experiences had natural touch points, like any good corporate merger the overlap and redundancy were minimal.

Michael, often having just concluded a talk with one Fortune 500 firm facing supply chain disruptions or another, would hop on our Zooms ready to share his frustration that countries are becoming overly reliant on the slenderest of economic threads. How one disruption in a far-flung territory – one Covid lockdown or one manufacturing facility fire – was unravelling whole economies. How if leaders chose to focus on long-term gains rather than near-term political wins – if they looked beyond the ribbon-cutting and into the future – they could grow their economy, reduce foreign overreliance and lower ladders of opportunity.

Mohamed, a frequent flier on CNBC's *Squawk Box* show and Bloomberg's *The Open* turned 'Fed Speak' into real talk, explaining how the Federal Reserve and other central banks being behind the curve translates to more people struggling to make ends meet and longer lines at food banks. How we've arrived at a place where there is an overreliance on central banks as essential policy actors delivering solutions that are beyond their reach. How policy co-ordination has given way to blame games.

Gordon would come off a call with one government leader or another and lament the failure to meet and master the challenge of getting the UK, Europe and the United States to deploy more of their Covid vaccine reserves to the developing world, and quickly we'd find ourselves discussing vaccine nationalism. How private–public partnerships that brought a vaccine to market in record time could only go so far before stalling out. How this was a global problem in need of global co-operation.

We shared our frustrations and fears on these calls. And we also shared our hopes. All of us are parents. And all of us are fearful of the world we're leaving for our children. What gift are we leaving for the next generation? The state of the world today is not something any of us are proud of when we think of tomorrow.

You don't need to know every part of the solution. But if you get going and keep an open mind, answers tend to present themselves. This book is meant to 'get going' – to frame the conversations that hopefully lead to answers and lasting solutions. At a certain point on our calls and Zooms, making the decision to put pen to paper seemed obvious and natural.

In writing, we hope we've kept this book out of the sleep aids aisle at CVS or Boots – that it's not a snooze-fest but rather something that provokes thought and keeps you up at night. Too many books exploring the state of the world are long on problems and a bit short on vision and specifics, an apparent aversion to nuance and complexity. This is not that book.

We've tried to thread the needle. Some pages are easier to read than others. Some concepts are more straightforward than others. Some observations and examples will seem more relevant to your life than others. But to speed ahead we have to take the turns slowly, so we ask that you bear with us. Buckle up. And we hope you enjoy the ride.

INTRODUCTION

PERMACRISIS:
THE 2022 WORD OF THE YEAR

Permacrisis (noun)
ˈpɜːmə͵kraɪsɪs
Word forms: plural -ses
Definition: an extended period of instability
and insecurity, esp one resulting from
a series of catastrophic events

In late 2022, Collins Dictionary announced their word of the year. Among the contenders were 'quiet quitting', 'splooting' and 'partygate'.[1] But there was a bigger geopolitical 'vibe shift' — also a word of the year contender — afoot. Enter the 'permacrisis'.

Russia invaded Ukraine. Tensions between the US and China surged. Inflation in the United States and throughout Europe was raging at levels not seen in decades. Energy prices forced some families to choose between gas and groceries. Covid continued to claim lives and livelihoods. And climate change's ceaseless trail of destruction grew with floods in Pakistan and heatwaves across Europe. On the Elbe River in the Czech Republic, a 'hunger stone' used hundreds of years ago to mark low water levels usually preceding famine revealed a message long-hidden underwater: 'If you see me, then weep.'[2]

These challenges, and many others, show no signs of abating — only accelerating. That's what happens in a permacrisis.

Do you feel like we're in a permacrisis? Think for a moment about the following: are the push alerts coming to your phone bringing good news or more doom and gloom updates on inflation and invasions? Around the dinner table, do your family and friends sound confident in their job security — or are they concerned the music could stop at any moment leaving them without a chair? As Ronald Reagan famously asked while campaigning for president in 1980, 'Are you better off today than you were four years ago?' What about one year ago, or six months ago? Do you feel the world is heading in the right direction?

Chances are you feel a bit of anxiety. There aren't enough green lights out there. Too many are flashing yellow or solid red. So how have we arrived at this dangerous intersection?

Well, we have to thank a combination of unanticipated shocks, poor policy responses, struggling co-ordination and bad luck. To be clear, this is not a mean-reverting situation where, with time, the world regains its footing. Quite the contrary — the longer the world teeters on the brink, the greater the likelihood for even bigger problems. That's just like in life where the longer a problem goes unresolved, the more likely it is to worsen. That balding tyre on your car won't just increase your stopping distance — it could burst when you're travelling at high speeds.

There's a generation, perhaps two, that thinks the relative stability of the last thirty years was normal, and this new period of instability is abnormal. They've got it backwards. The reality is the last three decades were the abnormal part of recent history marked by rapid growth in developing economies, massive injections of productive capacity and labour, and relative global stability with the US as the world's lone superpower. So, it's not enough to say a lot is changing. Our mindset is adapted to the old, and it doesn't adjust quickly to new realities. We have to adjust and add these changes up – the shifts and underlying causes that have come to define this permacrisis – and then go a step further with ideas to navigate this increasingly complex world.

Failure to act decisively risks taking many of the tensions undermining lives and livelihoods past the breaking point. And the consequences will extend far beyond harming this generation. The greatest risk is that these challenges persist and problematically interact with one another.

If we do not move quickly, inaction will condemn us to a low growth, low productivity and greater inequality future. The promise of high, inclusive growth will give way to the horrid combination of stagflation and financial instability worsening secular problems, such as climate change, that have long been in the making. Debt will mount, adding to poverty and instability, and financial accidents like the March 2023 cascade of regional bank failures seen in the US, leading to distress overseas, will become increasingly common. Inevitably, this will take social and political tensions from bad to worse. Trust in institutions, both national and multilateral, will prove harder to restore. First-best solutions will become more elusive, leaving us with an uncomfortable risk of collateral damage and unintended consequences.

This is not the path we want to travel – as households, businesses, countries and a family of nations. And it's a course that diminishes our ability to confront increasingly frequent shocks.

At the heart of these failures are broken approaches to growth, economic management and governance explaining everything from high gas prices to low wages. So how did we get here?

The World Changed

We are living through the greatest geopolitical seismic shift in a lifetime – new great power competition, protectionism and populist nationalism.

The ever-deepening list of global crises – and in particular, our inability to change direction – reveals fatal flaws in our decades-old thinking about how the world works. From models exploring how countries deliver growth, to the way we manage our economies and our integrated world, overcoming our greatest challenges demands new ideas.

There's no scarcity of evidence that old assumptions must go. Economic power has been shifting from west to east with jobs moving from manufacturing to services. The world is tilting from one divided between manual and non-manual workers to an era where the real division is between the education-poor and the education-rich. States which were relatively homogeneous are, thanks in part to increased mobility, becoming heterogeneous. Every day we are reminded that past views stating our environment was infinitely sustainable were horribly wrong. And the days when leaders were disinterested in inequality are over as concerns about social injustice are forcing issues of equity, access and participation onto the agenda. We see this issue taking shape around boardrooms with the Nasdaq setting new equity listing standards for publicly traded companies, and investors focused on environmental, social and governance (ESG) factors.

And let's not forget one of the biggest drivers of change – science – where breakthroughs in research and technology, arriving at a stunning pace, are waiting to be seized. Today we are failing to sufficiently secure innovation's myriad benefits at a cost to growth and quality of life. Innovative genius – from quantum computing to artificial intelligence – has the ability to change what we produce and how. And yet, instead of the high investment, high productivity and high growth decade in which the application of innovation makes us all better off, we appear condemned to a low growth, low productivity, low investment decade.

But there are signs of hope. The recent passage of three bills in the US – one focused on infrastructure, another investing in semiconductors and science, and a third addressing climate change, inflation and taxes – is an exception to the general trend. The bills can be seen as down payments on investment programmes for longer-term environmentally and politically sustainable growth. But down payments need to be backed up by recurring payments, and it remains unclear if those will be made in the years ahead as the world adjusts to new power dynamics.

Underlying these shifts is a simple yet powerful observation: while economics dominated political decision-making for decades, today politics is dominating economic decision-making. For most of the post-Cold War period, economics was the largest influence on international policy. With the Berlin Wall reduced to rubble, countries asked what they could do to expand their share of the economic pie – to cash in on new markets in a rapidly globalising world. Today that's all changed with nationalism and national security emerging as the dominant considerations. Countries are increasingly focused on what they can do to deliver military, defence, economic, food and energy security. Are we spending enough on our military and on technology to stay one step ahead of our adversaries? Are our food imports coming from allied nations? Are supply chains for critical inputs such as lithium and semiconductors vulnerable in a trade war?

And yet, notwithstanding setbacks, in the last thirty years the world has become more interdependent, more interconnected and more economically integrated. Logically, you'd expect there to be more co-operation as a result of this interdependence, but instead of co-operation we're seeing confrontations – socially, economically, militarily – all driven by nationalism.

Nationalism is how you explain Russia's attempt to rule Ukraine. Nationalism is the background noise to rising trade tensions between China and the United States. Nationalism is how you explain trade wars becoming tech wars marked by shifting supply chains, reshoring and ally-shoring – bringing business operations back to the home country or only linking with trusted partners and allies.

As we write, we're conscious of the nationalist headwinds buffeting our world. This 'us versus them' thinking has only served to add to instability and insecurity. If we are to overcome these obstacles to progress and exit this permacrisis, change is needed. And change is possible.

Any successful growth model hinges on co-operation, and yet mercantilism – advancing one country's interests to the detriment of others – is flourishing. Any successful approach to economic management requires recognising the interdependence of economies, and yet co-ordinated efforts to confront everything from inflation to sustainable investments have not emerged. And any successful attempt to create a more co-operative global order will, by definition, depend on collaboration, and yet governance is trending in the direction of becoming fully unco-operative in a world where every country's independence is constrained by its interdependence.

Taken together, we need a new growth model, a new model

for national economic management and a new framework for managing globalisation and the global order.

A New Growth Model

Let's begin with growth, an omnipresent abstraction in today's world. The inputs into growth — innovations, investments, incompetence — make headlines. But the sum total of government and private sector actions, not to mention conditions on the ground, are what shape the growth picture determining economic fortunes. It is easy to lose sight of the measures comprising growth from productivity metrics to income inequality and education levels.

Starting in the 1980s, growth models broadly fell into two camps. The liberalise, privatise and deregulate model exemplified the animal instincts of the neoliberal era. And there was the export-driven, manufacturing-led, low-cost labour model for industrialisation that led to an economic miracle throughout East Asia, giving rise not just to China but Korea, Japan, Singapore and other juggernauts.

These approaches had critical deficiencies — oversights that today are startlingly evident. These models of the past did not allow for or give priority to environmental sustainability, equity or national security. There was no accounting for environmental damage in the growth of economies. There was no regard for equity, a criticism often pointed towards globalisation in that it failed to live up to the promise of improving lives and livelihoods everywhere when, in fact, its effects were far more uneven. And supply chains were built without regard for the ground they were on and the vast distances they crisscrossed, leaving them vulnerable to ruptures.

Today we must think about growth in different terms. Our

13

understanding of national income will have to be augmented by other metrics that capture key dimensions of welfare. There will be new definitions demanded by shareholders and stakeholders for what constitutes 'sustainable' growth or acceptable investment. Value will be measured differently with social impact-weighted accounting taking its place – perhaps legislated as a statutory requirement – alongside traditional profit-and-loss balance sheets. This shift has the potential to change our idea of what 'value' is and give us, for the first time, the chance to measure and evaluate not just risk and rewards but results, particularly social impact.

The degrowth movement approaches the question of sustainability by acknowledging the finite nature of resources. And yet the movement's conclusion that economies should shrink to save the planet is akin to saying we should go backwards to move forwards. Philosophically it's provocative but functionally it's just a bad idea. Should we incentivise businesses to behave more sustainably? Without question as they are part of the solution. Should we encourage more responsible consumption of resources, both renewable and non-renewable? Absolutely. But if growth has given the planet cancer, then degrowth is humanity throwing up its hands and declining treatment.

There does not need to be a clash between growth and the planet.

You see, growth is progress. Growth is what has given the world the tablet you're reading this book on, the medicines by your bedside, the economic breakthroughs that have lifted billions out of poverty. The problem is how growth has been achieved, and the old, unsustainable 'profits over people' methods of the past have outstayed their welcome and today are not just failing individuals and our environment but national economies.

But for all the good there has been bad. For too many,

'growth' is a hollow word and a broken promise. You're told the economy is roaring, and yet your salary goes up by 3 per cent while inflation is 5 per cent. You're told growth is progress, and yet the wilderness has been replaced by a concrete slab for parking. You're told growth is bringing down consumer costs, and you see machines and artificial intelligence software threatening to push you out of work.

The way to counter low, exclusive and unsustainable growth is not by abandoning the quest for growth, but changing the path we are on. Shifting growth goals from expansion at all costs towards a focus on a trinity of ideals emphasising high, inclusive, sustainable growth can serve economies and individuals.

The nineteenth and twentieth centuries were a time when chemistry and physics were at the heart of innovation. The three previous industrial revolutions built around the internal combustion engine, electricity and computers depended on advances in chemistry and physics. Now all the sciences – from biotech to information technology – are ready to unlock a dramatically different future. That will not solve all our problems and meet all our needs, of course. But it holds an enormous potential to help meet medium- and longer-term growth challenges.

The biggest science-led transformations now in progress – in life sciences, energy and digital technologies – will so radically change what we produce and the way we produce that traditional growth models will have to be replaced. Growth models, which have focused too narrowly on privatisation and deregulation, have outlasted their use-by dates as they are now unable to guarantee the sustained levels of growth needed to ensure rising standards of living or the financing of public services.

The cost to generate a draft human genome sequence has

fallen from \$14 million in 2006 to around \$250 today, a rate of decline outpacing Moore's Law for semiconductors, and offering hope for a future where anyone, anywhere will be able to affordably and quickly get a diagnosis revealing underlying conditions.[3] Battery technology, most visibly in electric cars, continues to improve with ranges increasing and charge times decreasing and many new vehicles hitting the market offering more than three hundred miles of range.

These positive examples are not meant to overlook the bad. An overreliance on technology paired with a relaxed regulatory framework can end in disaster. Such was the case with the new Boeing 737-Max series of aircraft where an unaddressed design flaw would lead to two crashes claiming 346 lives. Larger engines on the new model meant the plane flew differently from earlier versions, and to win orders and to spare airlines from having to pay for costly retraining programmes, Boeing tasked a cockpit computer to provide control inputs in certain circumstances to help mimic the flying style of earlier 737s. The problem was, neither regulators nor pilots were fully aware the system existed. And when it activated on Lion Air Flight 610 and Ethiopian Airlines Flight 302, the pilots were catastrophically overpowered.

The success of finding a vaccine for Covid is another recent example of why we need a new model of growth. Yes, we needed inventors. Yes, we needed private industry. But we also needed the support and encouragement of government as the founding partner and purchaser to sponsor, risk-mitigate and deliver the new vaccine in such a short time and to a global audience. Public investment backed by appropriate financial risk-sharing and incentives, and where appropriate, more nimble regulation, matter far more than any neoliberal model has ever acknowledged.

'The Tragedy of the Commons' speaks to how we are headed down the wrong growth path.[4] Put forward by evolutionary biologist Garrett Hardin in 1968, the 'Tragedy' addressed resource consumption and self-interest. Looking to the past, Hardin noted how individuals would put their sheep and goats in a common area, and what happened next was predictable – the livestock would overeat, depleting the land of resources. This is a story repeated time and again, from fisheries to forests. Where we have non-co-operative settings and individuals are incentivised to act in their own self-interest, resource depletion and harm will follow.

Growth must account for a world constrained by finite resources, from the natural world to the man-made such as money. A new growth model recognises that technology can be harnessed to make the world better off, driving productivity. A new growth model accounts for the human being in artificial intelligence and emphasises augmentation and not automating people out of jobs. And a new growth model addresses a new world defined by supply constraints. In this world of new growth models, the mantra isn't growth *at* all costs but growth aware *of* the costs – to people and the planet.

But new growth models alone will not get us out of a permacrisis. We also need better economic management policies to unleash the potential of these new models. And if our growth models are failing us, so too are our traditional models of economic management, not just because they were unable to prevent the Global Financial Crisis of 2008 and the low and unequal growth that followed, but also because, through lack of sufficient reform, they floundered in the face of complex crises in the early 2020s.

A New Model for National Economic Management

Later on, we'll look at how the way we manage our economies is crying out for a new approach. And we'll do this by offering a blunt assessment of how failures in economic stewardship, both domestic and multilateral, have harmed prospects for growth and prosperity, as well as the need to move beyond the Washington Consensus.

The Washington Consensus is widely associated with a neo-liberal approach to economic management where government was increasingly written out of the script and growth was to be achieved just through the private sector. In fact, John Williamson had something broader and more sensible in mind when he wrote the defining paper coining the term in 1989. It was never meant to be a one-size-fits-all growth strategy, nor a prescription for minimal government, and Williamson chose the name 'sublimely oblivious to the thought that I might be coining either an oxymoron or a battle cry for ideological disputes for the next coup'.[5]

A new model for economic governance demands that we rethink the relationship between monetary and fiscal policy. Monetary policy addresses efforts of central banks to achieve some combination of price stability, job stability, financial stability and growth. Fiscal policy addresses the tax and spending policies of governments, and also has an important redistribution dimension. These terms have risen to celebrity status as of late with governments and central banks worldwide working to ease surging inflation in pursuit of a 'soft landing' where price rises recede without the consequences of high unemployment and low growth.

From the US Federal Reserve, we have seen inadequate analysis, poor forecasts, inconsistent communication, lapses in regulation and supervision, and belated policy responses.[6] In real terms, that has meant real pain for real people paying more for everything from goods to gas who don't care about the Fed's alphabet soup of inflation trackers from Core CPI to Supercore, Trimmed Mean PCE and ECI. They want relief and they're not seeing it fast enough. It has also meant worries about the safety of households' life savings held in banks, as well as companies' working capital there.

Moving forwards, it is clear that new forms of co-ordination and accountability between policymakers and central banks – as well as between countries – will be necessary to avert crises like the one we're in now. The benefits of central bank independence are well known and include the expertise, technical skill and ability to take a long view in setting interest rates month-to-month. It also means they are freed from the day-to-day pressures of partisan politics. But governments cannot afford to entirely subcontract such a critical part of their nation's economic policy to a group of bankers without modernising central banks' mandates, enhancing accountability and expanding cognitive diversity within those institutions.

Reforms will not lead to the end of central bank independence or a downgrading of the importance of expertise, but will instead emphasise the need for greater national leadership and oversight in the setting of monetary and fiscal objectives. This approach can help bring an end to the era of central banks being thrust forwards as the only game in town.

Monetary policy can do a great deal, but central banks are not – and should not be – seen as the only game in town. In recent crises, the lapses of fiscal policy activism attempting to stimulate the economy have become clear, as has the insufficient attention devoted to the supply side.

Talk of 'the supply side', which has seen an uptick thanks to the pandemic and a growing cost-of-living crisis, encompasses the entire structure of production and distribution of commodities, labour, natural resources and energy flows. For years, arguments have raged over the relative importance of supply and demand, and we must now rethink the balance between supply-side and demand-led economics and understand that investment and high levels of innovation command as much importance as the pursuit of low inflation and open competition. And just as growth must be understood in the context of environmental and social ob-jectives, the same must be true for the management of economic policy. We must also focus much more on talent development and deployment, as well as career retraining/retooling and better harnessing the power of exciting innovations.

There's a common refrain advocating for expanded par-ticipation of government in the economy – as an investor, co-ordinator, creator of incentives and so on. But acting alone, government easily makes mistakes or gets captured by special interests; think back to the 737-Max disaster. As a result, outcomes are worse when government shows little interest in economic management. This dilemma speaks to the impor-tance of better public sector management, and a crucial part of that involves recruiting and retaining top talent.

Economic policy used to be narrowly viewed through the lenses of growth and, to a lesser extent, social cohesion without regard for factors such as the environment. Economic policy must now be assessed on a trinity of objectives – economic growth, social justice and sustainability. This steady growth must also be inclusive, and that means we don't just talk about social justice but reflect it in budgets. And policies must be focused on sustainability. What is the point of having robust and inclusive growth if, sometime down the road, there isn't an economy to nurture due to climate catastrophes?

As the second section of the book will show, an integral part of this is rethinking the relationship between finance and industry. An understanding of the 2008 credit crunch requires us to question traditional views, in particular the assumption that the real economy always takes precedence over the structures of global finance, with changes in the former driving outcomes in the latter. Despite our knowledge of the scale and importance of financial institutions, finance is still naively treated as an appendage and not a force capable of both transformational opportunities and disastrous damage to livelihoods.

In 2008 and 2009, we found that what was once relegated in our thinking to be secondary players, secondary practices and secondary dynamics were at the heart of the global crisis. Hiding in plain sight, banks embarked on irresponsible risk-taking all while a non-bank shadow sector – largely unregulated and unsupervised financial institutions – recklessly expanded. In other words, the neoliberal model that presumes the most important reforms are deregulation, liberalisation and privatisation no longer captures sufficiently well how an economy prospers.

Sensible national economic policies require a reconstitution of central banks, a clearer picture of their role, new ways of co-ordinating monetary, fiscal and regulatory policy at a national level and the integration of environmental and social justice priorities into economic decision-making. Taken together, these shifts are but one part of a broader effort that can deliver a return to prosperity. We will need far more radical supply-side policies, and we will have to find ways to re-establish the financial sector as the true servant of the economy.

A New Global Order

New economic and growth models will only take us so far. The global order and how it can be reformed is the basis for our third and final section. The challenges we face cannot be solved by economists alone but instead demand co-operative domestic and global action.

In the wake of the Global Financial Crisis, the international community had the chance to reset and build a new path to more sustainable growth, but it failed to do so. In turn, when 2020 brought a pandemic, medical protectionism including vaccine nationalism was more visible than any sustained effort at international co-operation. The year 2021 saw the global order further erode at the COP26 climate summit as many countries did not agree to a carbon net zero future. And as we write, global co-ordination and even a spirit of co-operation has been limited as we deal with the ongoing impacts of Covid, climate change, inflation, conflict in Europe and rising tensions with China over trade, finance, technology, spy balloons and Taiwan.

Our challenges cannot be written off as unconnected, narrow national problems hitting countries in isolation. These are global problems in need of global solutions, but these solutions have yet to emerge.

For years the issue was presented as a binary: you were either for or against globalisation. This framing missed the real issue, which was always whether we managed globalisation well or badly, and the extent to which we co-operated to make globalisation work. But today the reality is that, despite living in an economically integrated, socially interconnected and interdependent world, we manage co-operation unco-operatively.

That wasn't always the case. When the world was on the

brink of a banking collapse in 2008, a new global economic forum building on the convenings of G20 finance ministers emerged – a leaders' G20 convening heads of state and government that proved critical to preventing a devastating global depression. When we faced an oil shock in the 1970s, a G7 comprising the West and Japan was created with a plan to recycle oil surpluses and stabilise destabilised currencies. In 1945, out of the rubble of war, entirely new institutions from the UN to the IMF and World Bank were created to rebuild, alongside the Marshall Plan, to root out poverty, hunger, desperation and chaos. Close to eighty years on, faced with multiple crises that also threaten death and destruction, there is no modern Marshall and no plan.

Today's crises from famine to inflation cannot be pigeonholed as one-off events whose causes can be pinned down as aggression, the spread of disease or the difficulties of an energy transition. As we have suggested, underlying these multiple emergencies are seismic economic, social and technological shifts that are moving the world away from its familiar moorings that anchored the last thirty years: a unipolar world where America was the sole superpower; a hyperglobalist world where global connections continually brought humanity closer together; and a neoliberal world marked by deregulation and free-market capitalism.

The danger now is that in the face of these challenges, the global economy will fracture into separate pieces producing economic blocs based on distinct ideologies and political systems. In turn, this rupture will lead to differences in 'technology standards, cross-border payment and trade systems, and reserve currencies,' as IMF chief economist Pierre-Olivier Gourinchas has warned.[7]

As adherence to existing rules fades, the needed

23

balance between competition and co-operation has been lost. Understanding the threat to the rules-based international order, and adapting the rules to a new international reality, are essential if we are to arrest a disastrous dissolution which will lower our quality of life and increase national security threats.

Our Manifesto

Don't let the perma prefix fool you; there's nothing permanent about a permacrisis.

Imagine a world in which high growth and prosperity are not just durable but also inclusive and environmentally responsible. Imagine a world in which leaders have a good understanding of where the economy is heading. Imagine a world in which policymakers domestically and globally co-ordinate well with each other.

That can be our world.

We believe that it is possible to reset many of the current unfavourable conditions and place domestic and global economies on the path to high, inclusive and sustainable prosperity. That's the power of reinvigorated growth models, improved approaches to economic management and enhanced governance.

Together, these three shifts constitute a departure from half a century of neoliberal dominance and offer a foundation on which co-operation, growth, stewardship, equity and self-interest can all stand.

These are the three structural reforms covered in the following pages. Our initial focus is on what is desirable. We show how actions in each area can make a material difference to inclusive wellbeing, and how simultaneous movement on all three results in multiplicative gains that quickly compound. Once we set out the key variables, we discuss how best to turn the desirable into the deliverable. We recognise that practical and political considerations favour an incremental approach rather than a big bang. We show how incrementalism can quickly compound and build momentum, turning vicious cycles into virtuous ones and favouring co-operation within and between countries.

The world is changing before us. And we must grasp the significance of the shifts now under way: first from a unipolar to a multipolar world; second from hyper-globalisation to a managed globalisation-lite; and third from a neoliberal era in which economics dictated political decision-making to a neo-nationalist one where politics and national security now dictate economic decision-making.

While the world is changing, what that change looks like is up to us.

SECTION ONE

GROWTH

I

TAILWINDS TO GROWTH

The $1.50 Hotdog

It's not healthy, but it is cheap. At Costco, $1.50 will get you an all-beef hotdog and a 20-ounce soda. Not a bad deal in a world of surging inflation and corporate cost-cutting. And that's the way it has been since 1985. Costco's chicken bake wasn't so lucky in 2022, with the price increasing from $2.99 to $3.99 alongside a ten-cent hike in soda prices. But the hotdog is special.

It doesn't take an auditing wizard to know Costco is getting the short end of the bun on their hotdog deal. That's why Costco CEO Craig Jelinek reached out to his predecessor, Costco's co-founder Jim Sinegal, for a blessing to raise the price of the dog. Jelinek told Sinegal, 'We can't sell this hotdog for a buck fifty,' to which Sinegal replied, 'If you raise [the price of] the effing hotdog, I will kill you. Figure it out.'[1] And figure it out they did.

As they do with many other products under their signature Kirkland brand, Costco took the step of bringing hotdog manufacturing in house. As Jelinek explains, 'By having the discipline to say, "You are not going to be able to raise your price. You have to figure it out," we took it over and started manufacturing our hotdogs.'[2] As a result, the dogs are no longer a loss leader.

The bulk of Costco revenues comes from recurring

membership subscriptions, not product sales. The hotdog with the tantalising $1.50 price gets people in the door. And when they're in the door, that's when they see the knife set, backyard patio set or the vacuum they can't live without. And this business model has been a winner helping Costco reach a value in excess of $200 billion.

Costco's hotdog is a powerful and tasty reminder that growth isn't always achieved by innovations developed in a Silicon Valley garage. Sometimes it's as simple as keeping the price of a hotdog and soda steady — a decision that advances social goals by feeding those seeking an affordable snack, all while helping to power the growth of one of America's largest companies.

Costco's chief financial officer was asked in late 2022 how long the $1.50 price would last. His response? 'Forever.'[3]

The Four Global Tailwinds

Don't let the innovations of the past fool you — ours is a growth-constrained world. Every tenth of a per cent of growth doesn't come easy. Growth is a battle. And growth isn't easy.

For all the blood, tears and sweat that birth innovative breakthroughs, so much of this growth potential is quickly undone by a lack of global co-ordination and economic mismanagement. And so, the picture that has emerged is of a world defined by slow, supply-constrained growth, and whatever growth is achieved is hampered by policies to rein in inflation via suppression of aggregate demand, as well as secular forces constraining supply that will not fade. In turn, inflation will remain a concern well into the future and real interest rates will be higher than in the recent past.

Fortunately, there is yet more to the story than the emergence of supply-constrained growth. Those are our headwinds, but there are also tailwinds that have the potential to restore growth and help economies take flight.

Shift 1: Emerging economies catch up

Successful development programmes have driven tremendous growth in emerging economies. In the last four decades alone, we have seen advanced economies' share of global GDP shift from roughly 60 per cent to 40 per cent while emerging economies have experienced the opposite shift and now account for roughly 60 per cent of the global economy.[4] Catching up is hard, but much of the world managed to do just that. This feat was enabled by the successive rounds of opening of the global economy, and by the transfer and adaptation of technology from advanced to developing countries. Cross-border flows of knowledge and technology mattered then and still do now – they are vital to achieving everything from a clean energy transition to broader sustainability goals.

Over the past four decades, the global economy experienced strong deflationary pressures with the rise of low-cost manufacturing capacity from developing countries. China is the largest element in this process, but by no means the only one. This deflationary shift began in Japan in the early post-war period. It then spread to Hong Kong, which at the time was independent from China and became an early entrant in textiles and apparel. With a push from the textile quota system, low-cost manufacturing spread to Singapore and then South Korea. By the time it reached there, Japan – which kicked off the cycle – was moving on to higher value-added activities to go with its higher incomes. And the cycle then repeated as underdeveloped countries became developed, and developed countries became advanced economies.

In Asia, this passing of the baton became known as 'the

flying geese model'. By the 1980s, Korea had moved into middle-income status and the baton was passed again, this time to Indonesia, Thailand and Vietnam a little later. But the big new arrival was China, mainly in the 1990s after the reforms associated with Deng Xiaoping's Southern Tour took hold when China came to dominate large portions of global manufacturing. China's share of global manufacturing surged from 3.5 per cent in 1990 to 30.5 per cent in 2021.[5] However, the effect of this surge in manufacturing capacity is now fading. With China's per capita income north of $12,000, it is impossible to maintain an unending grip on low-cost labour-intensive manufacturing.[6] So the baton is being passed once more.

The overall effect of the flying geese pattern was the introduction of a massive amount of previously unused productive capacity into the global economy – both manufacturing and labour capacity. And the impact has been dramatic. The graph below depicts the evolution of various components of the consumer price index in the United States between 1996 and 2017, and during this period the consumer price index (CPI) rose 55 per cent.[7] Non-traded services like colleges and medical care rose at much higher rates. Meanwhile a range of consumer goods barely rose at all or even fell, from toys to televisions, the latter of which is a labour-intensive good from a manufacturing point of view.

The rise of emerging economies has driven a huge decline in the relative price of manufactured goods. If we go back to 1954, the first colour TV for consumers, the RCA CT-100, sold for $1,000. (That's $11,000 today adjusted for inflation.[8]) It offered a not-so-crisp, somewhat snowy 15-inch screen – the latest whiz-bang technology. Today, any Costco or Best Buy will happily sell you a high-resolution 40-inch TV for a couple of hundred bucks. We can play this same cost-saving game

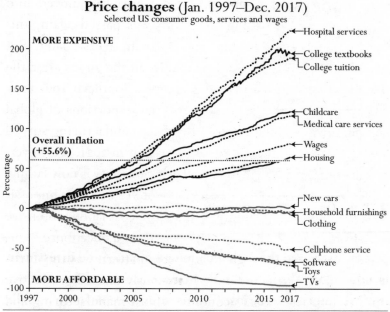

Price changes (Jan. 1997–Dec. 2017)
Selected US consumer goods, services and wages

Source: Mark J. Perry, 'Chart of the Day (century?): Price Changes 1997 to 2017', American Enterprise Institute, 2 February 2018

with computer prices, cell phones and scores of other pieces of technology.

But deflation wasn't confined to manufacturing. The deflationary trends spilled over into the non-tradable sectors – think government services, education and healthcare. In the non-tradable part of the economy, we deal with goods or services that are produced and sold in one location. And so, in advanced countries, the displaced labour in manufacturing sought employment elsewhere, especially in the very large non-tradable part of the economy. That shift increased labour supply conditions across the entire economy which, in turn, reduced the cost of labour, spreading deflationary forces well beyond their origin in tradable goods.

The implications of the global economy shifting towards emerging economies is profound in many ways. Economic

33

GDP based on PPP, share of world (1980–2027)

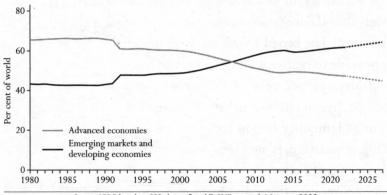

Source: 'GDP based on PPP, share of world', IMF, accessed 4 January 2023

power, exercised through technology, finance and investment, is now more dispersed as is market access. Governance in critical international institutions must adapt more rapidly, comprehensively and genuinely to this new power structure, and without a governance renovation, consensus is unlikely to be achieved. Driven by the shifting location of final demand and powerful digital automation technologies that diminish the importance of labour in manufacturing and logistics, supply chains are shifting. Trade patterns are quick to follow these shifts. And perhaps, most importantly, pressure on the environment and natural resources rises – along with the risks of operating beyond ecological breaking points.

Shift 2: The digitisation of everything

The multidimensional digital transformation of all aspects of the economy, the financial sector and even society presents numerous opportunities to advance productivity and inclusive growth patterns. Digital technologies, for the most part, are general purpose technologies which have the potential to increase productivity across all sectors. Sector specific technologies can have a very large impact on that given sector, but if that sector is a small part of the economy, it won't by itself alter the macroeconomic picture. Digital technologies are different. The broad-based reach of digital technologies makes it possible to realise widespread growth and productivity gains.

Today, 56 per cent of the world's population, 4.4 billion people, live in cities or urban environments.[9] The other 44 per cent of humanity live in the countryside or in small villages. This population is nowhere near the array of services that those of us in advanced economies take for granted in urban life. Moreover, there are many new and expanding cities in which the full range of service development is far from complete. Urbanisation is rising and estimates point to 70 per cent of the world living in cities by 2050. This move to cities and subsequent entry into the modernising part of the economy are promising signs for growth and development. Digital technologies have a crucial role to play in accelerating service accessibility to low-access populations which, in turn, accelerates growth by advancing economic integration at a pace that exceeds that of urbanisation. Giving a cell phone to someone in a rural area is much easier than building affordable housing – although both are social goods we should work towards.

Digital access improves the inclusiveness of growth patterns by reducing disparities between urban and rural populations. You can see these effects in many dimensions. E-commerce brings richer retail and consumption options while at the same time expanding the addressable market for smaller rural businesses. A 2019 study, which Mike co-led, out of Alibaba's Luohan Academy found that in China the average distance between buyer and seller in the offline world is a few kilometres while in the online world it is more than 1,000 kilometres.[10]

E-commerce doesn't just expand the addressable market

for businesses. It helps unbanked individuals enter the digital economy for the first time. It helps a disabled individual who can't make the trip to a convenience store get the goods they need to survive. It creates new forms of exchange while at the same time increasing digital literacy.

All powerful, general-purpose technologies reshape industries and economies. But the transitions are bumpy, not to mention the negative impacts and downside risks that go along with longer-term benefits. There are questions surrounding the future of work with the rise of automation and artificial intelligence. There are questions of regulation, privacy and market power, social media being the poster child there. And there are national security questions with worries about backdoors that foreign governments can exploit. The impacts of digital technologies, and specifically the internet, go well beyond the conventional boundaries of economics and touch social and political structures, and national security.

At a time when productivity is lagging and labour is in short supply, digital technologies have the potential to power a surge in productivity. They also have the potential to produce significant improvements in the inclusiveness of growth patterns. Finally, such technologies are important tools in the advancement of science and technology, including the two transformations described below: the sustainable energy transition and biomedical life sciences revolution.

Shift 3: The energy transition

The third transformation, which has the potential to be a tailwind if properly handled, is the challenge to achieve sustainability in the global economy, including what is known as the energy transition. Similar to the digital transformation, the energy transition is multidimensional, demanding the world

36

reduce the energy intensity of the economy while shifting the energy mix away from fossil fuels and towards green technologies. Unleashing wind, solar, geothermal, hydroelectric, nuclear, hydrogen and, perhaps in the future, fusion technologies will only get us some of the way there as greenhouse gas-capture technologies are deployed. We are already seeing the emergence of direct-air-capture technologies that scrub the air of carbon emissions to help bring our atmosphere back in balance. A prototype plant in British Columbia aims to scrub 1 ton of CO_2 from the air annually.[11]

Global CO_2 emissions currently stand at around 36 billion tons – way above levels consistent with limiting climate change to 1.5 degrees Celsius. What is more, global emissions have not peaked. In the developed countries, CO_2 emissions have peaked, albeit at relatively high levels of per capita emissions. But let's be clear – it's one thing for emissions to peak; but the world urgently needs them to decline. When a doctor tells a patient they have high cholesterol, they're not asking the patient to keep that number from going up – the doctor is saying drop that number before you have a heart attack.

A 2021 report from the International Energy Agency charts a path downwards to 26 gigatons of CO_2 by 2030 – an emissions decline of roughly 6 per cent per year.[12] Now let's assume a conservative estimated annual rate of 2 per cent growth for the global economy over that period. So, if total emissions have to decline at the rate of 6 per cent per year, and if the global economy grows at 2 per cent per year, then carbon intensity has to decline at 8 per cent a year. The world has reduced carbon intensity, but never this fast. Between 1980 and 2021, carbon intensity fell by an average of 1.3 per cent per year.[13]

In major emerging markets, the picture varies. China is expected to peak emissions between now and 2030, a projection that was made before the major energy shock associated with Russia's war in Ukraine. India is at an earlier stage of growth with a per capita income roughly one third that of China, and as a result its CO_2 emissions will certainly rise for more than a decade before peaking. A shorthand for understanding the magnitude of the challenge is comparing economic growth with the rate of decline of the carbon intensity of the economy. For high-potential growth economies like India, growth is likely to exceed the rate of carbon intensity reduction for years to come – unless there is a massive acceleration in the rate of decline of carbon intensity globally.

Emissions are concentrated in the developed economies and a few large emerging economies. According to the United Nations, the top seven global emitters – China, the United States, India, the European Union, Indonesia, Russia, Brazil – accounted for roughly 50 per cent of global emissions in 2020.[14] When that group is expanded to include G20 countries, the figure increases to 75 per cent.

As climate reports time and again make clear, we will either have an inflection point in the energy transition or move into higher levels of global warming and its consequences.[15] The shift to a renewable future will come at a cost – roughly \$4 trillion annually is the going estimate. But this price is nothing compared to the cost of inaction. And yet in an environment of high sovereign debt levels, rising inflation and interest rates and ageing populations, governments will probably face diminished capacity to invest and are unlikely to sufficiently co-ordinate to deliver the needed funds.

Even though the world is unlikely to reach the 26 gigatons of CO_2 target by 2030, that doesn't mean we shouldn't try. Crossing the threshold in 2032 is much better than crossing it a decade later, or not at all. The challenge is that we are not fully using the tools and technologies that we have. The US stubbornly continues to refuse to put a price on carbon, and when America rejoined the climate battle through the Inflation Reduction Act, it did so with subsidies and not taxes. Similar blockages and slow walking characterise international agreements and actions, although the 2022 Treaty of the High Seas protecting ocean biodiversity is an example of important progress.

Shift 4: Today's scientific revolution

There is a fourth transformation under way, one that is perhaps less visible to the general public and yet as important as the other three — a revolution in biology, biomedical and life sciences.

Like the digital arena, it is being driven in part by the widespread availability of powerful tools whose costs have declined and are now low enough to allow thousands of scientists to participate in the process of scientific advancement and producing innovative applications. The time path of the declining costs of DNA sequencing, advances in gene-editing, and progress in determining the three-dimensional structure of proteins using artificial intelligence, advances that were out of reach less than a decade ago, are now commonplace today.

The likely impacts of today's scientific revolution are wide-ranging and profound. The speed with which Covid vaccines were developed provided a glimpse into the power and potential of our scientific resources and know-how. Impacts will be felt in health outcomes, the prevention or treatment of infectious diseases, mitigation of diseases and disorders with genetic origins, longevity, as well as our ability to deliver food security.

Synthetic biology may also transform aspects of manufacturing and contribute to our sustainability goals. As with digital technologies, here too there are serious risks and potential misuses of science and technology. Progress in both areas will require a combination of innovation and adaptive regulation. With these rapid technological developments, there is an understandable and inevitable lag in needed regulatory structures. And responsible management and regulation of the security and uses of data is an essential ingredient across all these technologies.

Coup de Tech: Tech and Tools Driving Growth Tailwinds

From the present biological and life sciences revolution to the clean energy transition and the digitisation of everything, all of these transformations are being advanced by powerful technologies and tools. Not only do the tools exist today, they are widely available and increasingly affordable.

Consider photovoltaic electricity, or solar panels. The cost of solar generation of electricity has dropped by roughly a factor of five over the past decade making it competitive with, or even superior to, fossil fuel alternatives. This decrease in costs opens the door to smart grids and advances in storage and batteries. Similar advances in efficiency and cost reductions can be found in wind generation of electricity as well.

Or consider semiconductors where Moore's Law – a prediction first made in 1965 claiming the number of transistors on a chip would double every two years – has held true up until this day. Semiconductors continue to increase in power while they decline in cost. The density of transistors on the current generation of chips is astonishing, with Taiwan Semiconductor Manufacturing Company (TSMC) producing 3-nanometre spacing on chips – that's roughly 290 million transistors per square millimetre. These chips unlock the door to lower energy consumption and heat generation as well as massive increments in affordable computing power. More efficient chips mean less energy is required, in turn helping to advance our sustainability agenda. And not surprisingly, they are crucial for the development of AI – so crucial, in fact, that the US has restricted exports of certain chips to China.

Advanced AI and machine learning requires immense amounts of computing power, especially for the training phase. And at the moment, that computing power resides mainly with US tech giants – think Microsoft and Alphabet. Overseas or privatised computing power creates a walled garden making it difficult for everyone from scientists to scholars to access computing power only available to tech firms and governments. There are growing calls for a national research cloud opening up government and tech giants' data centres to researchers.[16] This kind of public sector investment would help to accelerate the responsible development and implementation of AI applications, not to mention social goods stemming from these innovations.

And artificial intelligence is no longer a science fiction talking point but a reality at our doorstep. A striking example of advanced technology comes from DeepMind in London, now a division of Alphabet and one that has gone well beyond game-beating innovations. DeepMind is among the leading centres for advanced AI research. Using a system called AlphaFold, DeepMind has developed methods for predicting the three-dimensional structure of proteins from the amino acid sequence that defines the protein. Finding the 3D structure has been a labour-intensive lab-based process that historically took weeks or months. The new technology they have pioneered is set to significantly increase 'productivity' in important areas of life sciences research and development. This may sound abstract but it isn't – it's elemental. Protein modelling may even save your life one day. The 3D structures of molecules are needed to determine how they bind, which is crucial for the development of vaccines, drugs and other life-saving treatments. AlphaFold has predicted the 3D structure of all 200 million known proteins and has made the results open-source so that any scientist can access them at no cost – a feat of private engineering that has created a global public good.

And then, of course, there's ChatGPT. In late 2022, the ChatGPT application by OpenAI launched quickly gaining millions of subscribers eager to have the chatbot answer questions. From what Christopher Columbus would see if he came to America in 2015, to writing a pitch sheet for the third season of HBO's hit series *White Lotus*, ChatGPT comfortably breezed through many queries. AI tools like ChatGPT don't get it right all of the time – just ask the lawyer who used ChatGPT to prepare a brief in a suit against the airline Avianca. The chatbot spat back case law such as Martinez v. Delta Air Lines and Zicherman v. Korean Air Lines as noteworthy precedent.[17] The only problem was ChatGPT made everything up.

AIs have become powerful detectors of patterns and prediction machines. And they are fast. They have vastly expanded the array of very basic tasks that humans perform that are now accessible

User   Tell me about when Christopher Columbus came to the US in 2015

ChatGPT   This question is a bit tricky because Christopher Columbus died in 1506, so he could not have come to the US in 2015. But let's pretend for a moment that he did!

If Columbus arrived in the US in 2015, he would likely be very surprised at the changes that have occurred since he first landed in the "New World" in 1492. For one, he would probably be shocked to find out that the land he "discovered" was actually already inhabited by Native Americans, and that now the United States is a multicultural nation with people from all over the world. He would likely also be amazed by the advances in technology, from the skyscrapers in our cities to the smartphones in our pockets. Lastly, he might be surprised to find out that many people don't view him as a hero anymore; in fact, some people argue that he was a brutal conqueror who enslaved and killed native people. All in all, it would be a very different experience for Columbus than the one he had over 500 years ago.

Source: 'Introducing ChatGPT', OpenAI.com

to machine learning. Image recognition is a good example. As little as ten years ago, AIs were not good at recognising images. A 2012 project at Google's 'X' division had a 16,000-computer neural network assess ten million images from YouTube videos for images of cats.[18] It was an interesting experiment to see if machines can teach themselves, but an imperfect one. When was the last time you went through an explicit checklist to determine if an object is a cat, an exercise that recalls the comical 'Not Hotdog' app in HBO's series *Silicon Valley*.

Machines utilising rapidly expanding computing power and access to millions of digital images can now detect patterns in the digital versions of the images. The figure below shows AI progress in object detection from an annual competition conducted by ImageNet, called the Large Scale Visual Recognition Challenge.[19] As we write, AI performance hasn't just surpassed human performance in object and image detection alone; there's an ever-growing list of tasks from coding to poetry composition where an AI can do the work more quickly.

And artificial intelligence has helped spur the rise of robots, broadly defined to include anything that performs tasks with some degree of autonomy. We see robotics touching everything from vehicles with self-driving functions, to industrial robots monitoring building perimeters, and automated logistics systems such as those found at major ports. Boston Dynamics' Atlas robot can do the twist and mash the potato to The Contours' 1962 hit 'Do You Love Me', and their Spot robot resembling a dog has applications for everything from building security to battlefield operations.

When it comes to robotics and AI, we're all just like a fish who, for the very first time, came up from the deep and poked its head above the surface of the water. We've only just scratched the surface of machine learning and its applications,

Object detection, LSVRC competition

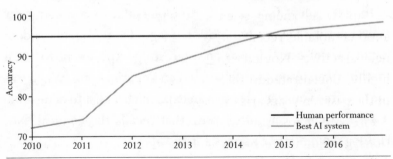

Source: Louis Columbus, '10 Charts That Will Change Your Perspective On Artificial Intelligence's Growth',
Forbes, *12 January 2018 (via AI Index)*

and relatively soon we will begin to see major advances in productivity using these tools. Think back to ChatGPT. This is not just about imagining a student farming out a term paper to the AI or a salesperson turning to it for a draft promotional email. AI's advances are quickly ushering in a tsunami of accessible, affordable tools for scientists, technologists and entrepreneurs to use to develop new products and services. And these advances will only arrive more quickly as vast sums are being spent in the robotics and AI arms race,

Source: Boston Dynamics, 'Do You Love Me?' [Video], YouTube, 29 December 2020

44

especially with respect to the knowledge and information side of the economy.

Rapidly advancing science and technology have spawned another notable recent trend: the globalisation of entrepreneurial activity. Not long ago, entrepreneurial ecosystems were highly concentrated in the US. They have spread dramatically in the past ten years and can now be found on every continent. Addressable market size matters because many of the applications of the digital technologies have high fixed and low variable costs, and also scale easily. As a result, China and India have joined the US in becoming major centres of innovation and entrepreneurial activity. Now one can find growing numbers of valuable startups in Latin America, Europe, the Middle East and throughout much of Asia. Africa too is not missing in action and will accelerate as digital infrastructure gets built out.

As of late 2022, the US is home to the most startup companies worth a billion dollars or more, also known as unicorns, with China, India and Europe home to sizeable numbers as well. Many of these high-growth companies' business models rely on serving underserved populations in finance, commerce, healthcare and education – an aim that aligns with broader economic and social inclusiveness objectives. These strides would not be possible were it not for the dramatic global growth of the internet, especially the mobile internet. In 2023, approximately 6.8 billion people used smartphones – that's close to double 2016's 3.7 billion.[20]

The expansion of digital access across India touches on several of these issues. In 2010, data plans for cell users across India were so costly that very few individuals had access. Around this time, a small upstart firm, IBSL, which was later purchased by Mukesh Ambani's Reliance and renamed Reliance Jio, began building a data infrastructure. When voice and data services

45

Which countries have the most unicorns?
Comparing the top-ten nations by total number of unicorns

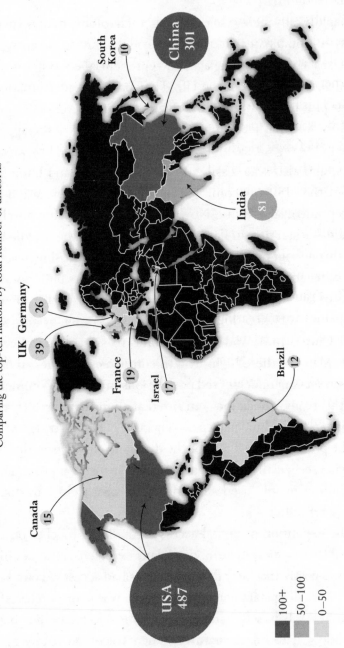

South Korea 10
China 301
India 81
UK 39
Germany 26
France 19
Israel 17
Brazil 12
Canada 15
USA 487

100+
50–100
0–50

Source: 'Which countries have the most number of unicorns?', Finshots, 3 January 2022

launched on the Reliance Jio network in 2016, people signed up in droves. Six years later, more than 400 million people across India subscribe to this service, all while data costs have fallen from around $3.50 per gigabyte to less than $0.30 today.[21] In turn, lower costs and dramatically expanded access to the mobile internet spawned a widespread entrepreneurial ecosystem across India. This has been complemented by India's biometric identity system, Aadhaar, providing citizens and resident nationals with a unique 12-digit identification number, as well as the Universal Payments Interface. These initiatives have contributed to India's digital acceleration and highlight the power of technology to be part of the growth solution for emerging economies.

While the unicorn phenomenon has become global, it remains a distinctly local and interpersonal activity. Many of the unicorns in Germany are in Berlin, with a few in Munich, and in France most call Paris home. That said, high-growth companies are increasingly targeting international markets such as Lagos, Nigeria and Nairobi, Kenya through e-commerce, fintech, health and education. This potential contribution to inclusive growth should not be ignored. These positive trends need to be accelerated if we are to overcome the substantial headwinds to growth.

2

HEADWINDS TO GROWTH

A Logistical Nightmare

We have a supply chain joke, but you might not get it for a while.

In all seriousness, the supply chain of the recent past is less of a joke and more of a logistical nightmare.

Before 2020, the words 'supply chain' were reserved for executives, students in business school classes, procurement teams, suppliers, shippers and cogs in vast networks that brought parts, goods and commodities to the market. Musing about supply chains was likely on the 'ten best' list of how to get out of a conversation at a dinner party. But that all changed in 2020 with the onset of the Covid pandemic. To go to the supermarket, to place an order on Amazon, to fill up a tank with gas, all of these things quickly became a study in the complexity – and costs – of the global supply chain.

What did you want to buy during, or in the wake of, the pandemic that you couldn't? Maybe that new car you wanted wasn't on dealer lots, so you had to compromise on features. Maybe the green iPhone you wanted was backordered so you opted for black. Or maybe that bedroom furniture set was so delayed, first by factory closures in Asia and then by shipping delays, that you just gave up on that part of the home remodel.

And it wasn't just expensive products that were impacted. If you liked Samoas or S'mores Girl Scout cookies, at the height

48

of the pandemic you were out of luck. 'Supply chain and labour shortage issues' meant the Girl Scouts of Greater Los Angeles were out of some of their most popular items.[1] It's rare for folks to get angry at Girl Scouts, but Americans were.

And the chocolate chip shortage wasn't the only kind of chip disruption.

Semiconductors, or chips for short, manage the flow of current in electronic devices. Without them, we'd be living in an analogue world. And for a brief moment during the pandemic, we got a glimpse of what that world might look like.

We may think of cars as mechanical devices, but increasingly they are computers on wheels. A fifth-generation F-22 fighter jet has close to 2 million lines of code, while a Mercedes S-Class circa 2009 has approximately 20 million.[2] At the start of the pandemic, automakers suspecting sales would fall off a cliff cancelled orders from suppliers – they needed less of everything, from sun visors to semiconductors. So, when consumers flush with stimulus dollars or furlough money went to dealer lots, there weren't enough vehicles.

Here's the thing: when you're short on semiconductors, there's no one-day shipping option. Orders are placed months, if not years, in advance. According to McKinsey, production lead times can exceed four months for well-established semiconductor products, while switching manufacturing sites adds six months and moving to another manufacturer adds a year or more.[3] Ford's solution was simple – sell vehicles with missing chips. For a time, you could kiss rear seat air conditioning goodbye.[4] Seat warmers – gone. Wireless charging pads in General Motors cars – adios.[5] Tesla CEO Elon Musk described his factories in Austin and Berlin as 'gigantic money furnaces' unable to complete a profitable volume of cars due to parts shortages.[6] And right around the time Ford achieved a steady stream of semiconductors, they experienced a new shortage – this time they didn't have enough 'blue oval' logos adorning the hoods of their cars.[7]

Published in 2014 and adapted into a limited TV series in 2021, Emily St. John Mandel's novel *Station Eleven* takes place in a world ravaged by a pandemic, one far more lethal than Covid-19. In a flashback scene in the series, one of the leading characters, Miranda, interviews for a job in logistics with her future boss. During that first sit-down, he asks her the following:

Leon: Do you know the meaning of logistics?

Miranda: The path things take?

Leon: Not the path. The *right* path.[8]

Throughout the pandemic, we learned things can take many paths. But in times of chaos, that is often the wrong path – the one that is most winding and costly. We need to heed the lessons born out of the pandemic so everything from Girl Scout cookies to semiconductors takes the right path – not just in good times, but in bad times too.

The End of the Demand-constrained World

From the late 1990s through the pandemic, there was no sign of inflationary pressure. In the period following the Global Financial Crisis, inflation remained persistently below targets even with low interest rates and large-scale asset purchases by central banks designed to lower interest rates on longer maturity bonds. That brew of easy money usually breeds inflation, but throughout the 2010s it did not. Of course, these easy money monetary policies had other impacts. Asset prices soared with low discount rates, and with monetary policy in the form of quantitative easing (QE) where the central bank stepped in to buy longer maturity fixed-income securities including government bonds, the return was lowered on 'safe assets' driving increased demand for riskier ones just as abundant liquidity was sloshing around in the financial system.

This was a demand-constrained pattern of weak economic growth. And that pattern came to a halt as countries emerged from the pandemic. All of a sudden, the demand-constrained world was gone. In the post-pandemic world, the balance shifted – and quickly – to supply-constrained growth patterns. The demand was there for TVs, cars and homes, but the inventory was not. And with that shift has come inflationary pressures not seen in decades.

This long post-war period of global integration marked by vast increases in accessible productive potential is unusual, perhaps even unique. There has never been a period of elevated global growth at the levels experienced since 1945. In the early decades of the industrial revolution, the 2 per cent growth witnessed was nowhere near the post-war developing country and global experience, which averaged around 6–7 per cent growth.

And we know why. Once the global markets were opened, lower-income countries had access to global technology and could participate in vast markets that for a small developing country are essentially limitless. Only China has reached a scale at which the size of the global market was a containing factor, and it took two decades to get there.

Rather than thinking of the recent past as normal in terms of growth in manufacturing, trade and wealth, history shows us it is, in fact, abnormal. The abnormal part was the surge in productive capacity that relaxed what would otherwise have been more stringent supply-side constraints. This surge was always going to be time-limited as demand would eventually catch up with productive capacity. The reservoir of unused or underutilised productive capacity and labour was large but not infinite. Now, as the power of that surge fades, growth – whatever it turns out to be – will mainly be enabled by direct productivity growth within sectors and across the economy. We have lived for so long in the world of relatively rapid, inclusive globalisation that it has come to seem like the normal case. But it is not. This new era requires a different mindset, one focused on finding inclusive ways to enhance productivity growth. And the alternative, as some have forecast, is a lengthy period of stagnation.

The Post-Covid Reset

While inflation has sent the prices of certain goods sky-high, other asset prices have collapsed. Already we have seen demand for speculative meme stocks and other fad assets impacted as people save their money to make mortgage payments that are double what they were at the start of the decade. In a supply-constrained economy, it is likely that once inflation is reined in via monetary policy targeted at eliminating excess demand, the 'new' equilibrium will have higher interest rates. Some of these shocks and impediments to growth are temporary, while others are more permanent, or secular, in nature. And while the temporary shocks born out of Covid are starting to fade, the secular ones are not. This shift has implications for long-term asset prices, and it also means that fiscal space in every economy will contract. Elevated debt levels that emerged from the Global Financial Crisis and jumped again in the pandemic, in conjunction with now-higher interest rates, will cause pockets of fiscal and financial distress and market malfunction. And these shocks are already starting to appear.

Denial is only natural, particularly as we say goodbye to what were the good times for many in the past. We are not going back to that low-inflation, easy money world of the past.

There was perhaps an initial natural tendency to assume this dramatic shift would not last and that we would revert to some version of pre-pandemic patterns. The pandemic was a huge global economic shock, one that eventually subsided. Global supply chains were congested and dramatically out of equilibrium, and those bottlenecks ultimately eased. The pandemic put many companies in survival mode, which meant cutting staff and inventories and anything else that increased the chances of emerging intact, and as a result fewer companies failed.

These shifts – the buffers we built into the system to accommodate unexpected shifts in demand – changed the DNA of the global economy. And these shifts could not be reversed overnight. So, when demand surged, the whole system was caught flat-footed. Airlines that had laid off pilots and cabin crew now scrambled to hire them back. Companies that had cancelled semiconductor orders could not get them in time leaving finished goods unfinished and unusable. Still, policymakers, central banks and markets clung to the idea that these supply constraints to expansion and meeting surging demand were 'transitory' and would fade.

History will show they were wrong. There was a collective misreading of what is going on in the global economy, and a disregard for secular supply-side headwinds that will not fade soon.

Without question there are transitory supply-side constraints. The Chinese economy's weak performance has multiple causes, but by far the largest negative pressure came from the 'Zero Covid' policy that suppressed supply, both for domestic market consumption as well as trade. With policies lifted, manufacturing hubs reopened, and consumers allowed outside to spend, China's economy surged. This pattern is well established more than three years into the pandemic.

Similarly, bottlenecks in global transport as economies emerged from the pandemic were dramatic. Major ports in

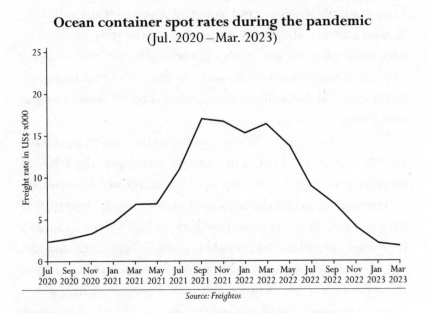

Ocean container spot rates during the pandemic
(Jul. 2020 – Mar. 2023)

Source: Freightos

Southern California, the East Coast and the Gulf saw ships backed up and waiting weeks to offload containers. A major cause was a labour shortage at ports to offload containers, a space shortage to store containers and a trucker shortage to move containers. But these bottlenecks subsided. Ocean shipping rates that peaked at $10,400 per container in late 2021 fell to $2,400 – but were still well above the pre-pandemic January 2020 watermark of $1,700.[9] An expectation that these significant supply-chain bottlenecks would not be a permanent feature of global trade going forwards was reasonable – a belief now largely confirmed by the data.

From shipping containers to pilot shortages, these conditions reduce the supply elasticities in multiple sectors as well as the overall global economy. There may be fewer flights, and the flights that are available are more expensive, or getting that specific toy in time for Christmas may prove to be impossible as they're stuck at the port. While these disruptions fade with time as pilots are hired and ships are offloaded, not all of the accompanying inflation fades with it. Inflation becomes embedded. It's sticky.

Pandemic-era shocks distract from the real global economic shifts under way: an underlying set of secular and structural trends that are adversely affecting global supply conditions and costs and reducing the elasticity of the supply side. These shifts are not transitory. They will not fade. And their impacts will increase over time.

The evidence, and the reasons, for this secular shift are not hard to find. And together they show us our future – one of a fundamentally different, supply-constrained global economy. So, we will begin by describing the trends that have reduced the supply elasticity of the global system. From there, we will turn to the implications, and following that to the need for different growth models to restore productivity, enhance growth potential and achieve our global goals.

Trends, Dear Boy

British Prime Minister Harold Macmillan was once asked what the greatest challenge for a statesman was. He famously replied: 'Events, dear boy, events.'

Events are without doubt a major challenge to supply chains, but they are just one challenge. Asked the same question about the value chains linking our world, the more appropriate answer is perhaps 'secular trends'. Reinvigorating growth models and the global economy first demands a brief exploration of these secular trends that are unlikely to fade anytime soon.

THE DEVELOPING ECONOMY EFFECT: Fareed Zakaria called it 'the rise of the rest' – the third in a series of great power shifts following the rise of the Western world and then the US.[10] Other economic powerhouses besides China have emerged, from Brazil to India. But after decades of growth, now the deflationary tailwinds caused by the introduction of huge amounts of previously unused productive capacity – land, labour, entrepreneurship and capital – in developing economies is fading. This fade comes even as the global economy's demand has swelled with the addition of tens of millions of new middle-class consumers in emerging economies. The reason is straightforward: the reservoir of unused productive capacity is finite, and much of it has already been introduced into the global economy. What is left is not easily accessible for reasons we will come to.

Today, a majority of people in emerging economies are at middle-income levels. Consider China where the middle class has grown from 39.1 million people in 2000 to more than 700 million in 2018.[11] That's hundreds of millions more people looking to trade up from Toyotas to Teslas. In China and elsewhere, throughout the ecosystem of emerging economies, purchasing power has increased dramatically. It's not surprising that with this surge in wealth has come a decline in the labour pool. Those same people who moved into the middle class are less likely to take low-wage factory jobs. In turn, the long period of deflationary forces associated with what at times appeared to be an inexhaustible supply of low-cost productive labour is coming to an end.

AGEING: More than 75 per cent of the global economy comes from countries that are ageing. That means fewer workers on assembly lines. That means increased stress on social welfare systems. That means increased burdens on the youngest members of society caring for the old. And that means new sources of demand. In top-heavy societies where the old make up the largest population segment, demand for headstones is likely to be higher than for school tutors. A 2016 study by the National Bureau of Economic Research found that in the United States 'a 10 per cent increase in the share of the population that is age 60 and above decreases growth in GDP per capita by 5.5 per cent'.[12] Ageing isn't an asset for supply chains and growth. It's a liability.

DEBT RATIOS: Sovereign debt has risen steadily since the Global Financial Crisis, with another large uptick stemming from pandemic economic conditions and policies. Global sovereign debt currently stands at more than $71 trillion, up from $62.5 trillion in 2020 and $27 trillion in 2005.[13] And just like household debt, the global credit card has steep interest rates. In a rising interest rate environment, investment-driven growth models, especially those that are required to transition to a sustainable future, suddenly seem unaffordable. Not surprisingly, high debt environments are more fragile and less conducive to growth.

LABOUR SUPPLY: Beyond the ageing of the workforce, there appear to be fundamental changes in the labour market. The pandemic shifted how we work and made the 'work from anywhere' model attractive to both employees seeking flexibility and employers in search of lower worker expenses. At the same time, it has left sectors where employment was stressful, dangerous or both short of people willing to work. The labour shortage has become so acute in the UK that some firms are paying a 'five days in the office' premium.[14] Not surprisingly, labour's bargaining power has increased as a result of a tight labour market. Labour shortages have appeared and persisted in huge employment sectors like education, healthcare, retail and hospitality. And just like semiconductors, these shortages are unlikely to abate soon as it takes time to rebuild the pipeline of skilled nurses and educators.

A recent study indicates that the US workforce is shrinking in part because of what the authors of a National Bureau of Economic Research working paper call 'long social distancing' – a preference for work that avoids frequent close contact.[15] In the study, 10 per cent of those surveyed will continue to social distance while 46 per cent will take a modified approach with both paths pointing to more hybrid work or people dropping out of the workforce altogether. But of course, not everybody can work from home as the hybrid work model is only possible in the knowledge sector of the economy. In the hospitality sector, estimates suggest less than 5 per cent of jobs can be done from home.

DIVERSIFICATION: There have always been shocks to the global economy. But their frequency, severity and global nature has increased dramatically. And these shocks are coming from all directions due to their multiple sources: climate change and resulting severe climate events, pandemics, war, the weaponisation of trade and investment sanctions and geopolitical tensions leading to the expanded use of economic instruments as tools – or weapons – of international relations and national security policy. No one expects a decline in the frequency, severity and geographic impact of these shocks. It is a secular trend that will not be reversed anytime soon.

There are two consequences of the rising shock trend. The first is straightforward: the shocks are sufficiently frequent and severe to have become a major macroeconomic headwind. This is particularly true of climate shocks. Much attention is rightly devoted to longer-term existential risks. But in addition, there are immediate and rising adverse consequences. Destruction of assets and crops, supply chain disruptions, the list goes on. This is climate change in action.

The second consequence is that companies and governments are changing their behaviour to mitigate the impact of these shocks. Businesses are adapting their supply chains to increase resilience by diversifying their sourcing, financing and choice of markets. Governments are following suit by intervening directly in what were formerly market-driven choices by creating policies that push global interactions in directions that are perceived to enhance economic resilience as well as economic and national security. This pattern of diversification, increasingly manifested through reshoring, where a business operation that was moved overseas is brought back to the original home country, and friend/ally-shoring, where operations and supply chains link trusted partners and allies, is just starting. And it is an expense that shifts the supply curve upward and inward, which is to say it increases the supply-side constraints to growth. Since this diversification process is being carried out in a highly decentralised fashion, results are likely to fall short. A co-operative approach to enhancing security and partially shock-proofing the global economy would almost certainly lead to superior results.

GEOPOLITICAL TENSIONS: Russia's war in Ukraine has led to a process in Europe of diversifying away from Russian oil and gas. This is a very expensive and disruptive process, and made even more so because of its speed and urgency. But less dramatic versions of it are occurring on a broad front, from semiconductors to assembly facilities. Rising geopolitical tensions have led to a growing shift away from economic dependencies with trading partners viewed as unreliable or hostile and towards those countries viewed as allies, sometimes referred to as friend-shoring. The Ukraine war is relevant for another reason: the conflict has been a major contributor to global inflation through sharp increases in energy and food prices.

RISING INDUSTRIAL CONCENTRATION: This is a reasonably well-documented trend that goes along with a widening divide between superstar firms and others – the best and the rest. And less competition makes it easier to pass along cost increases in the form of price increases to consumers. Research published in May 2022 found that since the 1930s, the share of the US economy controlled by the top 1 per cent of companies measured by assets has increased from 70 per cent to more than 90 per cent.[16] Think of it this way – you might see 20 different varieties of cereal on a supermarket shelf, but 18 of them may be owned by General Mills.

PRODUCTIVITY: Since the early 2000s, there has been a persistent downward trend in the rate of growth of labour and total factor productivity in virtually all the advanced economies. In the United States alone, the Bureau of Labor Statistics estimates that since 2005, $10.9 trillion in lost output in the non-farm business sector has occurred due to the labour productivity slowdown – a loss of $95,000 in output per worker.[17] There are two defining features. First, the decline in productivity is much more pronounced in the most recent decade covering most sectors of the economy. And second, the productivity growth problem is more pronounced in most of the high employment non-tradable sectors, all while productivity growth in the manufacturing and tradable high-end service sectors is much higher. As a result of falling productivity, potential supply is not rising fast enough to counter the other secular contractionary pressures.

PARTIAL DEGLOBALISATION: In international economic relations, there is a distinct drift towards nationalism and an aggressive competitive approach. The flip side of this drift is flagging support for co-operative structures and arrangements, as well as the institutions that develop and implement them. The result is a much more complex, and to some extent fragmented, global order than previously witnessed.[18]

Multinationals and global investors find themselves dealing with inconsistent or contradictory rules and standards, not to mention heightened legal liability. At the centre of this trend is great power competition between China and the US where national security and technological superiority are overriding goals. The trajectory of the US–China competition will have a first-order effect on the global economy. How this competition will evolve and its impacts is a source of great uncertainty in the global economy.

The Net Effect: Inflation, Low Growth and Accidents

From geopolitical tensions to rising debt ratios and ageing, the combined effect of these trends is a reduction in the capacity of the supply side to respond to increases in aggregate demand. When there is a surge in demand as we have seen coming out of the pandemic with relatively healthy household and corporate balance sheets, supply can't keep up. The slack is taken up by price increases driving inflation. That pressure persists until one of two things happens – either supply eventually responds, or rising prices choke off the excess demand.

The problem is that one person's price is an element of another entity's cost. When supply shortages and constraints are widespread, price increases don't bring markets back into supply–demand equilibrium but rather set off successive rounds of wage and price increases. And once this process starts, unless supply conditions change quickly across the board, the only circuit breaker is reducing demand.

Enter central banks. Through interest rate increases – sales of previously purchased assets and reserve requirements that rein in bank lending out of an abundance of caution – the central banks reduce credit, consumption and investment: that is aggregate demand. From the start of 2022 through much of 2023, aggregate demand and employment were resilient, though interest rate-sensitive sectors like real estate and construction experienced more pronounced contractions.

The state of balance sheets, in part, explains the persistence of aggregate demand. One might have thought that the pandemic would have left a trail of weakened balance sheets as business revenues declined and household incomes were lost. That was not the case thanks to pandemic policies designed to limit financial damage in households and the business sector. This feat was achieved by partially replacing shortfalls in income for households and businesses with government support through massive fiscal transfers, creating debt on the sovereign balance sheet. This is almost exactly the opposite of what happened during, and after, the Global Financial Crisis. In that case, the mortgage and subprime crisis produced extensive balance sheet damage in the household sector that took years to repair, suppressing consumption and investment. The period that followed was defined by demand-constrained growth.

POST-GLOBAL FINANCIAL CRISIS	POST-COVID
Demand Constrained	Excess Demand
Excess Supply	Supply Constrained

But it's different this time. Supply-side constraints and excess demand are perfect conditions to trigger inflation. But central banks have another concern – what we might call the second part of the inflation story.

If inflation persists, then wage and price increases develop a life of their own. In central bank speak, inflationary expectations become 'embedded'. During periods of embedded inflation, higher prices linger even when the demand–supply imbalances that triggered inflation in the first place are eliminated either by demand suppression, a supply response or some combination of the two. In the past, the embedding of inflationary dynamics was augmented by institutional arrangements such as indexing – think recurring cost-of-living adjustments in unionised wage contracts. That kind of indexing is less prevalent now in most economies in part because moderate to severe inflation hasn't been observed in decades, although the US Social Security system continues to have built-in indexing features.

Central banks will eventually succeed in reining in aggregate demand. Their credibility depends on it. How much of a slowdown will be required to get the job done and for how long is the great unknown, the concern being that demand will fall only when central banks 'break something' in the broader economy – perhaps a systemically important bank will fail or unemployment will quickly rise. Indeed, when you add rising interest rates to combat inflation into a world accustomed to and configured for low inflation and low interest rates, financial accidents follow as the system tries to adjust to a new reality. And as debt service costs rise in a high debt environment, including sovereign debt, fiscal capacity and flexibility decline. The implosion of Silicon Valley Bank in March 2023 and stresses faced by US community banks, events which will be explored in greater detail in the book's second section, offered a glimpse of how quickly things can change when interest rates go from zero to sixty. All of these pressures could be mitigated in the medium term if there is a broad-based surge in productivity.

Without question, the secular factors constraining the supply side are not going away anytime soon. The short- to medium-run prospects for the global economy include declining growth. Fiscal space, that is the capacity of governments to borrow or in some cases even to sustain existing levels of debt, will contract – a trend that is far from ideal when there are large public sector investments required to engineer the energy transition needed to restore sustainable growth patterns and deal with climate change. And real interest rates will be higher with asset prices at a significantly lower value than in the past.

This isn't all bad news. Asset prices that more realistically reflect underlying fundamentals create a more favourable and efficient investment and resource allocation environment. Bonds offer more attractive return potential, as well as portfolio risk mitigation. And with asset prices returning from stratospheric pandemic heights and less speculative investments coming into favour, manias marked by excessive exuberance are likely to be less common occurrences. A slow deflation of speculative assets such as cryptocurrencies is preferable to a bursting bubble leaving countless investors wrecked. If you had FOMO – fear of missing out on the cryptocurrency gold, or should we say pyrite, rush in 2021 – then chances are the sector's implosion in 2022–3 suddenly makes good ol' cold hard cash look more appealing.

Ageing Economies

The global economy is going through a midlife crisis. In the early post-war period, there was a huge supply of labour – a supply that has only increased with time – in the part of the world that was poor. As the global economy opened and producers sought reliable and low-cost sources of supply, primarily in labour-intensive manufacturing, many of these economies entered the global economy leaving behind a state of semi-isolation. Of course, there is a great deal more to the connectivity story than just getting plugged in. Among other things, countries require investment in education, infrastructure and production facilities, not to mention reasonably effective and non-corrupt governance. And most of all, countries need a growth model recognising the huge potential of connecting to global markets through exports and technology.

Not all countries have followed this path and succeeded. But over the last century, many have and as a result the productive potential of the global economy grew rapidly. This surge in productive potential caused the decline in the relative price of much output from the manufacturing sector and drove powerful deflationary forces.

This process of moving from poverty to a developing economy has its limits. The supply of underemployed labour in

Long-run supply conditions

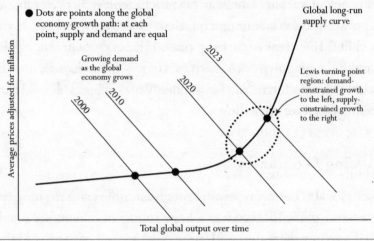

Source: Courtesy of the authors

Note: The period up to 2020 is characterised by low inflation and huge additions to global productive capacity. As we move to the right, the ratio of quantity to price shifts: less quantity and higher prices.

disconnected economies and underutilised productive potential is not infinite. The graph above illustrates this reality with the supply curve becoming steeper as you approach the limits. But the key question is how close we are to those limits, and thus how close the global economy is to reaching the point where the supply curve turns upwards and deflationary forces fade.

The long, flat portion of the supply curve corresponds to the introduction of incremental productive capacity from emerging economies. Think of this as the early days of a country engaging with the world economy with a deep bench of untapped labour. As global demand grows and the accessible store of previously unused labour declines, the supply curve eventually turns up. The easy gains go away and things become more expensive.

Much of the growth in the early stages comes from moving surplus labour in traditional sectors such as agriculture into the modernising urban sector. Productivity jumps as people cross that boundary. But eventually any country, no matter the size, runs out of surplus labour. The range in which the declining supply of surplus labour produces an upturn in the supply curve is called the 'Lewis turning point', named after the Nobel Laureate economist Sir W. Arthur Lewis, whose work illuminated these patterns. At this point in the development journey, countries either slow down or they find new growth models and sources of productivity growth and continue accelerating. When they slow down, they are in what is usually called the middle-income trap, so named because this turning point occurs when the economy enters middle-income ranges.

From a global perspective, when one wave of countries hits the Lewis turning point and moves on, other countries enter. In theory, the global upturn should occur when the reservoir of productive potential in countries yet to enter is not large enough to keep up with the growth of global demand.

Is that where we are now? Yes, but with a caveat.

Let's revisit demographics to illustrate. Ageing reduces labour supply and produces other stresses and imbalances. A reduction in the growth of the working-age population limits the supply potential of the economy, while also producing imbalances in pension and social security systems. Higher dependency ratios increase the burden on younger working people. And ageing also drives inflation. As people age and drop out of the workforce, they stop being part of the supply side of the economy. But the elderly do not stop buying and spending whether it's for cars, golf clubs, food or medication. Ageing produces a decline in productive capacity with little to no decline in consumption or spending. This, in turn, creates inflationary pressures and adds to the vicious cycle of supply-side constraints to growth.

Ageing economies account for the vast majority of the global economy today, delivering 78 per cent of global economic output with only 34 per cent of the global population. What about the rest of the world, which is relatively young? Consider the African continent, which has a median age of 19.7 years with a population of 1.3 billion, roughly the size of China or India. There is a very large and growing potential workforce across a range of African countries, but at this point these economies are not sufficiently integrated into the global economy's supply chains outside of natural resources and agricultural products to have a large effect on supply conditions.

And then there's India where the median age is 28.4, making it also a relatively young country. There's no shortage of labour with a population in excess of 1.3 billion. India has already emerged as a high-growth country in the middle-income category, and its potential growth may be the highest in the developing world at present. And yet huge swathes of the population, especially those in rural areas and traditional sectors, haven't felt the country's economic emergence and are waiting for employment engines to kick in. India's development path has always diverged from that of China and other Asian countries, being less reliant on manufacturing exports. This seems likely to continue as India relies heavily on digital economy drivers of growth, and a growth path tipped towards services. But change is possible. Diversification against shocks and geopolitical tensions could draw India more deeply into manufacturing sectors. In an effort to diversify away from China, Apple is investing in production facilities in India, and more companies are likely to follow suit.

If the goal is to delay the arrival of the global version of the Lewis turning point – a moment when economic growth gets trapped, slows, or worse, declines – then the biggest opportunity to restore global growth momentum lies in lower-income countries, many of which are in Africa. In a supply-constrained world, this would be mutually beneficial for both consumers seeking price relief and African economies hoping to grow incomes and enter into the global economy.

The Lower-income Country Challenge

More than two decades into the twenty-first century, there remain two distinct groups of people gripped by poverty. The first are the poorer citizens of countries that have experienced growth and have average incomes that are rising, albeit not fast enough. And the second group live in countries whose average incomes are low and stagnant, most having not experienced extended periods of high growth.

India is an example of a country in the former group where growth has been experienced, incomes have risen, but far too many people remain impoverished. In India as well as many other countries that are at or near middle-income levels and have successful growth trajectories, there is good reason to believe poverty levels will decline as more people are drawn into the modernising part of the economy. Historical experience in a range of successful developing countries, from Korea to China, supports this view. This is not to dismiss the considerable challenge that these countries face in pushing growth patterns towards broader inclusiveness and reducing inequality and poverty. But they have going for them momentum and rising incomes.

The second group is much more problematic: it is the world's 28 lower-income countries — home to more than 700 million people.[19] Across these countries, per capita income averaged $759 per year, recent growth stood at 1.9 per cent, and only 19 per cent of the population is connected to the internet. Looking at demographics, the population growth rate is very high at 2.7 per cent which, in combination with real growth of

1.9 per cent, means that per capita income is falling. The carbon footprint of these countries is negligible while the impacts of climate change are large and growing. Not surprisingly, the African continent is home to many of these countries.

Several decades ago, most of the developing world fell into the low-income category. But they achieved escape velocity by shifting to high investment and savings dynamics, connecting with the global economy, sound macroeconomic policy and stability, and through good governance.[20] Unfortunately, today there's reason to be less optimistic about the remaining group of low-income countries – a group which represents the largest question mark for the inclusiveness of growth across the entire global economy. The big story in the post-war period is the convergence of developing economies towards high-income economies. The side-story is that low-income countries are exceptions to the broader trend, at least thus far. And today's middle-income countries experienced their growth in a much less challenging global environment. They didn't have to deal with destabilising shocks from climate change to pandemics, forces that continue to hobble lower-income countries that need help in jump-starting the development process.

They may just be late in getting started on the growth and development paths that characterise much of the developing world. But the problem looks deeper than just a late start. If you look at population growth rates across the entire global economy, low-income countries prominently appear in the highest categories.[21] The correlation isn't perfect, but it is high. The combination of low growth and high population growth means that, if this economic divergence continues, a growing part of the world's population will be in countries that are poor and offer limited future prospects for their citizens.

Desperate outmigration is one predictable outcome and is

Population growth (2012–2021)

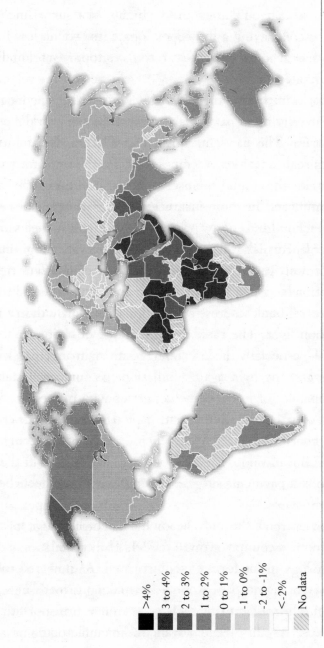

Legend:
- >4%
- 3 to 4%
- 2 to 3%
- 1 to 2%
- 0 to 1%
- -1 to 0%
- -2 to -1%
- <-2%
- No data

Source: 'Population growth 2012–2021', worlddata.info, accessed 6 June 2023

already evident. Another is the potential for future pandemics originating in countries that lack the resources to enhance public health outcomes. And climate change, while global in scope, is having a disproportionate impact on low-income countries who have the least resources to mitigate, and adapt to, climate disasters.

Shocks impacting the global economy with rising frequency and severity are a particular problem for the world's poorest countries. The pandemic produced a sharp deterioration in their fiscal capacities. Vaccines took a very long time to reach countries who found themselves at the bottom of the vaccine pyramid, and in some instances shots still have not reached people. Food and energy prices, already high and then sent even higher by Russia's war in Ukraine, disproportionately impacted poor countries forced into the global marketplace seeking to fill the gap left by Ukrainian grain supply disruptions.

Central bank interest rate policy is the key element in the inflation fight. The rapid surge in value of major global currencies, especially the US dollar, resulting from rising interest hikes and the fight against inflation has further destabilised the finances of low-income countries who cannot borrow in their own currency. In turn, capital outflows accelerate as they borrow in foreign currencies, and as those currencies appreciate in value, the cycle worsens while debt in the form of interest payments surges. Very quickly, those debts become unserviceable.

Those aren't the only headwinds, which brings us to the low-income country growth model. The capabilities of digital technology in the form of sophisticated, AI-powered robotics are advancing quickly. Robots are making inroads in a growing set of manufacturing sectors, as well as transportation and logistics. As this trend advances, manufacturing processes become less labour intensive. The availability of low-cost labour may delay the pace of change, but not the ultimate outcome.

The conventional source of comparative advantage for developing countries – labour-intensive process-oriented manufacturing and assembly – is in the crosshairs as digital substitutes advance. It is not clear at this stage, in a world in which economies are being reconstructed on digital foundations, what alternatives there might be for driving growth and employment in low-income countries.

As manufacturing moves from nuts and bolts to ones and zeroes, it becomes footloose in the global economy – largely unconstrained by the location, quality and cost of labour inputs. What does seem clear is that part of the answer for low-income countries has to involve a shift to services and the use of digital platforms to access the rapidly growing global trade in services. The digital infrastructure deficits that characterise many of these economies, not to mention the low level of internet penetration, represent major obstacles to alternative growth models.

For a wide range of developed and middle-income economies, they will be able to muddle through thanks to a combination of sound economic management and the availability of resources to buffer shocks and adapt to changing technological conditions. This is not the case for lower-income countries. In addition to the 'normal' internal requirements for jump-starting and sustaining growth, there appear to be a host of external headwinds creating a perfect storm. According to the Mo Ibrahim Foundation, recent trends in democratic governance are pointing towards a rise in coups and a decay in democracy, freedom and institutional strength, to some extent mirroring changes elsewhere in the world.[22]

To restore the possibility of development, the world's

poorest countries need help. And questions of sustainability –
the steps we take to address everything from climate change
to gender equity – have the potential to help every country
regardless of income status. Sustainability can be a headwind
or a tailwind to growth, and which direction the wind blows
is largely up to us.

3

SUSTAINABILITY AND SECURITY

A Letter to the Future

In August 2019, an unusual funeral took place in Iceland. Close to a hundred people trekked to the top of a volcano to mourn the death of Okjökull – a 700-year-old glacier now reduced to a vastly smaller patch of ice. At the ceremony, on a rock once buried under 50 feet of ice, the group placed a small plaque titled 'A letter to the future', which reads:

Ok is the first Icelandic glacier to lose its status as glacier. In the next 200 years all our main glaciers are expected to follow the same path. This monument is to acknowledge that we know what is happening and what needs to be done. Only you know if we did it. August 2019. 415 ppm CO_2.[1]

Where will that plaque be in two hundred years? Perhaps under a sky choked with pollution and in a climate several catastrophic degrees warmer. And where will we – humanity – be? Will we have met and mastered the challenges before us, or continued to defer action to the detriment of future generations? We know how to mourn. But will we act?

That plaque is just one of the more obvious signposts of the challenges before us. With footprints as vast as the glaciers of the past, around us today are the slums in which people left

75

out and left behind by progress have to live. For every hospital and health clinic in America and Europe ready to administer a flu shot, hospital shelves in less developed countries sit empty. And technologies at our fingertips that have the power to smooth the jagged edges of an unequal world seem to only make them sharper.

We need to distinguish between signals and noise – specifically, the longer-term signals about global transformations from the accompanying noise associated with increasingly frequent disruptions.

What makes this period feel unusual, at least relative to the recent past, is the multidimensional nature and sheer intensity and complexity of the economic transformations swirling around us. Sustainability is a topic worthy of special consideration. Everything from how we come together to confront the climate crisis to infant mortality rates and pay equity is linked to sustainability in the broadest sense of the term. And how we respond to these challenges will determine whether they are headwinds or tailwinds.

Towards Sustainable Development

The world excels at setting goals. Meeting them is another story.

After the 15-year time horizon for the Millennium Development Goals (MDGs) lapsed in 2015, the world once again came together at the United Nations with a new global goals initiative – this time titled the Sustainable Development Goals (SDGs) – comprising an expanded set of 17 goals and 169 targets. Taken together, the SDG's aim is inclusive and sustainable growth and wellbeing, where growth is understood to go beyond traditional indicators of national income and per capita gross domestic product. And for good reason. The SDGs are supposed to be about what people care about – what you care about. The quality of the education you or your child receives. Your ability to not just get a job, but to be treated equitably there. The right to not have to worry about where your next meal is coming from. Obviously, there is a long way to go in this work. And as put by the then United Nations Secretary-General Ban Ki-moon, achieving the SDGs requires 'action from everyone, everywhere'.[2]

It would be a mistake to characterise the SDGs as a continuation of the MDGs; the SDGs are different in content and focus. While the MDGs principally focused on growth, development and progress in developing countries, the SDGs – while not ignoring the developing world – take a more holistic approach by targeting multidimensional progress across all countries in the global economy. Targets go beyond eliminating poverty, which is the first goal and a carryover from the MDGs, and include good health and wellbeing, clean sanitation and water, affordable and clean energy, life below water.

Millennium Development Goals:

Source: United Nations Development Programme

77

Sustainable Development Goals:

Source: United Nations

There were reasons for the shift in messaging and goals, chief among them the success witnessed in developing countries. In 1990, close to half of those in the developing world lived on less than $1.25 a day, a dollar amount pegged by the MDGs, and by 2015 that figure improved to 14 per cent – a wholly insufficient increase even when generously accounting for cost-of-living increases and inflation.[3] The world saw a tripling in the number of citizens in the working middle class – a tectonic shift with people who previously took home $1 a day now living on $4 or more.[4]

To be clear, poverty had not been eradicated. As has been discussed, more than one billion people had been lifted out of poverty, most notably within middle-income countries. The Brazils, Indias and Chinas of the world continue to chip away at this figure in their efforts to avoid the so-called middle-income trap. At the same time, the world's low-income countries appeared largely unable to jump-start the process of sustained high growth, which is a necessary condition for widespread poverty reduction. And advanced economies began to encounter new challenges.

78

Enter the Sustainable Development Goals, or SDGs. The expansion of the SDGs to include a wider set of goals and a broader set of countries reflected an evolving global reality. During the 2000 to 2015 period, advanced countries received the worst economic and financial shock since the Great Depression – first in the form of the Global Financial Crisis, which in the Eurozone quickly morphed into a sovereign debt crisis. A core assumption underpinning the MDGs was challenged. Contrary to conventional wisdom, it became clear that growth and stability problems were not confined to the developing world but could be found in advanced economies as well as the global system.

And throughout the MDG period, issues of inequality began to move from an afterthought to a guiding lens through which to view trends in income, wealth and opportunity. Indeed, these trends preceded the MDGs with some of them dating back to the late 1970s when labour's share of national income in many advanced countries stopped rising and instead began a long decline.

Negative trends that persist for a long period of time turn worrying trends into big problems. Consider inequality in growth patterns. Time and again, from wages to government policies, growth has benefitted the few over the many – what John Kenneth Galbraith called 'private opulence and public squalor'.[5] But now, in the post-MDG era, equity and its many dimensions have been elevated as an economic and social priority. That is an important breakthrough in its own right. While the MDGs largely viewed equity as a barometer for gender empowerment, within the SDG framework equity extends far beyond gender and receives its own dedicated goal looking at everything from discrimination to health and migration.

And then there's the matter of climate change, which emerged as a global priority during the MDG era. Scientific warnings about the long-term economic and social consequences of climate change came half a century earlier from scholars such as Charles David Keeling and Wallace Broecker identifying changing carbon levels and ocean circulation patterns. As is often the case with global warnings, early calls to action to address global warming went largely ignored, or perhaps more accurately did not lead to significant policy attention until the late 1990s with the introduction of the 1997 Kyoto Protocol.

Surveys in the pre-2000 period show a widespread lack of awareness, and in turn concern, about the problem and its magnitude. In 1990, roughly 30 per cent of Americans surveyed worried a great deal about climate change, a figure that rose to 45 per cent by 2017.[6] Not surprisingly, fossil fuel subsidies were ubiquitous in the developing world with a 'drill, baby, drill' mindset reigning largely unchecked. Fast forward to the 2020s, and the world has changed with normally short-sighted markets placing a premium on electric vehicle makers, governments investing hundreds of billions of dollars in green infrastructure, and a climate change awareness gap that has entirely evaporated.

From 2006 to 2010, Mike chaired the Commission on Growth and Development, a group focused on development strategies and learning from the experiences of the world's poorest countries in the fifteen years following the Washington Consensus that first appeared in 1990. It was an exciting, fascinating time to study growth. China's historic growth surge lifting hundreds of millions out of poverty was well under way while India had broken out of its low-growth equilibrium in the early 1990s and began a growth acceleration that persists today. Through conversations with numerous leaders and policymakers in developing countries, it was clear that while sustainability had just started to emerge as an issue, it wasn't a high priority. General awareness was low. Severe climate shocks were less frequent, and when they occurred links with greenhouse gas emissions were often not drawn.

One of things the Commission discovered is that energy subsidies supporting fossil fuels were ubiquitous among developing countries. Governments told energy companies, which they either controlled or had direct influence over, to sell below market value. The concept of taxing fuel to generate revenues for education or healthcare was foreign. Instead, governments opted to deliver benefits in the form of lower prices without spending money. Of course, they were 'spending' potential revenue in exactly the wrong way.

So, the Commission came out and said these policies were bad – they were regressive from a tax point of view, they created strong incentives to build inefficient energy infrastructure, and they did less than nothing to advance the global climate agenda and air quality issues.

After the report's release, one of the foreign leaders Mike met with was the then President of Indonesia, Susilo Bambang Yudhoyono, or SBY for short. In the meeting, SBY said, 'You know, Professor Spence, I understand why these energy subsidies are not good policies. But they are very difficult to reverse politically, once in place.' Mike nodded that he understood and noted it would take time, patience and political skill to bring change. But it was a dramatic first-hand lesson about how policies come to be entrenched, even when leaders know better.

Fortunately for the planet, we've come a long way in a short time. Awareness of the climate emergency, and a broader set of environmental challenges that threaten economic growth and security, has become fully global. And this heightened awareness has been met by action in growing numbers of countries pursuing everything from carbon taxes to incentives to adopt electric vehicles – or better yet, hop on a bike.

While countries may still be slow to take climate action, a lack of awareness is all but impossible now. Take Pakistan. In the summer of 2022, severe floods put roughly one third of the country underwater. The floods were so vast that they destroyed 27,000 schools, 1,500 public health facilities, and pushed 15 million people into the ranks of those needing food assistance.[7] If there was any lingering doubt about the seriousness of the sustainability agenda, the floods in Pakistan hopefully opened the eyes of the climate-blind. To be clear, climate shocks are a huge negative for growth. And preventing them by reducing carbon emissions is, in its own right, a growth agenda. Sometimes people think of sustainability as somehow different from growth. But it is not. Sustainability is, among other things, a long-run growth agenda. And catastrophic failures to address climate change will certainly lead to negative, non-inclusive growth.

Chances are climate change has impacted your life in noticeable ways. Perhaps where you live it's rainier or drier than it used to be, or you experience power outages more frequently due to extreme weather shifts that stress the electric grid. Or maybe you don't feel climate change at all – you see it, witnessing melted snow caps or increased migration bringing climate refugees to your community.

The dramatic rise in the frequency and severity of climate events including storms, droughts and floods has further elevated sustainability as a priority for policy, business and society more broadly. But as with central banks fighting the 2022 inflationary environment, we are dangerously late in changing course. It's two minutes to midnight – climate Armageddon – and we've only just started to take action, and even then that action is proving to be slow.

The growth in both the size and market share of emerging economies has shaped how we approach issues of sustainability. Twenty years ago, some emerging economies were growing at high rates – think 6 per cent or more every year. But they were still small, and even in the aggregate did not account for most of the global economy. Consider China, which in 2002 was growing at close to 9 per cent[8] but accounted for a modest 4.4 per cent of the global economy.[9] Today, China's share is above 18 per cent.[10] And with that increased share of the global economy comes an increased share of global emissions. With two or more decades of sustained growth, the International Monetary Fund's basket of 20 developing countries accounts for 34 per cent of the world's nominal GDP and 46 per cent in purchasing power parity.[11] Emerging markets and developing countries now account for two thirds of greenhouse gas emissions – and that share is only growing.[12]

How Far We've Come

Since the Millennium Development Goals were launched more than two decades ago, performance has been mixed.

Growth and poverty reduction have been largely an unqualified success. Between 2000 and 2020, adjusted for inflation, global poverty rates tracking those living on less than \$1.90 per day were cut by half, and in September 2022 the World Bank adjusted the per person, per day poverty line to \$2.15.[13] Poverty reduction in high-growth emerging economies runs in the billions. In December 2020, China controversially announced it had ended poverty. And estimates from the Washington-based, non-profit public policy organisation the Brookings Institution suggest that 'by 2030, the only Asian countries that are unlikely to meet the goal of ending extreme poverty are Afghanistan, Papua New Guinea, and North Korea'.[14] In turn, the income and wealth gap between emerging economies and advanced economies has declined. According to the World Bank, the period between 2008 and 2013 saw global inequality fall for the first time since the industrial revolution two hundred years earlier.[15] This represents major progress in terms of growth, wellbeing and inclusiveness on a global basis.

The picture is not all positive, however. As discussed, there are low-income countries, representing a significant fraction of the world's population, that have not succeeded in finding high-speed growth models that leverage the global marketplace and technology. Many of these countries now face a perfect storm: climate shocks, precarious fiscal and balance of payments positions made much worse as a result of the pandemic, and uneven vaccine roll-outs undermining already fragile health systems. And yet these are the very countries most vulnerable to climate change, financial shocks and health emergencies. In addition, advances in robotics and digital automation threaten to displace labour-intensive manufacturing and assembly, undercutting the traditional early-stage growth model's source of comparative advantage, namely relatively cheap labour deployed in labour-intensive manufacturing processes.

In addition to substantial growth and poverty reduction in much of the developing world, there are other bright spots. Notwithstanding epidemics and the recent pandemic, some health outcomes around the world have advanced. Neonatal infant mortality tracking the first 28 days after birth has seen dramatic strides with deaths falling from 5 million in 1990 to 2.4 million in 2020.[16] Between 2000 and 2019, global life expectancy increased from 66.8 years to 73.4 years.[17] Polio cases have declined by more than 99 per cent since 1988, with poliovirus type 2 eradicated in 1999 and type 3 in 2022.[18] And since 2000, 2 billion people who previously lacked safe, contamination-free water now have access to this most basic resource and human need.[19]

Education is a more mixed picture. Literacy rates have risen from 81 per cent in 2000 to 87 per cent in 2020.[20] And with increased literacy comes better earning power and rising incomes. But while input measures like spending or years of schooling have moved up, output measures coming from international tests of cognitive and non-cognitive skills acquisition have lagged, and in some cases have even regressed, including in the world's wealthiest countries. By 2030, 825 million children are on track to reach their adult years without the skills needed to succeed in the workplace.[21] And this doesn't account for the pandemic which, when all the data is in, is likely to have shut even more children out of the classroom, or set back their educational progress in a major way – and done so in a manner that worsens the inequality of opportunities both at the domestic and global levels.

Inclusiveness marks another step down in global progress, especially when viewed at the national level. Yes, global incomes have increased. But within countries, there is little evidence to suggest any kind of reversal of the trends of rising income and wealth inequality; and with that often comes a worsening inequality of opportunity.

As of late 2022, more than 70 per cent of the global

population live in countries where inequality has grown.[22] According to the 2022 World Inequality Report, the richest 10 per cent of the global population accounts for 52 per cent of global income and 76 per cent of all wealth, whereas the poorest half of the population earns 8.5 per cent of global income and only 2 per cent of global wealth.[23] To draw on and adapt Senator Dianne Feinstein's famous quote addressing female representation, 2 per cent may be good for fat content in milk, but it doesn't work when it comes to equitably sharing wealth.[24]

Just look at income inequality in Brazil, China and the US. As the 2022 World Inequality Report details, in Brazil the top 10 per cent accounts for 59 per cent of total national income while the bottom half takes around 10 per cent; in China, the top 10 per cent captures 42 per cent of total national income while in the US it is 45 per cent.[25] Events such as the Global Financial Crisis and Eurozone Crisis hit distressed advanced economies particularly hard. Between 2007 and 2019 in Italy, the bottom 50 per cent average incomes dropped by 15 per cent and national income per adult dropped by 12 per cent.[26]

It is important to note that while inequality *within* countries increases, inequality *between* countries has slowed over the past two decades – a trend helped, in part, by rising wealth in China, Indonesia and Vietnam as observed in the graph below. And inequality is so much bigger than a measure of income and wealth but also touches on gender and carbon, among other areas. The magnitude of the inequality measures varies widely across countries.

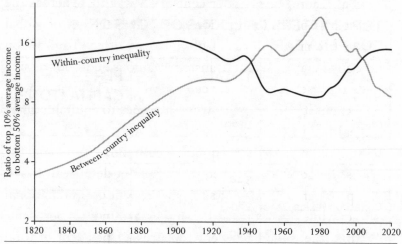

**Global income inequality:
between-country vs within-country inequality**
(1820–2020)

Source: Lucas Chancel, Thomas Piketty, Emmanuel Saez and Gabriel Zucman,
'World Inequality Report 2022', World Inequality Lab, 2022

The sustainability part of the global agenda is much bleaker. Global gross production-based emissions have risen steadily. The picture painted by per capita emissions is different reflecting population size and state of development. In the past 20 years, roughly the period of the MDGs and the first half of the SDGs, global emissions have almost doubled and now stand at 36 billion metric tons.[27] It can be hard to visualise a ton of CO_2, so the team at the MIT Climate Portal offered the image of a cube measuring 27 feet on all sides.[28] That cube represents one metric ton of CO_2. Now multiply that by 36 billion, and that's the world's output in just the most recent year. This figure is roughly 2.5–3.0 times what is needed to avoid the climate clock striking midnight. The Intergovernmental Panel on Climate Change (IPCC), the world's foremost authority on climate change, has identified 2025 as the cutoff for emissions to peak and then be cut by 43 per cent by 2030.[29] Even with creative accounting, it's hard to see how we get to the all-important 1.5°C target.[30] But that doesn't mean we should give up.

TOP EMITTERS (*BILLIONS OF TONS OF CO2 PER YEAR)		
	TOTAL*	PER CAPITA (TONS)
China	10.20	7.3
USA	5.30	15.6
EU	5.40	9.8
Canada/Mexico	1.20	10.0
India	2.60	1.9
Japan	1.10	5.5
World	36.60	4.9
Percentage of global emissions		71%

There is some good news. Both the United States and Europe, while remaining major sources of CO_2, have peaked their emissions and are declining. China is expected to reach a peak in or before 2030 – a significant achievement in a high-growth emerging economy. India, however, is a high-growth country with a population approaching 1.4 billion, and its future trajectory could easily look like that of China in the past 20 years.

A key question is whether the energy features of the growth model – in India and elsewhere in the developing world – can be changed enough to bend that trajectory down. It is certain that India's growth will entail rising energy consumption, even with state-of-the-art conservation measures. The issue then becomes the speed with which the carbon intensity of the energy mix declines. If you're India looking at China's incredible economic development and wealth creation over recent decades, it's logical to want to follow a similar path – a path that is carbon intensive. Getting India and other developing countries to see a different, more sustainable way forwards remains a huge challenge.

These trends are not the result of neglect, at least not in the two decades since the Kyoto Protocol. Awareness has become universal. Governments are engaged. And a sense of urgency is widespread. Under the United Nations Framework Convention on Climate Change, there have been more than two dozen annual Conference of the Parties (COP) summits where millions of businesses, non-profits, subnational governments, technology startups and ordinary citizens are engaged in the process of finding solutions and bending the growth models towards lower and greener energy production and consumption patterns.

Confronting climate change is a complex challenge involving global co-operation, differentiated roles, the creation of aligned incentives, new technologies, behaviour shifts and issues of fairness. And yet, in the face of this challenge, the world appears undeterred in word, and sometimes in deed. New growth models adapted for a rapidly changing global economy must include the requirements of sustainability. A failure to view growth through the sustainability lens will mean they are not long-run growth models, or even viable standing still models.

Achieving the SDGs does not fall on governments alone. Corporations, too, have an important role in this work. While environmental, social and governance goals, also known as

'ESG', is trendy, it's largely a hollow corporate buzzword that will burn out with each successive interest rate hike. But it speaks to the purpose of growth – making a difference and delivering broad-based prosperity. And it speaks to something that is very important for many of the companies' stakeholders.

If companies want to make a difference, they should focus on a specific issue, measure it, and get the government on their side to support the work. But a standardised ESG template that works for both Patagonia and Exxon simply does not exist. A diversity of values, as well as a diversity in the characteristics of businesses across sectors, presents a challenge for the development of measurement systems. Companies should 'choose their own impact' – build their own growth adventure. We all hold the widely shared value of 'doing good'. But go a layer deeper and there is a diversity of views. Inequality is a perfect example – most everyone agrees inequality is bad. For some only extreme poverty matters, while others object to all forms of inequality. The spirit of the ESG should be focused so companies, acting within their core competencies, deliver a meaningful impact.

From Sustainability to Security

The experience of the past few years has elevated another consequential dimension to the SDG framework: security. Security comes in many different forms: national security, economic security, energy and food security, personal safety and, in the aftermath of a global pandemic, health security.

The growing importance and relevance of security in policy, international relations, business, finance and society comes from our collective experience. Shocks and disruptions from climate events, the pandemic, the Global Financial Crisis, Russia's war in Ukraine and the sanctions that followed, geopolitical tensions and great power competition have become so frequent and severe to the point of having a major effect on overall economic and business performance as well as individual welfare. These shocks have changed our understanding of security and the global equation long believed to deliver stability.

For much of the post-war period, the global economy and its supply chains were constructed in a relatively open market-driven system. Their architecture was determined by open markets and incentives, and that meant efficiency and comparative advantage considerations. There were exceptions. Cold War interventions in trade and investment policy had different objectives.

For example, the quota system in textiles and apparel that eventually became the 1974 Multi-Fibre Arrangement (MFA) was designed to spread textile and apparel manufacturing across low-income countries and to prevent any one country, or group of countries, from controlling the market. Textiles and apparel are critically important sectors as they normally jump-start export-driven growth in early-stage developing countries. Think of textiles and apparel as the first rungs on a ladder leading towards economic prosperity for the world's poorest countries. Throughout the 1970s and '80s, textiles brought considerable wealth to Hong Kong, which remains a textile powerhouse to this day. But when Hong Kong reached its quota and textile entrepreneurs moved out to find places to expand, many set up shop in Singapore, which contributed to the country's early growth, wealth and development under Lee Kuan Yew.

When the MFA lapsed in 2004, the market was once again free and there was a large increase in concentration in these sectors, especially in China. The very monopolies and conglomerates the MFA sought to prevent emerged, and many countries have struggled to compete and thus move up the economic ladder. While leaving the MFA in place would have produced a less efficient and free global economy, it arguably would have led to a better distribution of growth across developing countries.

The global system based on market incentives, efficiency and comparative advantage was and is a powerful engine of global growth and progress. But that doesn't mean it is well suited for today's world of rising risks, disruptions and vulnerabilities. And it certainly is not suited to a world in which economic policies with respect to openness are increasingly viewed as tools in some larger process of strategic interaction, competition and national security.

So why is this multifaceted security agenda such a consequential addition to the growth, inclusiveness and sustainability agenda? First and foremost, security alters the incentives and architectural requirements of global supply networks. And security comes with significant costs. It is not a free good. If mismanaged, it is one of the secular headwinds to growth the global economy now faces.

To the extent there is still some kind of shared global agenda, whether through the SDGs or elsewhere, it must include the security agenda. In our new era, inclusive and sustainable growth needs to become inclusive, sustainable and *secure* growth. Whether and how these goals, and especially security in its various forms, are pursued is one of the central issues of our time.

4

PRODUCTIVITY AND GROWTH

Marsabit, We Have a Problem

A space race is taking shape, and it's not where you think.

If you want to put a satellite into low-inclination orbit around Earth, then you should consider a launchpad near the equator. Pick any point along the equator, and over a 24-hour period that point needs to cover the same distance as a point at a lower or higher latitude. Relative to Earth's centre, a point along the equator is moving at 1,650 kilometres per hour, while a point halfway towards a pole is moving hundreds of kilometres per hour slower.[1] As a result, a rocket launched from a pad along the equator needs less propellant to reach the 28,000 kph threshold needed to stay in orbit thanks to a 1,650 kph head start once in flight. But anywhere along the equator won't work. Launchpads and landing sites can't be near population centres in case disaster strikes. Add plenty of land, infrastructure, water and power, and a stable climate to the checklist of desirables for a launch site, and suddenly the location hunt becomes much harder. Enter Kenya.

Kenya is no stranger to satellite launches and space exploration. In 1964, Kenya and the Italian government established a launching and tracking base in Malindi, and between 1967 and 1989 more than two dozen rockets took off from Malindi station.[2] In December 1970, the world's first satellite mission dedicated to celestial X-ray astronomy began on the launchpad at

93

Malindi with the Small Astronomical Satellite 1 (SAS-1) named Uhuru, the Swahili word for freedom.[3] For more than two years, Uhuru peered into the cosmos in a way we never had before, contributing to our understanding of supernovas and galaxy clusters.

Throughout the late 1990s and the early 2000s, the Malindi station sat quiet. But with renewed interest and investment in space programmes, driven in large part by private citizens and corporations, Kenya is once again flexing its geospatial muscle. In 2017, the Kenya Space Agency was set up as a successor organisation to the National Space Secretariat. With more than 1,700 satellites expected to be launched annually by 2030, existing launch infrastructure – especially in the United States – is unable to keep up with demand.[4] Kenya has sensed this opportunity and is now courting governments and private firms to lift off from their country. The government is also exploring setting up a major spaceport for operations and has identified Marsabit County in Northern Kenya as the best spot for a major operations hub.[5]

But Kenya has competition. More than 20 African countries have active space programmes.[6] The African Union released a space strategy noting that 'Africa has significant potential for growth compared to the developed world, and this potential should be used to create a prosperous future for all' with 'space-based solutions' playing a part in this mission.[7]

In December 2022, Nigeria and Rwanda, at the first-ever US Space Forum, signed the Artemis Accords committing 'to principles to guide their civil space activities, including the public release of scientific data, responsible debris mitigation, registration of space objects, and the establishment and implementation of interoperability standards'.[8] The White House took the signing as an opportunity to celebrate the strengthening US–Africa space partnership highlighting ties to American businesses with

Nigeria becoming the first African country to get Starlink internet access and Kenya using Planet Labs' satellite imagery to assess drought risk prevention.

Countries across Africa are competing for this latest potential driver of growth and innovation. And one day soon, we may hear a control centre in Marsabit, Mombasa or Malindi call out the 'go/no go' for launch.

Elusive Productivity

Opportunities abound to restore growth. As the story that kicked off this chapter shows, sometimes all we have to do is look up. Back on the ground there are daunting challenges, from secular trends and structural shifts that are creating supply-constrained patterns of growth, to major technological transformations with uneven effects.

Not every country has leaped through the convergence window of opportunity. Mike predicted that the convergence process would take a century of sustained growth to reach completion. In 2023, we are three quarters into that journey — and that's bad news for the world's low-income countries. The numerous challenges they face, from climate change to financial shocks, may mean they are not able to converge. But these countries are the last large reservoir of underused productive capacity, so the global economy needs them to converge.

In a supply-constrained world, you don't have to be a highly trained economist to conclude that productivity growth is critical in avoiding a pattern of stagnation or stagflation. It is not the only instrument, but it is one of the most important ones. As discussed, productivity has been under stress. In the US, the overall trend is downwards despite a surge in the late 1990s and early 2000s. In fact, that pattern is repeated across most of the global economy. But if you look under the hood, the picture becomes clearer.

Any economy has two parts. One part consists of goods and services that are tradable internationally – from crude oil to cars. The other part of the economy is the non-tradable sector consisting of goods and services that do not trade internationally either because it is impossible – think services requiring proximity such as haircuts – or because it is not economically viable – take cement, where long-distance transport costs are prohibitive. A consequential part of manufacturing exists in the tradable sector. And job trends across these sectors are revealing.

If you go back to 1990, more than half the tradable sector jobs in the US economy were in manufacturing. By 1998, this figure had dipped to 43 per cent, and by 2021, despite occasional plateaus, manufacturing's job share had been ground down to 34 per cent. Over the same period between 1998 and 2021, the share of tradable service jobs grew from 57 per cent to 66 per cent. While manufacturing jobs did stop declining in absolute terms this past decade, the growth of tradable service sector jobs resulted in manufacturing's share continuing to decline.

These shifts are major upheavals. Overall, the US economy is tipping towards services in share of employment and value added at the expense of manufacturing. The non-tradable part of the economy is all services, so with services now dominating the tradable side of the economy as well, services dictate everything from employment trends to economic growth prospects. This is a tectonic shift representing millions of jobs moving from manufacturing to services. And it means that if productivity growth in services is low, it will drag down overall productivity even if productivity growth is respectably high on the tradable side in manufacturing.

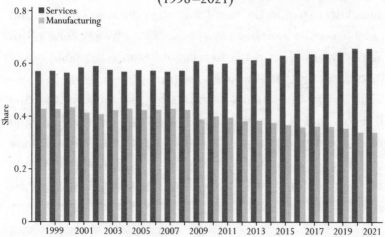

Tradables' real VA: services vs manufacturing share
(1998–2021)

Note: The figures show productivity measured in real dollars per person employed in these two parts of the US economy. The measure of productivity here is value added per person employed. Value added is a useful yardstick because it avoids double counting as value added across all sectors should add to GDP for the whole economy.

Labour productivity trends (1998–2021)

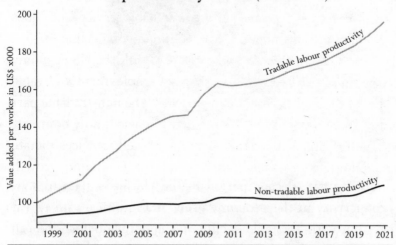

Source: Produced by the authors using industry-specific data from the Bureau of Economic Analysis (BEA) for employment (full-time and part-time employers) and real value added (in billions of chained 2012 dollars), where industry splits are based on the 2012 North American Industry Classification System (NAICS)

Productivity is higher in tradable sectors overall, and more importantly productivity is growing in the tradable sectors much faster than in the non-tradable sectors. In fact, the non-tradable sectors have been in a productivity backwater for more than 20 years. This rut is significant because the non-tradable sector is a huge part of the economy.

The tradable economy accounts for one third of the overall economy. The non-tradable sectors combined – think government, healthcare, hospitality, retail, education and construction – account for nearly 80 per cent of total employment and the remaining two thirds of the economy. And it is in this non-tradable sector where productivity is most lagging.

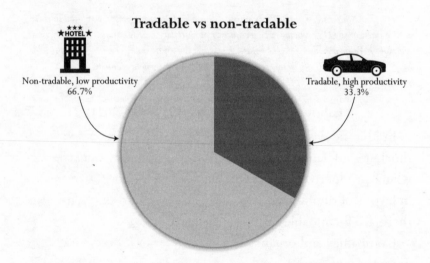

Tradable vs non-tradable

Non-tradable, low productivity
66.7%

Tradable, high productivity
33.3%

Over a two-decade period in the US leading up to 2021, productivity in the economy grew at an average rate of 1.47 per cent with a notable decline in the decade before the pandemic to 0.61 per cent. This decline is reflected in 66 sectors, everything from financial to legal services, while only rising in

18. Using 2021 employment figures, for the whole period, 46 per cent of those employed in the US worked in sectors with productivity growth below 0.5 per cent.

Share of tradable employment and real VA
(1998–2021)

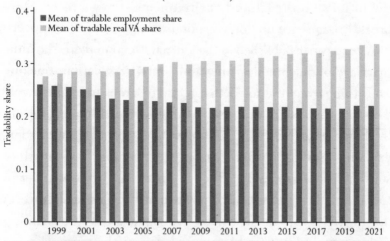

Source: Produced by the authors using industry-specific data from the Bureau of Economic Analysis (BEA) for employment (full-time and part-time employers) and real value added (in billions of chained 2012 dollars), where industry splits are based on the 2012 North American Industry Classification System (NAICS)

In this new supply-constrained world, there are striking shortages of labour in all of the large employment sectors where productivity has stagnated. The incentives have shifted in favour of digitally enabled, labour-saving productivity. And there are formidable obstacles in this shift.

Companies and organisations are starting to understand the potential, but don't really know how to proceed. Transformative digital solutions tend to have relatively high upfront investment costs, and if the benefits are uncertain, risk aversion slows the process – at least for companies and private investors. To date, AIs and robotics have worked best in structured environments, such as factory floors or fulfilment centres. With time, this too will change. But change requires major advances in AI and machine learning to bring the benefits to the unstructured environments in many service sectors such as healthcare, homecare, education and hospitality. We can already glimpse an aspect of that future in San Francisco with Alphabet's Waymo and General Motors' Cruise operating driverless cars in one of the ultimate unstructured environments – city streets. More breakthroughs are no doubt around the corner.

A 2020 paper published in the journal *Nature* explored how the marriage of machine learning and contactless sensors tracking everything from heat to depth can lead to 'ambient intelligence'.[9] The applications are limitless. At intensive care units, ambient intelligence can help us better understand, as the paper's authors explain, 'how patient mobilisation affects mortality, length of stay and patient recovery'. Today's smart watches are powerful tools, but they cannot discern when we receive assistance in day-to-day tasks. For the elderly living in assisted care facilities, ambient intelligence can fill this gap helping us better understand how many of those five hundred steps a patient took were on their own and without assistance, or if a patient's movement is unsteady suggesting an impending fall.

Not all productivity is created equal. There are leading and lagging sectors with respect to digital adoption. There are laggards within leading sectors, and leaders in lagging sectors. Productivity is correlated with digital adoption, and no one wants to become the next Blockbuster. Not surprisingly, the big employment sectors tend to be in the lagging category.

Technology and Productivity

The pandemic offered a glimpse of what digital catch-up in lagging non-tradable sectors could look like. Restaurants signed up to online ordering platforms. Booking systems for everything from rental cars to haircuts were updated. Contactless mobile payments became commonplace. And the shift to cloud software accelerated. This was driven less by opportunity and more by necessity as major parts of the economy shut down while other parts had to deal with pandemic-induced immobility in order to keep functioning. Fast forward to 2023, and questions surround the durability of this shift. Will major sectors revert to pre-pandemic models and patterns of behaviour, or will the pandemic lead to a permanent uptick in productivity due to increased digital adoption?

Consider education. Online education isn't a full substitute for in-class education for many reasons, not least of which is the importance of social interaction, which is especially important during early childhood. The pandemic did force virtually all education institutions to significantly upgrade their digital tools, many starting from next to nothing. These tools, now widely available and adopted, can be used as a complement – rather than substitute – to traditional education models with the promise of enhancing quality and outcomes.

In education, it is well known that students learn in different ways. When and where they encounter difficulties in mastering new concepts varies student-to-student. AI, as a complement to traditional instruction, can be used to tailor the programme of exercises for individual students, improving both efficiency and educational outcomes. In practice, algorithms are updated with student data and performance results, and get better in detecting blockages and matching learning programmes over time. Korea has been a trailblazer in this hi-tech and hi-touch approach to learning.

Healthcare is another example. Prior to the pandemic, there was no interest among suppliers and consumers of healthcare in online services. Investors who envisioned potential in this area found little receptivity in the marketplace. The pandemic changed that. Safety considerations and mobility restrictions forced both sides of the market to utilise online capabilities. Telemedicine surged. In the US in April 2020, telehealth utilisation was 78 times higher than a mere two months earlier, and a year later was still 38 times higher against the pre-Covid baseline.[10] You'd be hard-pressed to find a doctor that believes telemedicine will fully replace office or hospital visits, even if home-testing technologies expand their footprint. Fortunately, we don't live in a ten-toes-in, ten-toes-out world. Office visits do not need to be fully replaced by telemedicine. Instead, online consultations are an additional resource for routine consultations and economising the time of both service providers and consumers – a hybrid service model that is likely here to stay.

You're unlikely to ever hear the words 'government' and 'productivity' in the same sentence. That's not the start of a joke but rather an issue of measurement. Most government services are not sold in a market. Normally, in sectors where goods are produced and sold, value added is calculated by taking revenue or sales and subtracting the cost of purchased inputs, not including capital and labour, because it is labour and capital that create the added value. Of course, there are benefits to final consumers in excess of what they pay for the goods and services that they buy. This is called consumer surplus and is not captured in value added calculations. But in the case of government, there are no relevant revenues on which to base value creation. So, the assumption is that the gross value created is equal to the costs, again minus purchased inputs like energy. In other words, value added for government is the cost of labour and capital employed.

If wages for consular officials go up, does the gross value of your new passport or visa go up too? And therein lies the rub: we lack a market measure of quality-adjusted value creation in government. To make matters worse, there is no, or relatively little, competitive pressure that would produce benefits to those implementing productivity-enhancing measures. The incentives are weak.

We are not making an argument to charge for government services to better measure productivity, even in areas where that might be possible. In reality, taxpayers already cough up for these services. But there are digitally based survey methods that could be employed to assess the value and quality of service delivery, and these deserve more attention than they are getting.

Taken together, our belief is that productivity enhancements have the potential to blunt the impact of secular headwinds and to help deliver growth, increasing inclusivity, achieving sustainability and delivering security. But this shift won't happen automatically. It will require vision, new policies, different incentives, high levels of investment and changes in international relations. Our goal is to identify critical elements enabling these new pathways, routes which run through emerging technologies and smart government policies.

5

CHANGING THE
GROWTH EQUATION

From Model Ts to Briquets

It all started with a camping trip. Henry Ford, Thomas Edison and several other regulars of the annual 'Vagabonds' camping trip had a special guest in the summer of 1919. Joining them was Ford's cousin-in-law, Edward G. Kingsford, who owned a Ford dealership in Iron Mountain, Michigan.

Ford had a problem. More than a hundred board feet of lumber went into the Model T Ford, and he didn't have enough wood to meet demand. One million Model Ts were sold in 1919, and wood went into everything from the frame to the wheels and dash.[1] Kingsford had a solution – buy timber-rich land in Michigan's Upper Peninsula. Soon thereafter, Ford purchased 313,000 acres in the area and built a large sawmill and hydroelectric plant.[2] But then Ford had a new problem: wood waste. And once again, a new problem was met with a new solution.

His team came up with the idea for a charcoal briquet – a lump of reformulated wood that could be used as fuel for fires and cooking. The Vagabond brain trust leaped into action with Edison designing the factory and Kingsford managing it.[3] In that moment, American culture changed forever. The Kingsford briquet was born.

Go to an American grocery store today to pick up a bag of charcoal for a cookout, and chances are it'll be a bag of Kingsford. Or go to a barbeque with friends, pop the hood on the grill, and chances are what's under it will be those little Kingsford cubes of culinary goodness. Perhaps as much as the Model T changed manufacturing and gave rise to the modern-day assembly line, the Kingsford briquet symbolised the rise of 'industries within industries' while acknowledging the importance of sustainability. A 1924 Ford advertisement from the *Saturday Evening Post* with the headline 'For the People and Posterity' celebrated Ford's sustainability and ingenuity in recycling wood waste – how 'thirty-four valuable by-products are recovered from the 350 tons of scrap distilled daily'.[4]

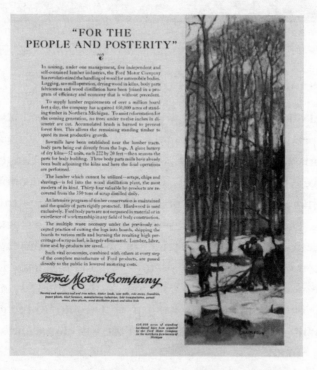

Source: '1924 Ford Motor Company Institutional Message Advertising
Campaign, "For the People and Posterity"', TheHenryFord.org

Ford's commitment to innovation created jobs. The fixation on eliminating waste created industries. Workers and consumers benefitted, all while the company sustainably reduced waste. From the humble briquet to the first brick cellular phones, innovation and technology have shifted, shocked and shaped the world around us. The story of the Kingsford briquet offers a window into how innovation can drive productivity leading to growth.

Overcoming Obstacles to Productivity

The US has a productivity problem. Which means the world has a productivity opportunity.

Tradable manufacturing is growing and increasingly productive. Tradable services, or the knowledge economy, is growing and increasingly productive. But the two thirds of the US economy that is the non-tradable sector is stuck. And the reality is productivity strides in one third of the economy that comprises the tradable sector cannot compensate for lags in the non-tradable sector making up the other two thirds. And even if they could fill that gap, that would lead to greater inequality with massive portions of the workforce and sectors left behind.

So how do we move forwards? Manufacturing offers clues as to how to restore productivity growth. After three decades of sharp decline, manufacturing employment stopped declining and in the past decade rose modestly. This corresponds exactly to the levelling off of global trade as a percentage of global GDP. To be clear, trade and interdependence are still very high, but it does appear that the period of hyper-globalisation in which trade dramatically gained share is over.

It all comes down to bits and atoms where atoms represent the hardware and machines that brought about the economic revolutions of the last century. But today we live in a bits world driven by information, analysis and transactions. Increasingly, bits are linking up with atoms powering productivity enhancements in manufacturing. Hardware and software are brought together, unleashing breakthroughs in manufacturing which, in turn, drive productivity in growth.

It doesn't take much to imagine what that looks like, from vehicle assembly lines turning out more cars at lower costs to textile factories producing higher-quality garments at no additional cost to the consumer – all while improving worker conditions. Now think about the non-tradable side of the economy, from schooling to healthcare, where technological strides are not as evident, or likely to be seized.

So why is the digital footprint larger in the physical part of manufacturing than in, say, construction or hospitality? If you ask experts in artificial intelligence and robotics, the answer is that these are structured environments in which autonomous and semi-autonomous tools like robots function well with respect to mobility, the range of required manual dexterity and the need for situational awareness and navigation skills. The challenge of situational awareness is much larger in unstructured and unfamiliar environments, the kind of environments one encounters in services. If you're in a classroom, you – a human being – know where the door is and have a good sense of what's beyond the door. A robot has no sense of this, and that is why most robots are presently confined to structured environments where they are bolted to floors such as assembly lines. But they may break through these boundaries sooner than we think.

Prior to the arrival of generative AI, the view among technologists was that AIs worked best in well-defined domains: a game, studying DNA sequences, or assessing financial data. But generative AI, through large language models, words and ideas, has demonstrated an ability to switch domains. Against this backdrop, one of the startling things about AI's large language models is that they appear to be able to determine the domain in response to questions, and then respond appropriately in that domain. If you ask a question about the Renaissance, you do not have to tell the AI this is history and art and architecture. If you are interacting about work and then switch to sports or mathematics, the AI follows along as a human would.

While there are major challenges associated with extending this kind of power to robotics, where the worlds of digital bits and atoms meet, generative AI systems operating on language, text, images and video have the potential to extend the digital footprint of robotics to increasingly unstructured environments.

Mainstreaming AI

With the arrival of generative AI, of which large language models such as ChatGPT are examples, the benefits and risks of the digital economy both leaped forward. The probability of achieving a widespread and large productivity surge went up due to the vast range of applications the technology can touch. Over time, hundreds of applications or use cases will be developed, and that is precisely what is needed to achieve the productivity surge in the second half of this decade and beyond. There will be bumps along the way – think back to the lawyer who fell victim to ChatGPT's hallucinations, made-up facts masquerading as real facts. But in some contexts, hallucinations are useful. In the creative arts and industries, facts are not crucial to value creation. New ideas and concepts are. The capacity of generative AI to produce things that not only are not 'real', but that no one has thought about before, is an asset.

Artificial intelligence has already hastened productivity in services that trade internationally almost exclusively in the high value-added part of the economy – think software and information technology. To be clear, the knowledge economy is not confined to the tradable sector – online legal advice, for example, isn't a globally tradable good, although it might be one day soon. The problem is that right now the progress in AI is creating the potential for large productivity increases in the knowledge economy, but the parts of the service economy that require physical presence are lagging behind.

One study published in April 2023 offers a window into AI's potential to turbocharge productivity in these areas.[5] Gradually introducing AI into the work of 5,000 customer service agents, the study's authors found that not only did productivity, measured by issues resolved per hour, increase by 14 per cent, but that low-skilled workers benefitted the most. Artificial intelligence accelerated these workers' journeys 'down the experience curve' by aiding them in greater mastery of their tasks.

AI tools are powerful assistants. And with time, technological breakthroughs are going to give many people – from software engineers to customer service agents – exactly that:

a highly competent assistant. This assistant will help them do their jobs better, avoid drudgery and boost productivity. That's a revolution, and it's certainly part of the solution.

Workers are justified in viewing AI as a potential threat to livelihoods. We don't know with any precision the magnitude and timing of the impacts, but we do know this is no time for complacency. As with early digital technologies, we will see a combination of automation and augmentation. If you automate certain job tasks with digital technology, then after the fact, it looks like the people are more productive working with digital assistants, which sounds like a reasonable description of augmentation. Some jobs may experience automation of enough tasks that define the job that the job effectively disappears, but such cases are likely to be exceptions.

Could the productivity surge be so large that we need fewer people to meet demand in various sectors? While this, too, is possible, it takes time for increased productivity to translate into higher incomes and demand. But when demand catches up, there is no reason to expect that labour and human capital requirements will be unchanged across sectors of the economy. A complex and uncomfortable transition seems likely, much like the digital technology transition we have been in for a couple of decades. The AI revolution is more of the same but with a wider economic footprint, especially in the knowledge economy and white-collar parts of the world of work. A continuing process of skills adjustment and new skills acquisition will be part of the transition. And, of course, there will be winners and losers.

There are answers out there to our productivity challenges. But artificial intelligence won't automatically bring huge productivity increases forward into the present.

ChatGPT and the large language model that underpins it

are a stunning advance in the knowledge side of the economy, with implications that are only beginning to be explored. Given the startling pace of innovation in AI, there is every reason to believe the scope for productivity-enhancing digital technologies could expand further beyond the boundaries of the knowledge layer. But for now, the rapid advances have by far their greater impact in the knowledge side.

As a historical note, it is of some interest to contrast present trends with the technology breakthroughs in the successive waves of the industrial revolution. Mechanisation brought huge increases in productivity in the physical part of the economy – those are our atoms at work. By contrast, in the industrial revolution, some two centuries before the digital era, there was almost no machine augmentation in the knowledge layer. Labour in factories, construction and transportation worked with new powerful machines. Accountants kept the books with paper and quills until the fountain pen rendered the quill obsolete. Banks and indeed the entire financial system continued to be largely free of any sign of machine augmentation.

The digital age is different. To be sure, an entire set of activities associated with information, knowledge, decisions and transactions has been transformed by digital technology and now prospectively by waves of advances in AI. The digital footprint in the worlds of manufacturing, logistics and the delivery of in-person services is not zero – and has the potential to expand further. But it will take advances in technology to get there.

So, what will it take for the non-tradable part of the economy to begin to realise productivity gains? What will it take for every school, hospital or company to have cutting-edge AI technology deployed?

There are three forces to contend with and overcome.

One is inertia, or the lack thereof — a feature found in individual and organisational behaviour that leads to under-experimentation. How many times at work have you heard the IT team say 'we'll look at it tomorrow' only for the software glitch to persist for weeks? The pandemic overcame inertia issues by necessity. With businesses going digital, if only for a period, the 'tomorrow' mentality was subject to summary execution. Delivering broad-based and inclusive productivity means businesses, especially those in the non-tradable part of the economy, need to overcome a kind of organisational conservatism and resistance to change. Even institutions under threat from competitors adapt too slowly. When you're running a company that has been around for a century, or a university that has been around for five hundred years, it's easy to fall into the 'this is how we've always done it' trap.

Part of the inertia challenge can be explained by questions concerning how to regulate this new technology. The regulation of data, privacy, security and control has been an important challenge for digital technology generally, and that challenge extends to the ever-expanding AI frontier. The arrival of these new powerful generative models should be met with swift and appropriate regulation, and every major economy is looking at AI regulations through the lens of national security, democracy and geopolitical concerns.[6] Generative AI can be used to produce messaging and text, video and images at a scale previously unheard of, and all are able to influence views in a political and social context. Here, deliberate, manufactured hallucinations are a serious concern.

A second obstacle we must surmount, and one that has justifiably received much attention, is skills training – or upskilling. The rate of penetration of productivity-enhancing technology can be impeded by skills deficits, and companies should be leading the charge with upskilling and reskilling programmes.

But these can only go so far – Google's scope for upskilling is different from global construction firm Bechtel's. While the rise of artificial intelligence tools like ChatGPT has the potential to enhance productivity, we have to be circumspect. As discussed, such advancements are good news for the 50–60 per cent of people who work in the knowledge economy. But what about the remaining working population in the physical world – in factories and on assembly lines – where ChatGPT alone won't help and they need robotic assistance to boost productivity? These physical tools for the physical world have not been as fully developed as large language models like ChatGPT, so while the knowledge economy reaps the productivity rewards, a productivity lag in lower-paying physical sectors such as construction may increase income inequality.

This work becomes even more important when, as currently is the case, skill mismatches are increasing and migration is becoming more difficult. In 2021, a Gallup survey commissioned by Amazon engaged more than 15,000 Americans and found that 48 per cent of those surveyed were 'extremely' or 'very' likely to switch jobs if a new employer offered skills training.[7] And that's in America where unemployment is low, wages are high – one of the drivers of inflation – and a social safety net, while with too many big holes, is in place. Think about what will happen if generations of workers in call centres across India or the Philippines are out of work due to the continued rise of artificial intelligence-led customer service.

And third, we need the breakthroughs to keep coming, especially in artificial intelligence. For robotics and artificial intelligence tools to reach the non-tradable sector, they need to get much better. ChatGPT and the growing list of competitors will have to expand their scope of services and do a better job of getting answers correct. Alphabet, the parent company of

Google, got a glimpse of this when a test run of its ChatGPT competitor, Bard, botched a question in a demo, which led investors to punish the company with a $100 billion wipeout in its market capitalisation. And robots will have to shift from tools anchored to assembly lines to resources that can move with human beings across sectors, but that will require addressing the situational awareness issue.

Why is this important? Up to this point, we have tried to make the case that the global economy has shifted to a new pattern of lower growth and declining productivity with a long and growing list of supply-side constraints. The short-run impacts include inflation, lower growth and an altered framework and set of options for macroeconomic management. But in our side mirror, we see transformative technologies developing that can blunt the impact of this new normal.

Taking these steps will go a long way towards restoring growth. And it will do a lot more than that. Productivity strides through technology can help to ease the global labour shortage, counter the impacts of ageing, move more people into the workforce, or help one person do the job of two during a 9–5 day. Productivity strides will address issues of equality helping to connect lower-income countries into the global economy, and in the process lifting people out of poverty. And productivity strides will make our energy transition and sustainability goals more achievable.

If structural, employment and productivity trends in the US persist, which tracks with global trends, they will almost certainly produce a continuation of high and even rising income inequality. The current pattern that includes digitally enabled rising productivity in the knowledge economy and manufacturing, which account for a third of the economy and 20 per cent of employment, alongside low productivity and low productivity growth for most of the remaining 80 per cent, is a prescription for having a dual economy marked by the have-nots and the have-a-lots.

The best chance to reverse this pattern is the expansion of the digital footprint in the economy to a much wider set of sectors. And we need to be smart about how we expand that digital footprint.

Augmentation, Not Full Automation

If you travelled during the summer of 2022, chances are your airport experience was chaotic. As travel demand surged – what many called a 'revenge travel' boom – airports and airlines struggled to keep up. Staff shortages in all categories were a major contributing factor. Chaos reigned: endless lines at security and border checkpoints, cancelled and missed flights, scores of lost bags.

At Amsterdam Schiphol Airport, security lines were so long they exited the terminal and temporary tents had to be set up with some people waiting more than six hours before they had the privilege of taking their shoes off and walking through a metal detector. The situation got so bad that KLM banned checked bags on connections through Schiphol.[8] Over at London's Heathrow Airport, things weren't much better with British Airways banning short-haul ticket sales to reduce congestion before the airport authority itself told airlines to cut their schedules.[9] And if you were looking to clear customs in the US, lines were so bad planes were held at gates with passengers onboard because arrival facilities could not physically accommodate the sheer volume of travellers.

So, who do we blame for this mess? The guilty party is

reactive, as opposed to proactive, management. In other words, laziness.

Even a blind squirrel could see a summer 2022 demand surge coming. And yet airport authorities, which had reduced their ranks as passenger volumes fell during the height of Covid, failed to rehire. They could also have more fully embraced image and facial recognition software, which is sufficiently advanced to be deployed in the screening of luggage and border security checks. These technologies don't eliminate the need for trained personnel who have to go through an often-lengthy security clearance process; but what they can do is increase throughput and quality.

Watching the contents of suitcases go by is boring. Lapses in concentration are likely, which means you don't get your bag, or worse, prohibited items from guns to batteries slip through. With an AI-powered assistant armed with image recognition capabilities – an assistant that doesn't suffer from boredom or fatigue – the results could be better with luggage arriving faster with a lower loss rate. And if AIs can do a reasonable job of recognising various types of lung or skin cancer in images – and they can – then they can certainly help identify problematic content in luggage.

This is not science fiction. Mike entered the airport in Toronto with a large crowd late one night, and if they'd each had to stand in front of a border officer who stared at their pass-ports and faces they would have been there for hours. Instead, a large number of machines scanned passenger passports and faces, confirmed their identity, checked with a central database for any warning flags, and produced a small piece of paper that confirmed the check was complete. Later, this paper was handed to a security officer simply as a way of ensuring the digi-tal check had been completed. Mohamed, who often transited through Newark Airport, neither had to insert his passport nor gather a piece of paper. Facial recognition cleared him and alerted the security officer.

Mike also went through Frankfurt Airport twice in the same period. In contrast, on both occasions there were endless lines at immigration caused by the presence of only one or two officers checking everyone without the benefit of any level of automation or digital support. With a passport full of stamps, further delays are caused by a search of the stamps.

Our point is not to compare Toronto and Frankfurt. In fact, Toronto also experienced significant blockages at check-in along with flight delays and cancellations. Rather, this example illustrates the usage of technology to augment capabilities, signalling a proactive approach to operational management – an approach where significant productivity improvements are possible, even in the absence of competitive pressure. Well, partial absence. If disruptions persist, experienced fliers won't take long to route themselves through airports that have a reputation for efficiency, and the best-managed transportation and airport authorities understand this and will benefit.

The keys to this kind of progress are incentives, management, talent acquisition and openness to potentially useful technological tools. These are the general inputs. There is no one-sentence solution to restoring productivity growth. It is the mindset that matters – the curiosity to search for better answers and better ways of doing things.

Only So Far

Towards the end of the drafting process for the Commission on Growth and Development report, one of the Commission members pointed out to Mike the report was boring because it focused on what should happen. Too often, reports that take years to produce are dismissed in a matter of minutes – often for reasons as simple as readability. So, Mike and his fellow commissioners had an idea. Rather than narrowly focusing on what you're supposed to do to deliver growth, they included a brief section on bad ideas.

Poor banking regulation, underpaying civil servants, measuring educational progress through new buildings, banning exports, imposing price controls – all of these actions, and others, were listed as 'bad ideas'.[10] And after the report was published, by far the most feedback Mike received was a bunch of gleeful emails on the bad ideas: 'I checked, our government is doing twelve of them.' 'We're guilty of six.' 'Our economic model is a carbon copy of the bad ideas list.'

Governments have tried every imaginable approach to delivering growth. And we know what works. A good first step begins with tackling lagging productivity, making smart investments and using technology responsibly.

But such actions alone are not enough to fix a world out of order. We also need better economic management and new approaches to co-operation in the global order. Without macro stability, we can forget about the growth agenda.

The stakes are high. If we don't get growth right, inequality will grow. If we don't get growth right, the world's poorest countries will fail to thrive. If we don't get growth right, unproductive industries will shrink leaving scores of people unemployed. And if we don't get growth right, we won't get the solutions to the climate change crisis right. More than any single metric, that is why growth, and hence productivity, are so important.

SECTION TWO

ECONOMIC MANAGEMENT

6

HOW QUICKLY THE
WORLD CAN CHANGE

Little Fires Spread

'Am I,' I ask, 'talking to the world's first trillionaire?'[1] That's one of many memorable lines from a 14,000-word profile that Californian venture capital company Sequoia Capital published in September 2022 on FTX's founder and then-CEO, Sam Bankman-Fried. When Sequoia posted the story, FTX was a seemingly thriving cryptocurrency exchange with Bankman-Fried, or SBF as he became known, worth an estimated $26 billion.[2] Less than two months later, he lost most of his fortune.

FTX's collapse, and with it SBF's fortune, will no doubt be the topic of many business school case studies for years to come. Whether it was ultra-loose monetary policy, stimulus checks, increased adoption of various coins, or idle and curious minds considering new investment possibilities during the pandemic, cryptocurrencies witnessed a historic surge in late 2020 and throughout much of 2021. And by November 2021, the cryptocurrency ecosystem that barely existed a decade earlier was worth more than $3 trillion – greater than the market capitalisations of Apple, Microsoft, Amazon, Chevron and other highly profitable companies.[3] It didn't seem to matter that much of the public couldn't explain what they were investing in. FOMO, the fear of missing out, had taken over.

It has been said that during a gold rush, don't dig for gold – sell shovels. FTX made a market in selling shovels, in this case through trading and storing cryptocurrency. Investors of all stripes, from institutions to retail investors, picked which cryptocurrencies to invest in, and FTX was one of a handful of firms that would process trades and store investors' crypto portfolios.

But SBF had an even bigger vision for FTX. As he explained to Sequoia partners during a pitch, 'I want FTX to be a place where you can do anything you want with your next dollar. You can buy bitcoin. You can send money in whatever currency to any friend anywhere in the world. You can buy a banana.'[4] He made that pitch over Zoom while playing *League of Legends*, and Sequoia ultimately invested. With this and other cash injections, FTX sponsored racing cars, ran a Super Bowl commercial and took over the naming rights of a Miami stadium – FTX Arena.

With time, all excesses come to an end or, as the American economist Herbert Stein famously wrote, 'If something cannot go on forever, it will stop.'[5] Rising interest rates from the Federal Reserve, rolled out late and initially timid but then massively increased, began to dry up liquidity and fuel a risk-off environment for speculative assets like cryptocurrencies before pulling the rug from under several other sectors including commercial real estate and certain banks with unstable and fluid balance sheets.

Slowly the crypto ice cube began to melt with buyers exhausted and sellers looking to lock in profits. In an unregulated, Wild West crypto gold rush, some segments of this market quickly broke down. Coins collapsed. Three Arrows

Capital, Celsius and Voyager filed for bankruptcy. And crypto's market cap fell from more than $3 trillion to less than $1 trillion. As suddenly and quickly as it seemed to rain down, money now evaporated.

Enter SBF who pledged $1 billion to rescue failing crypto firms, either buying them outright or propping them up with loans and investments made through FTX or his crypto trading firm, Alameda Research.[6] All told, these bailouts paired with bets made during better times led FTX to have 500 investments across ten holding companies valued at more than $5.4 billion.[7]

The bailout of the crypto ecosystem led to comparisons being drawn between SBF and JP Morgan who, during the Panic of 1907, famously lent funds to prevent the country from entering a financial crisis. But there were key differences. Morgan's bailout directed real money towards real companies with real earnings, such as the takeover of the Tennessee Coal, Iron and Railroad Company by Morgan-owned US Steel. SBF's bailout was of highly speculative assets often without profits or even revenues – an ecosystem built around what JPMorgan Chase CEO Jamie Dimon called 'pet rocks'.[8] And while Morgan had a well-developed risk management system, SBF relied on good fortune and some rather dubious practices and procedures.

By November 2022, the crypto carnage reached FTX. There was a run on FTX's own token, FTT. Complicating matters was Alameda Research, which was a major FTT shareholder. A $6 billion surge in FTT withdrawal requests created a liquidity crisis with neither FTX nor Alameda possessing the capital to fulfil withdrawals.[9] Interest from rival firm Binance to bailout FTX, only to then back away after seeing the company's financials, led to a further collapse in prices and the equivalent of a bank run. Within days, FTX and Alameda Research had filed for bankruptcy, client accounts were frozen and SBF was out as CEO. In the ruins were likely more than a million creditors waiting to be made whole, not to mention unaccounted funds raising questions of criminal activity.[10]

The episode recalls the lessons surrounding the stock market crash that ushered in the Great Depression. In his famous history of the economic disaster, John Kenneth Galbraith wrote: 'Men have been swindled by other men on many occasions. The autumn of 1929 was, perhaps, the first occasion when men succeeded on a large scale in swindling themselves.'[11] The lessons of a century earlier were not heeded. One can believe in blockchain technology and a decentralised Web3 while also exercising reasonable financial risk, but with FTX it wasn't a case of too big to fail – but too worthless, and perhaps too corrupt, to succeed. They swindled themselves.

As quickly as the collapse happened, history is already being rewritten with Sequoia's SBF profile no longer on their webpage. And for a time, Washington seemed to move towards crypto regulation. FTX is, in the grand scheme of things, a little fire. But the risk is that little fires spread and become something bigger, and domestic economic management is unable to respond.

The same kind of dangerous risk-taking we saw at FTX appears in other places – in certain exchange-traded funds, in segments of high-yield markets, and in areas of private equity and commercial real estate. Silicon Valley Bank saw $42 billion of deposits fly out in just one day, a shock it could not handle leading to its rapid demise. First Republic lost $100 billion of deposits over two months, turning a once highly envied bank that prided itself on industry-beating client service and best of breed customers into a fire sale that JPMorgan snapped up at a twentieth of its value just three months earlier. And both banks have now gone down in history as part of the hollowing out of regional banks that play important roles in local communities.

Are these shocks canaries in the coal mine indicating broader, deeper structural fragilities that can haunt the economy? We can wait to find out, or we can take action now to prevent future financial and economic fires becoming global firestorms.

Economic Management Challenges

The prior section in this book set out the importance of rethinking growth models, and doing so in a way that looks at tomorrow rather than just reapplying yesterday's thinking. This is a vital, necessary first step before individual measures can be rolled out to underpin prosperity with low inflation, financial stability and sound banking.

Better economic policymaking is only one piece of the puzzle needed to escape a permacrisis. Without revamped and effective growth models, economics will continue to disappoint and frustrate not just society's genuine aspiration for a better life for ours and future generations, but also the political system. The rich will get richer, the middle class will be hollowed out, and the vulnerable segments of our society will get even more so. Meanwhile, and as vividly illustrated by developments in a wide range of countries – not just very fragile developing countries but also more advanced ones – politics will impose itself even more assertively on economics and oversteer it. In the process, policymaking will continue to drift further away from the world of 'first best', with every action involving a broader range of collateral damage and unintended consequences.

It's unrealistic to ever expect perfect policymaking, and we certainly haven't been anywhere close to perfection overall with how economies are managed. Over the last fifteen years, there have been distinct highs and many more lows. The principal achievement has been successful crisis management, or the repeated ability to avoid major economic collapses whose effects would have been felt by both current and future generations. There's been pain, but it has been managed.

The high risk of multi-year depressions triggered by shocks such as Covid and the Global Financial Crisis has – for the most part – been short lived. That was not preordained but rather the product of courageous, and also at times lucky, national economic management. These successes in crisis management, where economies avoided falling off the precipice, are even more commendable given the otherwise ongoing failure to generate economic growth that is high, inclusive and respectful of the limits of our planet.

Instead of a bold shift to something different, policymakers have opted to continuously tinker with increasingly exhausted approaches. When we write of a permacrisis, we mean that unless an overhaul is put in place that extends to outdated national economic management models, crises that are avoidable will occur and recur.

Central bankers have been notably slow to analyse and understand threats; recall the Federal Reserve's initial and protracted claims in 2021 that inflation would be 'transitory', or as put by Fed Chair Jerome Powell, a belief that 'it will not leave behind permanently – or very persistently higher – inflation'.[12] The Fed's analysis proved to be incorrect with inflation running much hotter and for much longer, thereby undermining both economic wellbeing and financial stability.

Instead of being the highly needed stabilising force, an increasingly less credible Fed became more of the opposite, not only in its late policy reactions but also in its communications. Findings from the Centre for Economic Policy Research, for example, show that 'Market volatility is three times higher during press conferences held by current Chair Jerome Powell than those held by his predecessors, and they tend to reverse the market's initial reactions to the Committee statements.'[13] If, in reaction to the official Fed policy statement, the market is up in advance of comments from Chair Powell, chances are it'll be down after he speaks; and vice versa. That has especially been the case when the Chair has ventured away from the written responses prepared for him, sometimes also either confusing or negating the main messages of the statement from the Committee as a whole – a phenomenon that has been illustrated by the meeting minutes released a few weeks later.

Forward policy guidance, once a powerful tool of Fed central banking, lost its potency. As an example, for the first half of 2023, markets were actively betting against it. Rather than price in the Fed's repeated assertions that it will not cut interest rates in 2023, the markets were positioned for cuts starting as early as the end of the summer. At the time of writing in mid-2023, they had priced a Fed policy rate almost a full percentage point below where Fed Chair Powell had repeatedly signalled it would be by the end of the year.

Mohamed had never seen, over his many decades of market experience, such a divergence between market pricing and Fed forward policy guidance. One, and perhaps even both, would be proven wrong in the months to follow. You would think that the markets would converge swiftly on what the Fed was guiding given that the central bank sets balance rates. Yet this was not happening quickly enough as markets doubted the credibility of the Fed's analysis and forecasts. With that, either more market volatility would result, risking adverse spillovers to the economy, the Fed would lose more of its already eroded credibility, or both.

Lapses have come not just from monetary policy – meant

to deliver price stability, maximum employment and financial stability – but also from fiscal policy, taxation and spending of various branches of government. Consider the mini-budget the short-lived UK Prime Minister Liz Truss released in 2022 that caused a brief yet historically disruptive collapse in the British pound, a surge in borrowing costs and a meltdown scare in the pension system. We were all reminded of the old economics saying that macroeconomic stability is not everything, but without it you have very little.

Implementation has always been a challenge, but with a shift from economics driving policymaking to politics increasingly exerting its influence over economic logic, actions can be halting, frenetic and inconsistent. The Federal Reserve was quick to dismiss the need for a series of rapid interest rate hikes, let alone anything in the neighbourhood of 75 basis points, only to be later forced to do just that – and not just once. Instead, the Fed raised rates by 75 points at four consecutive meetings in 2022 – a record. The Fed was so behind the curve that even in the wake of Silicon Valley Bank's collapse and the subsequent regional/community banking turmoil, inflation was still running hot and they had to twice raise rates by another quarter point.

And inflation, a truly global phenomenon, was being addressed on a country-by-country basis with no co-ordinated plans emerging from any global bodies. This is a global problem without even an attempt at a global solution. And layered on top of these failures, there's inconsistent communication from central bankers and insufficient attention to behavioural shifts in markets – in the risk appetites, habits and reactions of consumers and businesses.

Taken together, we see too many sins of poor analysis, design, implementation, communication, supervision, regulation and co-ordination in economic management. Addressing these stumbling blocks is the only way to better navigate an increasingly shock-prone future. After all, the first rule for policymaking to get out of a hole that has been mostly of its own making is, well, to stop digging.

The stakes are high given the central role that the Fed plays at the core of the global financial system due to the dollar's present reserve currency status, the extent to which other countries outsource the management of their savings to the American financial system, and the influential – and often deterministic – role the Fed plays in key multilateral institutions such as the International Monetary Fund and World Bank. The more US policymaking credibility erodes, the higher temptation will be for countries to circumvent America in financial transactions, the greater the efforts will be to rewire international trade and payments, and the deeper the fragmentation of the international economic and financial order.

But it's not all bad and ugly. On three occasions in the last fifteen years, the systemically important regions of the world economy faced major crises that could have easily tipped the globe into catastrophic depressions. And on all three occasions, economic and financial crisis management responded in such a way as to avoid multigenerational destruction. It is what came before and what came after that have repeatedly let us all down – frustratingly, and we would argue, unnecessarily so.

7

THE GOOD OF ECONOMIC MANAGEMENT

Averting a Depression in the Global Financial Crisis

'Please go to the ATM and withdraw as much as the daily limit allows.' It was 2008, the markets were in freefall. Banks were tipping over. Mohamed, at work again that evening with his colleagues at PIMCO, the investment management firm, called his wife and asked her to withdraw $500, the maximum cash allowable at the ATM. When asked why, he responded that he wasn't sure banks would remain open. A 'bank holiday' was not out of the question, a possibility that was confirmed years later in memoirs by policymakers of the time.

In 2008, a deep crisis of the payments and settlement system erupted in the United States and threatened a global financial meltdown whose economic spillovers would have included, in all likelihood, monumental bankruptcies, distressing long-term unemployment and the annihilation of retire-ment savings, pensions and home ownership. This became known as the Global Financial Crisis, which ultimately gave way to a Great Recession and, in the UK, biting austerity measures that cut billions from public services. The onset of the crisis was so brutal, and the effects so widespread, that even basic cash and collateral management operations became problematic.

This was the equivalent of an oil malfunction in our cars. Without it lubricating all those small but mighty gears, the car will struggle – even if it has a powerful engine. There's no engine more powerful than the US economy, and with the oil light flashing, the engine began to sputter. With fewer and fewer banks trusting each other, and less overall trust in the banking system, every transaction became an adventure, a negotiation and a considerable risk.

The damage was real. The housing sector collapsed. Banks were bailed out to avoid a domino effect that would bring down the entire economy. US gross domestic product fell 4.3 per cent, the deepest recession since the Second World War took hold, while unemployment doubled from 5 per cent to 10 per cent.[1] But the outcome could have been far worse.

The immediate cause was, of course, the disorderly collapse of the American investment bank Lehman Brothers. Its final act was just one illustration of a financial system – and, in particular, banks – that had gotten drunk on leverage, credit and excessive risk-taking. At the time of Lehman's failure, its debt-to-equity ratio, a measure of a company's debt to shareholder equity, was close to 30:1.[2] That's $30 of debt for every $1 held. With leverage ratios like those, even a small drop in value of the firm's assets or investments will lead to enormous pressure. And that's what happened, and worse.

Lehman didn't exist in a vacuum. It and other distressed banks were part of a broader, highly integrated and interconnected global economy. So as these institutions started to suffer the consequences of their massive individual and collective irresponsibility, the payments and settlement system experienced major cracks, putting in doubt the ability of households and companies to undertake even the simplest transactions.

With the US coming very close to a financial collapse, unprecedented action was quickly taken to bail out banks that were deemed too large to fail. In the end, the Troubled Assets Relief Program (TARP) authorised and deployed hundreds of billions of dollars to stabilise troubled institutions, and the financial system as a whole. Recapitalising banks was what was needed most, and the Federal Reserve flooded the system with liquidity. But while the US was initiating this major crisis management response, the rest of the world found it almost impossible to do even the simplest of cross-border financial operations. Global trade crumbled 15 per cent, and global growth was quick to follow.[3] Confidence evaporated. Savings and wealth that took years to accumulate seemed to be on the brink of a sudden wipeout. Growth and employment collapsed around the world.

The resulting Great Recession was one of the deepest experienced in many decades. Yet as harmful as it was, and it was very painful especially for the more vulnerable segments of the population, it pales in comparison to what the world would have experienced had the authorities in several countries not embarked on historic rescue operations in April 2009.

As Prime Minister, Gordon met with President George W. Bush at the White House in September 2008. The Global Financial Crisis was in full swing, and a co-ordinated global response had yet to emerge. Gordon asked President Bush to back his initiative for a G20 bringing together the world's largest economies to forge a co-ordinated action plan. Bush memorably said that 'Hank Paulson is the only one who can make that decision, and he's very tired at the moment dealing with the roll-out of TARP.' To which Gordon replied, 'He's been very busy doing the wrong thing because TARP won't solve your problem.' Sure, bank rescue packages could stop the panic, but recapitalisation was needed and essential. The real battle – saving the global economy – demanded deeper action.

Gordon got his wish, and everything changed at the London G20 Summit. The global economy had been skidding for months, and while the US had managed to slow the slide towards catastrophe through national action, any meaningful recovery demanded co-operation. To hear Gordon tell it, his decade as Chancellor of the Exchequer before assuming the role of Prime Minister had prepared him to not just bring global leaders to the table, but to reach an agreement. Early on in the G20 meeting, French President Nicolas Sarkozy frustratingly questioned the ability to make a deal if 'we have no plan'. To which US President Obama replied, 'Gordon has a plan.'

The plan was simple, yet effective. The G20 leaders agreed to inject $1.1 trillion into the global economy to ensure orderly market functioning, sufficient liquidity, to restore confidence and backstop economic activity. The co-ordinated action would result in a much better outcome than unco-ordinated measures coming from individual countries. And this unprecedented policy co-operation was made more effective by central banks' willingness to also flood financial markets with cash.

The restoration of normal functioning to markets depended on much more than averting a global depression. The 'technicals' also had to be fixed. One of the simple ways of illustrating how such technicals work is to consider that, for quite a few market segments, there are two types of investors: residents and tourists. When the going gets tough, tourists head for the airport, causing disruption and at times panic. But residents stay and use periods of distress to retrench, refocus and react.

The promise made by global leaders to invest unprecedented

sums in the economy and markets signalled a bigger and more influential long-term resident in town prepared to backstop markets, calm other residents and slowly attract back the tourists. And this historic 'coming together of the world' was enough to not only stop the global economic slide, but also provide the basis for the global recovery that followed.[4]

It wasn't just the promise of $1.1 trillion that restored confidence. It was just as much the global determination to co-operate and seek out a solution. Strong, assertive domestic policy management was necessary but not sufficient. What was needed was the world's economic powers coming together. And they came together in a way that had not been seen for a long time – and has not been seen since.

Handling the Eurozone Crisis

The world had barely caught its breath from the Global Financial Crisis when the Eurozone Crisis erupted.

A similarly dramatic rescue, this time of countries and their banks in the Eurozone, was launched by the region's central bank – the European Central Bank (ECB) – just four years after the Global Financial Crisis market turmoil. In July 2012, ECB President Mario Draghi boldly asserted that the central bank he presided over was 'ready to do whatever it takes to preserve the euro. And believe me, it will be enough.'[5] Words have weight. And these words restored trust and brought confidence to markets. And once again, Europe was saved from a damaging multi-year depression whose spillovers would have undermined global growth and prosperity. But Draghi's announcement didn't happen overnight. It was a pledge built on decades of work.

On the eve of Draghi's call to action, the Eurozone had gotten close to dramatic economic, financial and social meltdown. What was at stake was much more than economic growth, financial viability, savings, pensions, retirement plans and the currency regime. At stake was the integration and interdependence of the region – a construct enshrined in the first line of the Treaty of Rome which birthed the European Economic Community pledging all members to 'lay the foundations of an ever-closer union among the peoples of Europe'.[6] The Eurozone Crisis threatened to burn down more than half a century of integration. Decades of work to create economic, financial, institutional, political and social co-operation were now on the verge of total collapse.

It was a time of great market and social turmoil. 'Peripheral' Eurozone economies such as Portugal, Italy, Greece and Spain were in the initial stages of a dramatic economic and financial implosion that was set to accelerate. The derogatory term 'PIGS' was coined referring to these countries hit hardest by the Eurozone Crisis – a pejorative that indicated a fracturing in regional cohesion between a wealthier and more stable northern Europe and a struggling southern half needing rescue. The very existence of the euro as a regional single currency was in play and, with it, all the economic and social linkages that had been developed through years of hard and systematic work.

So, with Europe on the brink, another conference was taking place in London – once again organised by the British government. Mohamed was in the room when President Draghi made his dramatic 'whatever it takes' pronouncement. For Mohamed and others present, it was not immediately clear the extent of the exceptional, unprecedented firepower that would be promised by the Eurozone's central bank to stabilise markets. The commitment, even on the eve of Draghi's announcement with all the market turmoil, would have been deemed highly unlikely if not unthinkable just a few days earlier. Indeed, as it came out later, even Draghi's colleagues on the ECB's Governing Council were unaware of the public commitment that he was about to make. Some would have opposed it while others, more open to such a bold commitment, would have doubted that the ECB had the ability, including the legal space, to deliver on it.

By setting out the facts and then quickly following up with bold operational announcements, President Draghi signalled a seemingly infinite willingness to use the ECB's apparently bottomless balance sheet on that occasion to absorb all the unwanted risk sloshing about in the financial system. And it worked – so well, in fact, that the markets looked past the obvious limitations governing a 'whatever it takes' claim. As a result, the ECB never had to use much of its balance sheet. A comforted and inherently risk-taking private sector did the Bank's bidding for it.

Despite the self-correcting role that the markets played, the amount of rescue financing that was deployed by central banks in the Global Financial and Eurozone Crises had never been seen before. Between the end of 2007 and 2012, the Federal Reserve's balance sheet grew from close to $1 trillion to $3 trillion[7] while that of the ECB expanded from $1.5 trillion to $3 trillion.[8] With some of this exposure backed by governments, sovereign debt also rose as did that of other segments of the economy. Yet few, if any, envisaged that these seemingly large numbers would pale in comparison to what would transpire a few years later.

What were once thought of as 'temporary, timely and targeted' emergency interventions proved impossible to unwind. Central banks, in particular, were slipping into what economists call path dependency and multiple equilibria – that is, an expansion of the balance sheet as banks flooded the system with liquidity was making another expansion more likely. In the case of the ECB, policy rates were taken negative – an outcome not covered in any economics or financial textbook at the time.

Markets became even more conditioned to believe central banks will always be their BFFs – best friends forever, always ready to protect markets from losses, even from unsettling volatility. The conditioning was reinforced by the subsequent tripling in the size of the Federal Reserve's balance sheet to an eye-popping $9 trillion as central banks themselves became hostage to the process. But as high inflation erupted in 2021 and persisted for the whole of 2022, even this strange codependency friendship hit its limits. After hesitating way too long, central banks were forced into aggressive interest rate hikes and started contracting their balance sheets, albeit timidly. But before that came the Covid crisis.

Dealing with the Covid Crisis

As large and as consequential as the Global Financial Crisis and Eurozone rescue operations were, they were overshadowed by the response to the economic 'sudden stop' caused by Covid in 2020.

The markets were in freefall. On 11 March 2020, the Dow Jones Industrial Average crashed 10 per cent – 2,352.60 points lower – in its worst day since 1987.[9] Five days later, the Dow collapsed another 13 per cent in its biggest-ever point drop – 2,997.10.[10] Pershing Square Capital manager Bill Ackman went on CNBC and said 'hell is coming' and called on the government to 'shut it down now', referring to the economy.[11] The Dow closed down another 1,300 points.[12] Efforts by the Federal Reserve to stabilise the economy by slashing interest rates to zero did little. Markets wanted a lot more cash.

As reported by the *Wall Street Journal*, Fed Chair Jerome Powell looked to history for a mantra for present circumstances. 'Get in the boats and go' from the British Dunkirk evacuations during the Second World War seemed fitting.[13] Powell would later reflect, 'We have a four- or five-day chance to really get our act together and get ahead of this. We're gonna try to get ahead of this. And we were going to do that by just announcing a ton of stuff on Monday morning.'[14]

By that Monday, the Federal Reserve had announced a resumption of its quantitative easing programme buying debt and securities. The pledge was historic in nature with the Fed vowing to use its 'full range of tools' with an open-ended commitment to 'continue to purchase Treasury securities and agency mortgage-backed securities in the amounts needed to support smooth market functioning'.[15] The market had found a buyer with a limitless appetite, a printing press in the basement and little sensitivity to market pricing. And, as a result, the market bottomed that Monday and would go on to rise more than 101 per cent over the next two years.[16]

The next day, the United Kingdom's then Chancellor Rishi Sunak announced a £350 billion package of loans and grants to stabilise the economy pledging to do 'whatever it takes' to minimise the pandemic's economic impact.[17] The Eurozone announced a similar aid package, and countless countries took action to confront the crisis.

Around the world, the level of co-operation between government and central banks was unprecedented with billions of dollars transferred to companies and households to ensure both lives and livelihoods were saved. One of the leading criticisms of the Global Financial Crisis bailout in the US was that it helped the rich and did far too little to help those most impacted by the recession. With history in mind, Congress passed close to $5.9 trillion in spending for 2020 and 2021, compared with an inflation-adjusted $1.8 trillion between 2008–9.[18]

Imaginations were stretched once again, and once again

the previously unthinkable became reality with governments making outright cash transfers to households and companies to compensate for their loss of wages, salaries, revenues and profits. Even those who largely avoided economic pain, such as better-off white-collar workers who were able to shift to remote work, received money in their accounts. And this support continued well after the worst of the pandemic.[19]

All of this 'easy money' came at a cost – a price that started to be felt in 2021–2 with surging inflation and is likely to be consequential in several other ways as well, including financial instability.

The Fed's balance sheet had moved ever higher to a 2022 peak of close to \$9 trillion[20] and the ECB's to more than \$8 trillion.[21] These increases are hardly surprising given that central banks flooded the system with money for more than a decade, well beyond what was strictly needed to counter market dysfunction, the freezing of credit, eye-popping borrowing costs and then a pandemic. With that excess liquidity also came collateral damage and unintended consequences – a financial sector that increasingly captured and steered monetary policy – something that Mohamed had warned about in his 2016 book on protracted central bank interventions.[22]

To be clear, central banks and governments had to take swift action to blunt the impacts of the Covid crisis, and that action is worthy of praise. There was thoughtful analysis on how to address the crisis, careful design of relief programmes, fast implementation and historic levels of co-ordination. But the speed with which central banks like the Fed moved to provide relief at the start of the crisis was not matched with the courage and wisdom to stop the liquidity injections when the crisis had subsided, or the agility to address the subsequent inflationary pressures. Just like in the Global Financial Crisis, policymakers found it easy to throw the money crack pipe at the markets, to draw on Andrew Ross Sorkin's striking analogy, but were once again reluctant to wean the markets off the easy money drug.[23]

Avoiding a global depression also came at the cost of distorting even more economies' resource allocation and financial behaviour. The market interventions that took place during Covid led to the unintended weakening of the structural resilience of the financial system. It worsened moral hazard, conditioning markets to believe that bailouts were automatic. It accelerated the migration of financial risk and excessive risk-taking from the large and highly regulated banking system to poorly supervised and analysed non-banks. It encouraged those non-banks to stretch ever wider for returns, including in poorly understood and illiquid segments of the markets. It helped balloon the balance sheets of some banks ill-equipped to deal with increased size. It supported zombie companies. It set the ground for an inflation problem that would erode central bank credibility, future policy effectiveness, and unquestioned political operational autonomy of key institutions. It also turned the classic dilemma of inflation-fighting – that is, the tradeoff between lowering inflation and maintaining economic growth – into a trilemma. Increasingly, the Fed would struggle to simultaneously lower inflation, avoid damage to growth and maintain banking and financial stability. And all this put off an important conversation leaders needed to have about both crisis prevention and putting in place the genuine conditions for high, inclusive and sustainable growth.

So even the good economic management responses were not purely good – they were incomplete. And if the good is just okay, then looking to the bad and the ugly we see far worse outcomes.

8

THE BAD AND THE UGLY OF ECONOMIC MANAGEMENT

From Confetti to Acid Rain

When the confetti decade of ultra-low interest rates and easy money yielded to the acid rain of high inflation and forced interest rate hikes, financial accidents followed. And accidents happen fast.

It took less than 48 hours for the 16th largest bank in the US, holding more than $200 billion in assets, to collapse in what became the second largest bank failure in the country's history, only to be surpassed soon after by First Republic Bank's failure. The failure of Silicon Valley Bank (SVB) is a tale of avoidable incompetence – by bank executives and policymakers, particularly the Fed as it painfully acknowledged in its own review.[1]

Over the years, SVB had grown into a respected financial institution carving out a lucrative niche as the go-to lender for startups and the high-net-worth individuals behind them. And like the startups they bankrolled, SVB thrived in a low inflation, floored interest rate world flush with money. But that world abruptly drew to a close in 2022 as the Federal Reserve attempted to course correct for their transitory inflation call by rapidly hiking interest rates.

The tech ecosystem felt the crunch as easy money stopped

flowing, and SVB's depositor base stopped growing. Ordinarily this wouldn't be a problem, but SVB was no ordinary bank. Its depositor base wasn't a cross-section of America as a whole, but rather a cross-section of tech-heavy Silicon Valley; some 95 per cent of these deposits exceeded the $250,000 ceiling for FDIC deposit insurance. It helps when a bank's depositor base is, for lack of a better word, sleepy and doesn't pay attention to day-to-day market gyrations, but in many respects SVB's clients *were* the market. And making matters worse, the bank held an unhealthy concentration in long-dated government and mortgage-backed securities subject to interest rate risk.

Bank balance sheets are split between assets, everything the bank holds from treasury bills to real estate, and liabilities which include consumer deposits. In recent years as deposits swelled, SVB took client money and stocked up on tens of billions of dollars in treasuries and mortgage-backed security bonds. When interest rates – and in turn yields – go up, bond prices fall. If these are short duration bonds, the risk is minimal as scheduled principal repayments enable holders to move out of them fairly quickly. But SVB's bonds were long dated, meaning they matured in, say, ten years.

In part comforted by the Fed's repeated assertion that inflation was transitory, the bank didn't see coming the dramatic 2022–3 change in the interest rate and liquidity regimes. With each successive rate hike these assets were worth a fraction of what SVB paid. And with each rate hike, we went from a year with a historically high number of companies going public to a year with few companies going public. We went from unprofitable startups commanding rich valuations to them being devalued. Silicon Valley went from a world of confetti to acid rain.

Having grown big very fast, SVB didn't pay enough attention to the critical need of configuring the asset side of the balance sheet consistently with the size and nature of the liabilities. That's banking 101.

The bank's announcement they were raising funds by selling billions of dollars of long-dated bonds at a loss was all it took for a bank run. Indeed, the run on SVB happened so fast no one had a chance to establish whether their assets would be able to cover depositor liabilities. Word spread throughout the Valley that they were in financial distress. Venture capitalists like Peter Thiel told startups to pull funds. Slack channels were abuzz with gossip. A full-on bank run led the FDIC to take over SVB less than two days after the rumour mill began swirling. And many wondered how a bank that had grown so large under the nose of the Fed had managed to escape proper supervision.

But it didn't end there. At the same time, Signature Bank was shuttered by the FDIC. Community/regional banks, like First Republic, caught in the muddled middle – not small enough to be invisible niche players and not big and diversified enough to absorb the hit of rising yields – found themselves in the crosshairs with a surge in depositor withdrawals. Share prices collapsed and the concern of widespread financial contagion caused markets to panic. A pooling equilibrium ensued with the public lumping a growing number of other banks in with SVB. Soon PacWest would be pressured even though only 25 per cent of its deposits were uninsured. Their only sin seemed to be location, location, location – they just happened to live in what was now perceived to be a vulnerable banking neighbourhood.

Citing 'systemic risk', the US authorities vowed to make all of SVB's depositors whole – even those beyond the $250,000 FDIC insurance limit. European regulators described the move as 'total and utter incompetence'.[2] Some worried that, if depositors are infinitely insured, what's the incentive to place your hard-earned money with a responsible bank as opposed to a fly-by-night operation offering irresponsibly high interest rates? And if banks themselves saw their deposits as comfortably insured and stable, what would stop them from taking excessive risks in pursuit of high profits and handsome executive compensation?

Meanwhile in Europe, the winds of banking system instability toppled over Credit Suisse, Switzerland's second largest bank and one of the thirty global systemically important financial institutions, or G-SIFIs, in the world. Long troubled by internal management slippages and regulatory problems, Credit Suisse was too weak to withstand a sudden loss in confidence. In a hectic weekend of negotiations, the Swiss government and central banks convinced UBS to buy its main rival at a price well below the market valuation. Thomas Jordan, the Chair of the Swiss National Bank, told the *Financial Times* that the alternative of orderly shutting down the failing bank 'would have triggered [a] bigger financial crisis, not just in Switzerland but globally'.[3]

Anyone reading this book who remembers 2008, which should be most every reader at the time of publication, is probably going, 'Gordon, Mike and Mohamed – didn't we prepare for this?' We could have, and we should have, but ultimately we didn't.

For example, the stress test system where the Federal Reserve runs recurring scenarios on banks to see if they can remain solvent does not include rate hikes on safe assets kept in some parts of banks, the trigger at SVB, but instead focuses on high default rates on loans – the last crisis. And even then, Silicon Valley Bank was below the $250 billion in assets threshold for a stress test thanks to 2018 legislation out of Congress relaxing requirements for certain banks. Adding to embarrassment, the CEO of SVB sat on the board of the San Francisco Fed, the entity responsible for regulating SVB, up until the bank failed, raising questions of improper oversight. There were so many accountability and governance missteps, even the White House wanted to acknowledge central bank regulatory failures in the March 2023 joint statement by the Fed, the Treasury and the Federal Deposit Insurance Corporation. That *mea culpa* didn't happen as Fed Chair Powell successfully 'blocked efforts to include a phrase mentioning regulatory failures'.[4] What he could not block, however, were the loud calls for external reviews of lapses in Fed supervision and regulation.

Reacting to these upcoming reviews, the Fed moved first, issuing in late April a more than 100-page brutal report looking inwards, for once, and acknowledging its role in the banking turmoil and the need to 'strengthen the Federal Reserve's supervision and regulation'.[5] And what turmoil it was. By 1 May, less than two months after SVB's failure, three notable US banks holding a total of $532 billion in assets had failed – more than the inflation-adjusted $526 billion held by the 25 banks that failed in 2008.[6]

US bank failures in each year, adjusted for inflation

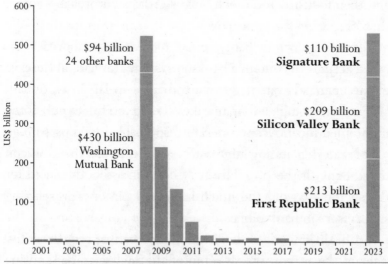

Source: Based on Karl Russell and Christine Zhang, '3 Failed Banks This Year Were Bigger Than 25 That Crumbled in 2008', New York Times, 1 May 2023

You see, this is what happens when you live in a volatile and accident-prone economic world. This is what happens when central bankers, in this case the Federal Reserve, wait too long to act and then, playing hectic catch-up, act too firmly for too long. This is what happens when the Fed conditions the system to expect either abundant liquidity or bailouts. And this is what happens when the Fed is confronted by a trilemma of its own making where it struggles to quell inflation, contain damage to growth and ensure financial stability. Not surprisingly, it risks failing at all three. And, once again, it is the most vulnerable – both at home and beyond – that are most at risk.

The Bad: Failing at Crisis Prevention

As admirable as the intentions of governments and central banks have been, the trauma and scars of intense crisis management have repeatedly failed to lessen the likelihood of future crises. As the Global Financial, Eurozone and Covid crises illustrate, the focus was crisis management – fighting the immediate fires and then focusing too much on yesterday's outbreaks – rather than preparing for tomorrow's.

Yes, after lagging badly, most regulatory authorities had taken actions to contain a banking system that had, at the core of the financial system, grown too large to fail in an orderly fashion, too complex to manage well, and too full of hubris and misaligned incentives to operate responsibly on its own. New guardrails demanding high and costly capital requirements, together with the prohibition of certain activities, de-risked the sector – as did the much-increased physical presence of supervisors in bank offices.

Yet in their work to de-risk the large banks, regulators lost sight of the way in which some of the mid-sized banks were changing and starting to pose a new systemic threat. And when some of them failed, the deposits ended up in the largest banks, which had already been deemed as too big to fail and too complex to manage. Meanwhile, risk continued to morph, with a growing part migrating to the non-bank financial institutions (NBFI) sector – a sector that, surprisingly, remained largely outside of their analytical curiosity and reach for far too long. This structural imbalance would repeatedly cause unsettling volatility whenever the markets' conventional wisdom shifted.

The new and growing sources of systemic risk – mid-sized banks and non-bank institutions such as asset managers, hedge funds, private equity and pensions – were insufficiently understood, analysed, supervised and regulated. And as illustrated by the near-collapse of the British pension system, the fraud in crypto that impacted millions of individual account holders, and the collapse of Silicon Valley Bank and financial shocks seen across the US regional and community banking space – all of which hit in 2022–3 – the possibility of systemically important financial accidents has continued to threaten economic, social and institutional wellbeing.

The impulse may be to blame leaders; indeed, they are often a good outlet for our frustrations. Brazil's then-President Luiz Inácio Lula da Silva told Gordon in 2009 how to most effectively point fingers. When Lula was a junior politician and constituents were upset, he would blame the government. Later, when he became leader of the opposition party, facing angry voters, he also would employ the tactic of blaming the government. But when he became the government as President, what did he do? Lula said, 'Blame the Americans.'

In October 2022, as policymakers gathered in Washington, DC for the annual meetings of the IMF and World Bank, the *Financial Times* ran a column by Edward Luce, its respected US national editor, titled 'The World Is Starting to Hate the Fed'.[7] Earlier that year, *The Economist* was even more brutal. The cover of its 23 April edition featured an embarrassed Benjamin Franklin with the searing headline: 'The Fed That Failed'.[8]

Source: 'The Fed That Failed', The Economist, 23 April 2022

The March 2023 US community banking crisis also had Europeans doing just that. The press conference where UBS agreed to purchase Credit Suisse vividly illustrated this 'blame the Americans' sport. Lined up behind microphones, it was a cast of characters who largely disagreed with each other. Regulators, longtime rivals UBS and Credit Suisse, politicians – none of them wanted to be there or seem to see eye-to-eye. And all of them took the time in their remarks to blame the US for financial instability spilling over into Europe. In their view, the Americans had mishandled interest rate hikes and been too slow to reassure depositors in the wake of Silicon Valley Bank's failure. And now, just like in the Global Financial Crisis, preventable failures had spooked global markets.

Time and time again, governments and central banks have failed to follow the often-repeated advice of Wayne Gretzky, the legendary ice hockey player, to 'skate where the puck is going'.

This failure to notably lower the threat and likelihood of future financial crises comes at a time when inflation has curtailed quite a bit of the scope for emergency interventions and made their deployment more likely to cause even more collateral damage. Governments and central banks have used up most of their ammunition to not just fight financial crises, but also economic ones. In turn, their approach to financial risk has, inadvertently, made future crises both more likely and harder to contain.

Crisis management often risks sacrificing longer-term wellbeing for shorter-term stabilisation, and that truth is not limited to financial issues. This is especially true when fundamental reforms fail to follow the deployment of emergency measures. The 2022 energy crisis triggered by Russia's invasion of Ukraine, for example, has made some countries not just subsidise the use of polluting fossil fuels but also reopen even more damaging coal mines. Instead of allowing the price mechanism to increase the incentives for the much-needed energy transition and accelerate it while also enhancing the protection of the most vulnerable segments of the population, too many countries went the other way.

The Ugly: Inadequate Growth, Inclusion, Productivity and Sustainability

While the crises and near-crises have attracted most of the popular attention, and understandably so, decisions made in the interim have been equally consequential. Repeatedly, governments, central banks and other regulators have failed to follow the 1962 advice of President Kennedy, a phrase often repeated by Christine Lagarde, the former Managing Director of the IMF and current ECB President, to 'repair the roof while the sun is shining'.[9]

In the run-up to the 2008 Global Financial Crisis, too many countries fell under the spell of finance and its innovations as uniquely powerful enablers of growth. Increasingly creative and complex product offerings emerged: securitisation, collateralised debt obligations, loan-tranching that pooled together different assets – you name it. It was all poorly understood and believed to be good, the kind of innovations that could reduce all sorts of barriers and generate a new era of wealth creation. Instead, left to its excesses, it ushered in wealth destruction as regulators' inclination to just let finance do what they thought it does best, including through a 'light-touch' regulatory approach, ended up detracting from growth rather than enabling it.

Most of the period after the Global Financial Crisis saw a combination of crisis management and political gridlock undermine the implementation of pro-productivity and pro-growth measures, let alone deal with a mounting climate crisis. Inequality – of income, wealth and opportunity – worsened.

In many advanced economies, talk of bringing down stubbornly high inflation became the dominant narrative in 2022, and any talk of a 'green' future was constrained by the immediate political need to preserve jobs and lower costs, even in the fossil fuel industry. From the insufficient modernisation of infrastructure and highly inadequate investment in human capital to wrong incentives and poor communication, policies failed to renovate inclusive and sustainable growth frameworks at precisely the moment the sun was shining. During the easy money, cash-rich 2010s, those investments in growth could have been made, but they weren't. At a time when major investments – of time, treasure and talent – were needed to transition economies to postures less damaging to the environment, the world largely missed the window of opportunity.

And then came Covid and the post-Covid inflationary spike. Central banks weren't talking about broader growth objectives. Their focus was to first save the economy, and then cool it off having horribly misread the inflation picture.

After too slow an understanding, central banks were forced by inflation to exit the very low interest rate, easy money paradigm they had stumbled into – a set of conditions that had made them the 'only game in town', driving policy and markets through quantitative easing, rock-bottom interest rates and highly comforting communication. Floored interest rates and seemingly infinite quantitative easing, policies which dominated up until the 2022 tightening period, boosted stock portfolios while doing little to help the economy in a sustainable manner. Ask someone in Los Angeles or Liverpool to tell you about quantitative easing, and they'll tell you how they struggle to survive on their paycheque. Ask financial asset holders, and they'll insist on the need for even more quantitative easing and low interest rates forever.

Not only was growth artificially promoted and repeatedly insufficient, it also aggravated inequality. As a result, younger generations risk inheriting a world of insufficient growth on top of climate calamities, high debt, political polarisation and destabilising inequality. It is also a world of diminishing trust in the effectiveness of institutions, such as central banks, and in their accountability. And it is a world in which a shrinking pie, both domestically and internationally, makes 'beggar-thy-neighbour' behaviours more problematic.

To draw on the lyrics of Taylor Swift's 2022 hit single 'Anti-Hero', central banks and policymakers should see that 'It's them, they're the problem, it's them.' Until the very nature of economic management is overhauled, there will continue to be bad blood poisoning lives, livelihoods and markets. But there is hope. We understand the root causes that have brought us to this point. Which means we have it within our power to change course.

9

THREE STEPS TO IMPROVE ECONOMIC MANAGEMENT

Admitting You're Wrong and Learning From Mistakes

The Battle of Shiloh was one of the most consequential of the American Civil War. Major General Ulysses S. Grant had the Confederate Army on the defensive following their losses at the Battles of Fort Henry and Fort Donelson earlier that year. A victory at Shiloh would give the Union control over a greater portion of the Mississippi River Valley while crippling the Confederates' supply lines and industrial strength. But a surprise Confederate attack early on 6 April 1862 pushed the Union Army to the banks of the Tennessee River and claimed staggering casualties.

The rain came down hard that evening. There were accusations that Grant had been slow to react, contributing to the disarray and heavy casualties, while other reports pointed to commanders in the field getting lost on unfamiliar roads. Whatever the cause, defeat seemed all but certain. The screams of the injured rang out as doctors used primitive tools for amputations. Grant returned to a log house used as his office, only to find it turned into a field hospital with limbs strewn about. He would write in his memoirs, 'The sight was more unendurable than encountering the enemy's fire, and I returned to my tree in the rain.'[1] The conversation that happened next would go on to become the stuff of legend.

Grant went out in the rain and took refuge under an oak tree. A soaked cigar was in his mouth, his Union bucket hat dripping with rain. One of Grant's top lieutenants, Brigadier General William Tecumseh Sherman, walked out to the tree to see him. 'Well, Grant, we've had the devil's own day, haven't we?' Sherman asked. 'Yes, lick 'em tomorrow though,' Grant replied.[2] And that's what Grant did, dealing an unexpected defeat to the Confederates. But this victory would come at a heavy cost with more men dying at the Battle of Shiloh than the combined totals from the Revolutionary War, the War of 1812 and the Mexican War.[3]

The 'lick 'em tomorrow' spirit is not just a tale of perseverance in the face of incredible odds. It's also an oft-told reminder about the ability to learn from our mistakes, adapt and move forwards, something that's all too rare when it comes to economic management. Time and again, central bankers and policymakers seem to fight yesterday's battle with yesterday's weapons, and not the one in front of us with the required degree of open-mindedness and agility.

Reimagining Economic Management

Counterfactuals are useful – not for wallowing in regret but rather for helping guide our understanding of the past and efforts to move towards a better, brighter future.

Imagine how different our economies would be if in the run-up to the Global Financial Crisis, governments, central banks and other regulators had not fallen hostage to the charm and self-interested narrative of the financial system.

Imagine if governments' response to that crisis had not been based on the assumption of it being just a temporary and quickly reversible cyclical shock, but rather a structural one that required a durable focus on inclusive and sustainable growth, as well as financial stability.

Imagine if, in the decade following the Global Financial Crisis, instead of continuously showering the system with cash and flooring interest rates, central banks had been able to hand off to governments the lead for driving economic growth, productivity, social wellbeing and prosperity – not to mention addressing distortions in the private sector.

Imagine if, led by the Federal Reserve, central banks had not spent almost the entirety of 2021 mischaracterising inflation as 'transitory', a confident yet false assertion that this quick-to-pass phenomenon would not alter behaviours and livelihoods.

Imagine if, once the Federal Reserve recognised its big analytical mistake, it had acted more decisively and honestly in countering inflation, and in avoiding the need to excessively slow the economy and cause financial instability in order to control a disruptive phenomenon that was eroding purchasing power and economic confidence.

Every one of these failures had important behavioural dimensions to them. Every one highlighted the tendency of policymakers to either deny or reframe evidence that took them out of their comfort zones. And each fell hostage to groupthink and old ways of thinking.

In *The Checklist Manifesto*, surgeon and writer Atul Gawande offers a framework for how, in the face of complexity, humanity can move forwards. Gawande explains that 'know-how is often unmanageable' as the 'volume and complexity of what we know has exceeded our individual ability to deliver its benefits correctly, safely, or reliably'.[4] That's certainly the case here considering the array of challenges. But we won't get overwhelmed. Instead, we'll take Gawande's advice and put together a checklist of reforms.

Step 1: Be open to new perspectives

The recovery from the depths of the Global Financial Crisis was anything but quick. It wasn't the 'V'-shaped recovery market watchers often hope for but rather a 'W' with charts whipsawing between peaks and valleys as the threat of an 'L' loomed.

Around this time in the summer of 2009, Mohamed went to Washington to discuss with policymakers the concept of a 'new normal' – the idea that the US economy had been hit not by a cyclical shock that would result in a rubber-band-like recovery, but rather was hobbled by structural and secular weaknesses that would severely undermine growth if not met by a forceful and long-lasting policy reaction.[5] The 'new normal' was defined by three features: low growth, increasing inequality and central banks beholden to the whims of the marketplace. Major structural measures were necessary to change the economic trajectory.

Mohamed's 'new normal' notion, developed with his colleagues at PIMCO, was dismissed as 'idiotic'; he was told that while developing countries 'live in structural space', advanced countries like the US 'live in cyclical space'. As time passed and growth consistently disappointed, the 'new normal' notion was again waved off as too 'fatalistic'. Yet a few years later, and in the face of overwhelming evidence, it was rebranded and broadly accepted as 'secular stagnation'.[6]

The lack of open-mindedness was in great part due to the fact that the vast majority of policymakers had lived their entire career in a cyclical space where economies bottom and then bounce back. Some had even been in love with the false notion that good policymaking had conquered the boom–bust business cycle. But rather than broaden their analysis to include the experience of other countries – or consider for a moment that the past is not always a mirror of the present and future – they instead reverted to prior experiences and let the comforting notion of a return to normalcy substitute for more rigorous scenario-based risk assessments.

A similar phenomenon took place when Mohamed and a few others, including former Treasury Secretary Larry Summers, economist Olivier Blanchard and historian Niall Ferguson, publicly warned the Federal Reserve throughout much of 2021 to keep an open mind about its transitory inflation call. From the remarks of companies in one earnings call after the other to how inflation was starting to spread beyond food and energy, there were enough signals to warrant a much broader scenario analysis. After all, growth, jobs and financial stability were at stake.

Instead of considering the possibility of persistent inflation, and therefore assessing the appropriateness of policy actions and risk-minimisation steps according to a range of potential cost–benefit outcomes, the Fed mistakenly opted for very high conviction in just one of them – that inflation would come back down in short order. The Fed chose the most politically comforting, calming assertion. And it chose poorly, held hostage by recency bias – emphasising recent events over historic ones – as well as an excessive focus on models that failed to account for changes in the global economy.

By the time it retired the 'transitory' word from its vocabulary, to paraphrase what Chair Powell told Congress at the very end of November 2021, the delay in its policy response had inevitably increased the economic, financial and social damage caused by inflation while also worsening the side effects of whatever medicine came next. The window for avoiding a recession, what was called a 'soft landing', had narrowed. And when the Fed did recognise inflation was sticky, initial rate hikes to tamp down inflation were far too small. This led it to slam on the brakes through a catch-up hiking cycle that was unusually rapid and concentrated, risking both economic and financial accidents. With that came the worrisome risk that the Fed could miss on every element of its trilemma – that is, fail to lower inflation to its 2 per cent target, push the economy into recession and trigger unsettling banking and financial instability.

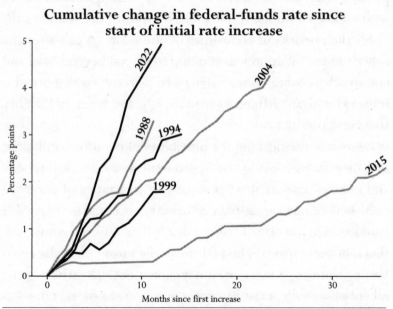

Cumulative change in federal-funds rate since start of initial rate increase

Source: Nick Timiraos, 'Federal Reserve Hikes by 0.75 Point, Signals Slower Increases but Ultimately Higher Rates', Wall Street Journal, 2 November 2022

Communication is one of the Federal Reserve's most powerful tools. Central bankers don't just guide and often calm the economy and markets with their policies, but also through their words. What markets hate most in the world is uncertainty, and the Federal Reserve can provide the clarity markets so

158

badly seek. In the process, it helps others in the economy adjust in a timely and orderly manner. This is particularly important at a time of monetary policy regime change.

Yet as obvious as the Fed's initial wrong call on inflation was, this mischaracterisation was not accompanied by making public an honest and comprehensive analysis of the policy mistake. Also absent was a timely revamp of a guiding policy framework that had visibly failed to take account of the possibility of higher-for-longer inflation and a profound shift in the global economy – from one of deficient aggregate demand to one of deficient aggregate supply. This too only exacerbated an already faulty and harmful policy response.[7]

Making matters worse, the Fed slipped in the regulation and supervision of a segment of the banking system – regional and community banks – that play an important role in local ecosystems. The more of these banks that fail, the lower probability that their funding role would be taken up by the large money centre banks like JPMorgan Chase and Bank of America. The resulting reduction in credit extension would likely hit small and medium-sized firms particularly hard.

Moreover, accountability has become warped in central banking. Yes, central bankers are of course accountable for their actions, especially when reporting to those who appointed them. And this is not a job anyone takes for the paycheque as all of these public servants could get a much larger salary in the private sector. But the simple fact is that by its very nature, the role of central bankers is so technical and sometimes so mysterious that proper and timely accountability is scant.

It doesn't help that the Fed lacked the cognitive diversity that, by virtue of their structure, is found in the Bank of England and the European Central Bank. Groupthink dominated – so much so that the number of public dissents fell to an unusually low level despite the fact that the economy, and therefore monetary policy, were navigating a highly uncertain and fluid environment.

In financial accidents, the public points fingers at policy-makers or businesses. No one has ever stood in a supermarket, looked at an expensive head of lettuce, and sarcastically muttered: 'Thanks, Federal Open Markets Committee.' They'll scold the president or their senator, people they can vote out of office, but there's little ire directed at central bankers.

Together, these cognitive, institutional and implementation errors severely limited the possibility of containing inflation with minimum damage to jobs, growth and financial stability. This 'first best' world was gone, leaving us instead with second best responses and outcomes where additional policy mistakes, collateral damage and unintended consequences become more common. And among those bad outcomes was the risk of recession and financial systems malfunctions as the Fed scrambled to catch up to the inflation dynamics that were getting more deeply embedded in the economic system as they spread from a small set of price disturbances – namely energy and food – to the goods sector and then to services and wages. One little inflation fire became a big firestorm.

Miles's Law famously states that 'where you stand depends on where you sit'.[8] We are often so rooted in our own thinking – where we sit – that the positions we take and what we stand for are anchored to this view. Central bankers, just like all of us, need to open themselves up to new perspectives and appreciate that past performance is no guarantee of future results.

Step 2: Strengthen the architecture for policy co-ordination

Where there's narrow analysis, inadequate co-ordination is often close behind. And when they fuse together, the consequences are catastrophic. Consider the 44-day episode that turned the perception of a mature G7 economy with respected institutions into one more closely resembling a developing country with weak institutions and poor governance.

We are talking here of a moment of economic and financial turbulence – some say madness – in the United Kingdom in 2022 that saw the currency plunge, borrowing costs explode, a public reprimand from the International Monetary Fund and a warning from a credit agency. It all began with Liz Truss taking over as Prime Minister, and it didn't take long for things to fall apart with the 'mini-budget' presented by her Chancellor, Kwasi Kwarteng.

This mini-budget, which was designed to give a boost to an economy straining under the weight of high inflation, out-trickle-downed some of even the most ambitious Thatcher proposals from decades earlier. The plan called for an unfunded £45 billion tax-cut package to stimulate the economy, disproportionately favouring earners over £1 million as well as corporations. It bypassed institutional checks and balances, including critical validation processes. No wonder the director of the UK's independent Institute for Fiscal Studies noted the plan lacked 'even a semblance of an effort to make the public finance numbers add up'.[9]

The markets took notice, and within 24 hours the British pound crashed to an all-time low against the US dollar. Interest rates skyrocketed, which had the knock-on effect of freezing the mortgage markets and destabilising pension funds leading to a full-blown second crisis. Bank of England Governor Andrew Bailey warned that the British economy was 'hours' away from a meltdown.[10] So the Bank stepped in with an emergency £65 billion bond-buying programme to stabilise markets. Truss sacked Kwarteng, and shortly thereafter the

Conservative Party sacked her. All told, Truss's tenure aged worse than a head of lettuce – an actual competition featured in a tabloid newspaper, which took place to see which would wither first. Truss did.

This cornucopia of catastrophe is a lot for any country, let alone an advanced G7 economy that plays an influential global role. An autopsy of the crisis reveals the confluence of three factors. First, Truss, by her own admission, went 'too far and too fast' in forcing unfunded tax cuts and more debt onto a financial system already unsettled by an ongoing change in the global liquidity regime.[11] Second, policymakers underestimated the fragility that exists in a system that had been conditioned for too long to embrace zero policy interest rates and massive liquidity injections by central banks. And third, Truss and Kwarteng ran an economic red light bypassing policy co-ordination and validation mechanisms that are in place to avoid this very type of crisis.

Were it not for the timely and swift actions of the Bank of England, the UK would have fared far worse. This was not just about the emergency intervention by the Bank to counter severe financial market malfunction, buying the highly destabilised government bonds that threatened the financial system and the economy as a whole. It was also about the Bank's very public resistance to capture by both the fiscal authorities looking for an easy way out, and some overstretched financial firms eager to play their 'too large to fail' moral hazard card. While policymakers' behaviour in Downing Street was destabilising the country's finances, the Bank of England was instrumental in avoiding catastrophe.

Better fiscal and monetary co-ordination would have likely prevented this moment of instability. Such co-ordination doesn't just help central bankers and policymakers arrive at the appropriate decision. It also puts whatever action is taken on a stronger footing. And, crucially, it need not result in 'fiscal dominance' where the central bank becomes subservient to the will of the government.

Maintaining the critical operational independence of central banks away from political interference is also the responsibility of central bankers themselves. Yes, they will occasionally slip in their analysis, forecasts, implementation and communication. Having the humility and honesty of owning their mistakes and explaining how they have learned from them, along with appropriate mid-course corrections, is critical to maintaining their independence.

After falling into the 'transitory inflation trap', the Bank of England was among the first central banks to admit its mistake and explain it. The Bank was analytically more honest with its narrative, something that proved politically uncomfortable yet necessary to send the right signals and incentives to an economy facing the clear and present danger of a deep and prolonged stagflation.

Notwithstanding severe criticisms for not doing enough to curb an inflation rate that was well above that in most other G20 countries, the Bank stood up to both fiscal dominance and market co-option. Having introduced a time-limited financial intervention to calm markets during the Liz Truss period of significant financial turmoil, the Bank came under tremendous pressure to extend its support. Yet rather than follow what the Fed had done repeatedly, the Bank's Governor Andrew Bailey came out on a Tuesday evening to remind everyone that the support would cease on Friday as initially signalled. And it did — an outcome achieved without causing additional turmoil.

None of this was easy — leadership often isn't. Indeed, almost every element of the course correction needed to compensate for central banks' initial inflation miscall was, and remains, a tricky one. The world of second-best policy-making is full of potential collateral damage and unintended consequences.

All of which takes us back to the issue of striking the right balance between accountability, autonomy and co-ordination. It is puzzling why more countries have not pursued the model of a formal 'national economic council' (NEC) that resides in the executive branch of government alongside less insular central bank decision-making. The key function of an NEC-like structure is to inform, influence and, in some instances, impose outcomes on the multiple agencies that implement bottom-up individual economic policies on a daily basis. It opens the doors wider for the important pursuit of multi-year policy initiatives that benefit from co-ordinated and self-reinforcing measures from several policymaking entities. What is more, the NEC model also facilitates interactions with the private sector as needed.

No one can deny the importance of timely information-sharing in ensuring better economic and financial outcomes. The right hand needs to know what the left is doing. By regularly convening meetings of the key economic agencies and ensuring everyone is operating in a 'safe zone', governments acting through an NEC could ensure that each agency is better informed in pursuing its individual objectives.

Such a safe zone also helps with cognitive diversity that tends to be absent due not only to long-standing institutional biases and rigidities but also the continuing lack of sufficient diversity of gender, culture, education and experience. Hiring doesn't lead to groupthink by design, but rather groupthink by default. An NEC can play a critical role in exposing fragilities and mis-understandings, as well as facilitating the kind of dialogue that has repeatedly proved critical for better policy understanding, alignments and more effective crisis management.

Through dialogue and co-ordination, a well-functioning NEC can also influence outcomes, especially when there is a particularly important policy objective that is not receiving deserved attention. And there have been many – from the importance of improving growth prospects coming out of the Global Financial Crisis to battling climate change, overcoming the supply chain disruptions caused by Covid, increasing labour force participation or lowering inflation. In every one of these cases, better inter-agency co-ordination would have helped deliver better outcomes. And in every one of these cases, an NEC acting as the hub connecting agency spokes would have lessened the likelihood of financial mishaps while raising the prospects for growth.

Then there is the example of the Treasury Borrowing Advisory Committee (TBAC) that advises the US government on its liability management. This is particularly important in a world of high debt, volatile capital markets and pockets of financial risk.

The structure and experience of the TBAC is a worthwhile case study. Composed of representatives from banks to hedge funds and insurance companies, the TBAC advises the Treasury Department on its funding plan. And this is a rare thing because policymaking is an exercise in power which is often derived from centralisation. Embracing input from external thinkers with a breadth and depth of knowledge and experience will only lead to better outcomes.

Think of the economy as a patient with chronic, and potentially life-threatening, conditions. Before being put on the operating table, would you be satisfied with one opinion, or would you want to consult another doctor for a second assessment? Bringing more voices into the fiscal and monetary policy decision-making process will lead to better, and more inclusive, outcomes.

Finally, there are the rare cases in which a big failure necessitates the imposition of certain policy actions on individual agencies. Think of the payments and settlement systems freezing and crashing during the September 2008 liquidity crisis, or the economic sudden stop when whole economies were shut down at the onset of the pandemic in March and April 2020. Without an institutionalised co-ordination structure, policy responses risk being too little, too late, and insufficiently aligned.

Pick your reason, and it is clear how the national economic policy architecture must be updated in some countries. Too many agencies, and especially those operating in isolation and overly paranoid in protecting their independence, have fallen victim to common behaviour traps.

There are blind spots where agencies fail to notice critical issues evident to others looking on from a different vantage point; think of that car in your blind spot that everyone else can clearly see and avoid but you can't. There's the issue of inappropriate framing as tends to happen when we are taken out of our comfort zone and seek to return to it regardless of the legitimacy of the underlying cause; think of the Federal Reserve clinging to the comfort blanket of transitory inflation when others said they needed to let it go based on a growing set of evidence. And then there's path dependency brought on by close-mindedness; even when they know they need to do something different, too often what results is simply more of the same – active inertia.

All this is made far worse when accountability is lacking. Taken together, the better co-ordination and greater accountability facilitated by open-minded institutional reforms can help to lessen the likelihood of severe economic disruptions and blunt the impact of inevitable speedbumps the economy encounters.

Step 3: Be ready to show leadership

Change is hard, so hard in fact that more often than not change is what you get back from a $20 bill and not something to be witnessed in policymaking.

Domestic economic management matters and leadership is critical. The wealthiest countries, which seemingly have all the advantages in the world, still face profound challenges born out of leadership failures, from homelessness and financial accidents in the United States to pension instability as we have seen in the UK. A country's economic record and economic future are increasingly determined by the strength of leadership rather than its overall level of wealth and development.

Some countries, such as Singapore, have achieved great levels of wealth and human development over a short period of time despite having limited initial economic advantages. Others, Nigeria for example, have failed to deliver economic, social or human development strides despite favourable conditions, in this case a wealth of resources. There are countries like the United Arab Emirates that have been blessed with resources and have managed to deliver for their citizens. And all too often we see fragile economies with poor endowments whose history, unfortunately, is one of going from one awful suffering to another together with negative spillovers for neighbouring states and the wider region.

So, this is meant to serve as a disclaimer. This lack of a unique and predictable relationship between endowments and outcomes must be kept in mind as we go through the needed policy adjustments. Even favourable initial conditions, better institutional setups and appropriately designed policies will fail to deliver if they are not managed well in a sustained fashion and if leadership is not open to ideas and held accountable for both the 'what' and the 'how'. There is no one-size-fits-all approach, but there is a one size fits many.

With weak leadership and poor economic management, the worst is possible and the best outcomes impossible. Recognising this helps explain the challenges we have faced and our condition – how battered and bruised we were – as we exited crises only to enter others.

And without leadership, these crises are likely to recur in an increasingly problematic fashion. Both the Securities and Exchange Commission and the Commodity Futures Trading Commission have no safety and soundness mandate – they act more as policemen spotting fraud, not referees flagging dangerous players. The 2010 Dodd-Frank Act created the Financial Stability Oversight Council to help fill this void, empowering the Council to designate unregulated financial firms or activities as risks to the system. As we write in 2023, zero have been flagged – a baffling statistic. Without accountability and oversight, we can expect little to change.

But good leadership is out there. Even if poor leadership and co-ordination led to the Global Financial Crisis, swift action to stabilise markets avoided a global depression. Even if rushed and misguided policymaking bordering on economic self-destruction caused a convulsion in the British economy, strong leadership from the Bank of England soothed unsteady markets and avoided an implosion of the pension system. And even if central bankers, especially those at the Federal Reserve, have a history of taking too long to act and then acting for too long – that certainly can change.

10

A BETTER WAY

Enter the Investment Committee

Everyone knew Monday, 15 September 2008 was going to be tricky. Blood was in the water, and Lehman Brothers was at the end of its life. That weekend, 13 and 14 September, Mohamed was with other members of PIMCO's Investment Committee (IC) at their Newport Beach headquarters, and together the group tried to predict what was going to happen next. Lehman's complete failure was anything but assumed at that stage – multiple suitors were kicking the tyres on the investment bank and there was even talk of a last-minute bailout. But nothing was certain, so the PIMCO team gamed out the three scenarios and assigned probabilities to each.

Scenario A – 85 per cent probability according to the average of the individual assessments of members of the IC – predicted Lehman would not fail and be a repeat of Bear Stearns. A stronger bank would come in, take over Lehman, and there would be no counterparty risk come Monday morning. Lehman had been in discussion with at least two banks, so this seemed to be a fairly likely outcome. Scenario B – 12 per cent probability. In this outcome, Lehman fails in an orderly fashion because no regulator would gamble with a disorderly failure putting the payments and settlement system in play, which would paralyse the economy and destroy livelihoods. If

Lehman were to fail – if it were allowed to fail – that would happen in an orderly fashion. And that left a 3 per cent probability for Scenario C calling for a disorderly collapse. No intervention from the Federal Reserve, government or private sector actors. A total, unmitigated implosion.

Scenario C was what happened. PIMCO didn't predict Lehman's failure, as some outside the firm continued to suggest despite explanations from Mohamed and Bill Gross, PIMCO's co-founder and legendary investor. The firm's success in largely avoiding client losses and subsequently growing assets substantially was due to quick repositioning precisely because they gamed out each scenario and, just as important, had detailed action plans for whatever the outcome. There was no mystery – everyone in the room and beyond knew who would be doing what and when. From delivering the notice of failure so that you can re-establish swap positions, to informing clients and changing portfolio postures before others work out their own actions, plans at PIMCO were instantly put into motion as Lehman's disorderly collapse came into focus very early on Monday morning.

Getting it right in economic management means not becoming paralysed when things break or decision makers face unusual uncertainty. Nor does it mean you stick to the 85 per cent probability outcome and ignore the 3 per cent scenario when so much is at stake. Getting it right demands doing the hard work of mapping out multiple scenarios and response plans, all while following the data even when the impulse is to track with long-standing assumptions. The effort and energy spent laying that groundwork pales in comparison to the costs born out of poor preparation.

When leaders are open to new perspectives, when they are willing to co-ordinate and be accountable, and when they show leadership, anything becomes possible. Here's what that looks like for economic management.

Aspiring for Resilience

Planning and preparing during the good times are critical to ensuring economies survive and bounce back quickly during the bad times. National policymakers urgently need to deliver a better set of measures to improve economic prospects and lower the probability of financial crises. This will, in turn, foster the resilience needed to deal with more frequent and violent external shocks.

At the heart of this challenge is generating high and durable economic growth that is consistent with climate realities, ensuring an equitable division of an expanding economic pie, and balancing that with low and stable inflation as well as financial stability – all of which is achievable only through greater open-mindedness, co-ordination and leadership. Remember, if we continue to fall short, the very fabric of society will tear as the middle class is further hollowed out, the rich get richer, and the most vulnerable experience yet greater insecurity seemingly from every direction.

Part of the problem has been the ill-fated romance with finance. In the run-up to the Global Financial Crisis, too many countries fell in love with finance and its seemingly magical innovations as the enabler of growth. One country after the other aspired to become a regional or global financial centre, including those with relatively small economies such as Iceland and Switzerland. While this romance ended in tears and tragedy, the needed pivot to genuine engines of growth has failed to materialise in most countries. Instead, they ended up shifting from private balance sheets to public balance sheets.

Central banks found themselves taking on the primary responsibility for delivering growth. Yet their policy tools were, and remain to this day, badly suited for this task. The most they can do is build a financial bridge – and even that is not without problems. They can't build physical bridges or other infrastructure, let alone improve the functioning of the labour market and overall productivity.

This reality is yet another reminder that financialisation was not, and is not, an answer to our growth challenge. Delivering the type of growth that we desperately need – one that is durable, is consistent with the environmental realities, and whose benefits flow to the many and not the few – requires the modernised growth models discussed earlier in this book and, within that, consistent effort to increase the productivity of both labour and capital.

But while economic conditions are perilous, policymakers are not powerless and have before them tools which will deliver greater resilience.

The Power of Partnerships and Infrastructure Banks

Well-functioning public–private partnerships are needed to enhance innovation and productivity. Without such partnerships, governments will find it very hard to resolve the climate crisis, navigate the energy transition, adapt to a changing globalisation and improve the functioning of the labour market. For their part, companies will struggle in their quest for greater resilience and operational effectiveness.

The twin ports of Los Angeles and Long Beach handle roughly 40 per cent of all containers coming into the United States.[1] And getting them to the US is the easy part. Once they arrive they need to be offloaded by port crane operators and carefully dropped onto trucks. Then drayage – the transportation of goods – takes place where the containers and goods are moved to a nearby storage point, often at or near the port. And at a later point in time, after clearing customs and other checks, the container can exit storage and head to rail cars for shipping across the country. That's a lot of steps, and a lot of contact points where skilled labour is involved.

But technology is catching up with automated cranes and trucks already making appearances at ports in Asia and the Middle East. Shipping through the Port of Los Angeles is a choice – the Maersks and Evergreens of the world can choose to ship a greater share of goods through other ports if they feel operations elsewhere are more efficient. Data from McKinsey suggests automation could lower expenses by 25–55 per cent while contributing to a 10–35 per cent productivity boost.[2] To port labour unions, automation is understandably viewed as a threat to livelihoods. But rather than fight the tide, the City of Los Angeles led in the creation of a first-of-its-kind labour–management partnership to not just provide advanced training, but also to deliver equity by hiring from communities immediately surrounding the port.[3]

There is no way for us to successfully surmount the infrastructure and innovation challenges we face without smart partnerships between the private and public sectors, and without better guidance – through information and, at the margins, influence – from what many too readily dismiss as industrial policy. Institutional mechanisms need to help with the heavy lifting.

There is a case to be made for domestic infrastructure banks that complement what better-managed regional and multilateral institutions can and should do. Rather than rely on direct public funding of projects and programmes, these new development banks would use public seed money as a catalyst to mobilise the significant amount of private funding that is already available and looking for long-duration exposure. Together they can spur private sector activity, not just through co-financing but also through intelligent risk allocation and joint expertise.

The United States has richly reaped the benefits of public finance and credit support through the Export-Import Bank (EXIM), nicknamed the 'Bank of Boeing' for its consistent financing support to purchases of Boeing aircraft. But while EXIM has been criticised by European regulators as a thinly veiled tool to subsidise sales to the detriment of Airbus, without the presence of EXIM acting as a credit window, Boeing's overseas sales would not be as high and thousands of jobs in America and at global suppliers would evaporate. The European Investment Bank (EIB) and European Bank for Reconstruction and Development (EBRD) also provide similar services. Now imagine how government investment through a domestic infrastructure bank could crowd in private financing, and what could be achieved – the jobs that could be created, the growth realised and the equity unlocked.

It is not just about public–private partnerships. Imagine if the UK government in 2021–2 had opted earlier for greater taxation of the windfall profits of oil companies to seed a domestic infrastructure bank that would not only accelerate the modernisation of the country's productive base, but also facilitate its transition to a 'technology powerhouse', to use the phrase of Chancellor Jeremy Hunt.[4] The more the balance sheets crowded in, the greater the scope for sustaining much-needed reforms. Nowhere is this more important than in tackling our climate crisis.

Of course, partnerships aren't limited to within countries. There is an old saying that it is hard to be a good house in a challenged neighbourhood. This should serve as a constant reminder that improved domestic policy management will only fulfil its considerable potential if it is accompanied by better regional and global policy co-ordination.

Many of the challenges we face are either global in nature – from the climate crisis to the rewiring of supply chains and the transition to clean energy – or significantly impacted by developments elsewhere such as inflation, financial stability and labour movements. Addressing these challenges demands co-ordinated global action, the success of which will depend critically on improving governance – an issue that occupies the third part of this book.

Balancing Fiscal and Monetary Policy

The use of fiscal and monetary policy has typically been viewed as levers to pull to manage the level of demand in an economy. While that is true, it's far from the whole story.

The first priority for demand management is to seek a better balance for fiscal and monetary policies – both within each of these important macroeconomic measures and between them. This is most urgent for monetary policy which, unlike fiscal policy, is subject to fewer checks and balances. With fiscal policy, the dominant party in power can advance its agenda and ultimately answers to voters, while in monetary policy central banks in advanced countries are politically independent and largely insulated from the actions and passions of public sentiment.

Central bank balance sheets have become unsustainably large, and it is time to pay down that balance – carefully.

Taking this step requires central banks being firm, and leaving no doubt in the minds of markets, not just through words but through consistent action, about their strong commitment to exit the protracted period of emergency balance sheet expansion and interest rate repression that has left us with widespread resource misallocation, excessive risk-taking as witnessed in meme stock surges and crypto crashes, holes in regulation and supervision, as well as pockets of worrisome financial fragility and excessive debt ratios. And these measures by central banks must be accompanied by more open-minded analyses, better forecasts and detailed what-ifs as well as more consistent communication. With time this will allow for a much-needed pivot from highly tactical approaches in decision-making to more strategic ones.

The mathematician Benoit Mandelbrot had a clever way of describing the interplay between good and bad times. Drawing on the Old Testament story of Joseph recounting seven lean cows devouring seven fat cows, Mandelbrot coined the 'Joseph Effect'.[5] His idea was elegant: a period of good times defined by 'Joseph effects' would be followed by leaner, more chaotic times known as 'Noah effects'. Years of excess by central banks are likely to yield to periods of increasing chaos and economic disorder. The economist Hyman Minsky developed a similar theory where complacency and speculation during periods of stability lead to instability and ultimately crisis. But again, reforms can do more than mitigate and instead fundamentally change this tug of war.

Any shift towards a monetary policy anchored to moderation and not excess is unlikely to happen without major institutional modernisation, especially at the Federal Reserve, which is the world's most powerful central bank. The actions the Fed takes inevitably lead to economic, financial, political and social spillovers and spillbacks domestically and across borders, so its impact is outsized relative to other central banks. But that also means it carries great influence, so any reforms could become an example for others.

The Fed's Unholy Trinity

First, the Federal Reserve must undertake a fundamental revamp of the monetary framework. Although recently adopted in August 2020, the current framework is designed for the world of yesterday – a world defined by insufficient aggregate demand and not that of today and tomorrow where supply-side constraints will play an important role in influencing growth and inflation.[6]

As characterised by St Louis Fed President Jim Bullard, two changes were at the heart of this 2020 framework. First, the Fed stressed 'that it will react to high unemployment but not to particularly low unemployment unless inflation is threatening the economy'; and second that it 'will aim for inflation to run moderately higher than the 2 per cent target for some time to make up for past misses of inflation to the low side of the target'.[7] The word 'supply' appears nowhere in the Fed's 'Statement on Longer-Run Goals and Monetary Policy Strategy'.[8]

Second, the Fed must hardwire better cognitive diversity in decision-making by opening up its most important policy making committee, the Federal Open Market Committee (FOMC), to highly qualified outside appointees – similar to what the Bank of England has done with its Monetary Policy Committee, which is targeted at countering the risks of both groupthink and over-determination by the Chair. Importantly, the Fed also needs an additional level of accountability between a relatively insular FOMC and high-level congressional oversight – a need that has been underscored by infractions within the Fed, most recently with several Federal Reserve officials violating personal trading rules and having to resign, as well as the SVB and First Republic supervision problems and the mistaken inflation call.

And third, the Federal Reserve must revisit, in a very careful and measured fashion, the path to sufficiently low and stable inflation. It should consider the cost–benefit of allowing inflation to run 'moderately higher' than its target for a period, as well as the longer-term appropriateness of the target.

The benefits of a 2 per cent inflation target are less certain given the multi-year outlook for the global supply side. The Fed needs to manage both its inflation path and target accordingly, a need that requires careful design, communication and buy-in, all of which are not just possible but also desirable for durable economic wellbeing.

The 2 per cent inflation target originated in New Zealand in the early 1990s and, over time, spread to several other advanced economies even though they differed in their conditions, economic flexibility and endowments. While that 2 per cent figure was arbitrary, it seemed to tick several boxes. It was viewed to be low enough to anchor inflationary expectations, yet high enough to grease the skids for resource reallocations, all while avoiding the lower zero bound for nominal interest rates. There are a series of possible transitions to be considered, including but not limited to the widening of an inflation band in a symmetrical fashion, and over an extended time frame.

Today, 2 per cent may not be high enough to enable the many ongoing changes on the supply side, and at the same time it has proven to be too close to the zero bound.[9] A higher inflation target of 3 per cent is worth discussing. The challenge, and it is not to be underestimated, is in making the policy transition at a time when the Federal Reserve has lost credibility for repeatedly failing to deliver on the inflation portion of its dual mandate.

The most likely path to a 3 per cent target would involve a period of de facto stable inflation around that level while the Fed continues to reiterate its desire to eventually reach 2 per cent, all while knowing full well inflation is likely to remain higher for longer. With the experience of stable inflation at the higher rate, the Fed could then make the formal target pivot without undermining expectations, including through the application of a transitional regime. It is a tricky course of action, but it is one that is preferable to either returning to the 1970s world of unanchored inflationary expectations or crushing the economy and destabilising finance to rapidly attain an arbitrary and outdated 2 per cent target.

Without a revised framework, greater cognitive diversity and a careful transition to a new inflation target, the Fed will find it increasingly difficult to meet its objectives. It will continue to be an inadvertent contributor to undue financial market volatility. And it will encounter growing political interference from Congress, jeopardising its operational autonomy, which is essential for successful monetary policies.

Managing Risk

An early warning siren should be going off. The importance and need for early action are amplified by the reality that additional policy mistakes will reverberate globally – not just threatening the US economy but other countries as well. Complicating policymaking elsewhere only accentuates the 'little fires everywhere' phenomenon as witnessed with Silicon Valley Bank's failure in March 2023 and First Republic a few weeks later, the subsequent stress faced by many US community and regional banks, and the shotgun marriage of long-troubled Credit Suisse with UBS.

A better functioning monetary policy won't just improve the balance of power between fiscal and monetary policy, but can also serve to reduce financial volatility and the risk of market malfunction. And policymakers controlling fiscal policy should remove anti-revenue and anti-growth elements of the revenue and expenditures systems. Examples include the favourable tax treatment of carried interest in the US, or tax exemptions for private schools in the UK that cater for just 10 per cent of the population and are often dominated by children from privileged backgrounds. Tax loopholes stifle revenue and growth, and the work of closing them falls to policymakers and not central bankers.

There must be a multi-year, if not multi-decade, effort to improve the impact of fiscal policy tools. First, greater emphasis should be placed on the funding of social sectors, particularly health and education, and in a manner that is productivity enhancing. Second, fiscal policy should gradually move away from funding consumption to funding investment – we need less of an emphasis on stoking the economy so consumers can go out and buy TVs, and more of a focus on government funding public goods from education to health. Third, fiscal policy should adopt more of a menu approach to crowd in private financing where targeted government involvement enables private entrepreneurship, innovation and funding. We saw this with the development of the Covid vaccine in which smart risk-tranching opened the way for critical innovations that saved both lives and livelihoods. And fourth, fiscal policy needs greater operating room so that during the hard times there isn't a default to the immediate hard choices of cutting spending on social sectors, hiking household and corporate taxes or growing debt through deficit spending. This is particularly important for Europe where a rethink of fiscal rules is becoming even more urgent, raising questions of referring to assets, as well as liabilities, when measuring debt sustainability.

Such shifts can be made sustainable. They are good policies. And they all contribute to growth and greater fiscal viability.

Protecting People and the Planet, Not Just Profits

Economics and growth shouldn't be about the bottom line, but the bottom up. And yet too often we have seen an opposite – an emphasis on profits over people.

The inability to generate high, inclusive and sustainable growth has alienated and marginalised too many members of our society, raising consequential economic, political and social issues. And this uneven growth has also worsened the climate crisis, fuelling the false notion of an inevitable clash between growth and the wellbeing of our planet. Putting both these considerations front and centre is critical if improved domestic economic management is to achieve its full potential.

How to – and how not to – undertake income transfers is one of the lessons of the pandemic. Suddenly forced into frantic crisis management, many governments deployed direct cash transfers to citizens, most notably in the US through stimulus payments and in the UK with furlough payments. Higher earners were included in initial rounds of stimulus checks, a decision that ultimately contributed to other problems. But for individuals suddenly out of a job and unable to make ends meet off of unemployment payments alone, the stimulus checks helped to smooth the financial rocky road and add needed capital to bank accounts. The personal savings rate in the US went from 8.9 per cent in March 2019 to a record high of 33.8 per cent in April 2020.[10] That surge in savings encouraged consumer spending and helped the economy get going again. And this is a tool that can be used tactically outside of a once-in-a-lifetime pandemic.

Income transfers are an important tool because, in many though not all ways, they are the most effective and efficient way to protect the most vulnerable, especially as this digital age has rendered identification and targeting easier. Importantly, unlike during the pandemic, such transfers need to be targeted and can be combined with 'nudges', the behavioural science term referring to incentives, to overcome challenges to future earnings and wellbeing.[11] The more such income transfers are used efficiently, the less policymakers need to reach for short-term solutions that are detrimental to, and at cross-purposes with, long-term objectives.

Just think of how some governments reacted to the energy crisis triggered by Russia's invasion of Ukraine in February 2022. While committed to a gradual energy transition away from fossil fuels, several governments, including in the European Union most notably, opted to subsidise fuel prices in order to shield households and businesses from a cost-of-living crisis.[12] Pressure was placed on oil companies to increase production. A few governments around the world went even further in reopening coal mines marking a major step backwards from climate change emissions pledges.

A much better approach, for both the short and long term, would have been to allow the price mechanism to do its work while enhancing the use of targeted income transfers and safety nets. This would succeed in protecting the most vulnerable by providing the funds needed to avoid a choice between gas and groceries, while at the same time letting prices shift consumption away from fossil fuels, and in encouraging a faster development of alternative energy sources. And income transfer aid could have been reinforced with additional nudges[13] to influence – and lessen – energy use beyond efforts encouraging residents to wear turtlenecks as Tokyo's Governor Yuriko Koike suggested.[14] Perhaps leaving market prices intact, and not subsidising energy costs when prices spiked, would have been the greatest nudge of all to reduce consumption.

Income transfers also align with the broader issue of centring the climate crisis in domestic economic management. Climate change shouldn't be an afterthought but our first thought alongside equity considerations. Without a stronger institutional mechanism that asks the climate question when a range of policy decisions are being considered, it will prove hard to reconcile bottom-up developments with the top-down goal for sustainability. We don't need to choose between economic growth and the wellbeing of our planet. Only when we consider both goals together can we achieve both aims.

We Cannot Fail

'Failure is not an option.' The movie *Apollo 13* immortalised those words – a can-do spirit and rallying cry which embodied NASA's tireless commitment to bring a stricken spaceship home against the steepest of odds. Those words hold renewed meaning today as the world stares down more crises than we can count, the permacrisis that has come to define our world. But for the sake of future generations, we have to get it right. Without improved domestic economic management, we will find ourselves pushed further and further away from our goals and into a whirligig of wrecks that only multiply in an increasingly destructive manner.

We are not living in a cyclical, mean-reverting world where the bad is temporary and the effects reversible. The distribution of our potential economic and financial outcomes is not a normal bell curve with a high probability of certain outcomes and 'thin tails' at the extremes denoting terrible or exceptionally good outcomes. Instead, ours is a world of many possible outcomes with what economists call 'multiple equilibria' in which a shift to a bad situation makes an even worse one more likely. Outcomes aren't arranged neatly on a bell curve but rather lurk behind the lines of a chaotic painting – think a Jackson Pollock.

We already live in an extraordinarily complex world. At the time of writing, for example, we could think of three plausible outcomes for each of growth, inflation and monetary policy. If that three-by-three matrix were not complicated enough, just think of the scope of interdependencies that would also be in play.

The longer we wait to take action to improve domestic economic management, the deeper the hole we will find ourselves in – economically, financially, geopolitically, institutionally and socially – a long list that reflects the type of adverse interactions we have seen too many times in recent years. And this is an unsustainable situation that renders it difficult to maintain the mix of resilience and nimble agility that is essential for dealing with increasingly frequent and violent shocks such as the pandemic and war in Ukraine.

The good news is that the recommendations outlined here are not just desirable but also achievable. To make them effective, we need visionary leadership from both politicians and central bankers, strong and honest communication, popular buy-in, inter-agency co-ordination, better public–private partnerships and self-reinforcing domestic, regional and global interactions.

There is more good news. Multiple equilibria dynamics open the door not just for vicious cycles but also for virtuous ones. The more the positive policy momentum gained by an economy, the easier the path for further reforms and the greater the scope for aligning and expanding private sector support. And the more countries that take such a path, the bigger the scope for policy co-ordination making superior global outcomes more probable. The possibilities and their power are enormous.

We find ourselves on a bumpy and unsettling journey to an unusually uncertain destination. This comes at a cost — loss of social cohesion, economic and financial insecurity, pain for the most vulnerable segments of our society, and accelerating damage to our planet. It is our awful reality. Our challenge is to ensure that this journey ends up at a better destination — that we break free from this permacrisis. Fortunately, the path we're on is not the only one.

SECTION THREE

GLOBAL ORDER

11

THE NEW ABNORMAL

Getting Unstuck

On 23 March 2021, a sandstorm hit the Suez Canal.

Sandstorms are a common occurrence on the flat, dry and dusty Sinai. But this storm was different because of what it left in its wake. When the dust settled, a ship as long as the Empire State Building, the *Ever Given*, found itself wedged across the Suez blocking traffic.

Fifteen per cent of all global goods pass through the Suez.[1] And with the blockage, all of those things – everything from toilet paper to tennis balls – came to a halt. To make matters worse, this accident came at a moment when supply chains were already in disarray due to Covid.

With every Covid outbreak, factories in China slowed or stopped production. The world's largest ports did not have enough dockworkers to unload cargo or space to store the containers that were offloaded. And through it all, the insatiable demands of the consumer – propped up by government stimulus – never waned.

Enter the *Ever Given*. Images of a lone excavator pushing at dirt to try and dislodge the ship looked like David standing beneath Goliath, a diminutive yellow dot under an endless green hull.

The world had a problem with the ship holding up billions of dollars in goods. Onboard the *Ever Given*'s 18,000 containers

189

were snuggly blankets, furniture and laptops.[2] On other ships behind the stuck vessel, everything from vital personal protective equipment needed in the fight against Covid to landscaping decorations were stalled. The United Kingdom, which had seen garden gnome sales boom during the pandemic, now found itself in a gnome shortage with raw materials caught in the logjam.[3]

The lone excavator was not going to cut it. So many countries and companies had a stake in the ship, and everyone had an idea how to get it freed. The ship was managed by a German operator, owned by the Japanese, leased to a Taiwanese firm, helmed by an Indian crew, insured by a British broker and flying a Panamanian flag.[4] Dredgers and tugboats were quickly mobilised. Millions of cubic feet of mud and water were moved. Two of the world's biggest and most powerful tugs, the Dutch *Alp Guard* and the Italian *Carlo Magno*, joined the fight.

What experts feared could be a weeks- or month-long logjam was resolved in only six days. The spectacle was over, the bottleneck sailed away, and goods could again head to their destinations. Without global co-operation, the outcome would have been far worse. For those six days, the *Ever Given* was the most vulnerable link in the global supply chain – a broken link – and only co-ordinated global action could mend it.

In an interdependent world, we are only as strong as our weakest link. And that interdependence creates great new opportunities, but also unforeseen vulnerabilities whose challenges can only be addressed through co-operation.

The Co-operation Question

Different versions of the *Ever Given* take place every day – global problems that require global solutions, and global threats – such as infectious diseases or polluted environments – that require co-operation to remedy.

Previous chapters have explored the national dimension – the need to repair our models of what brings about growth, as well as models for national economic management shifting away from purely finance-driven economies and central banks as the only game in town. But many problems cannot be written off as exclusively, or even primarily, national problems hitting individual countries in isolation. Pollution is not neatly confined to national boundaries. A banking crisis in one country rapidly spreads to another, hence the term financial contagion. Wars and conflicts in one country inevitably impact neighbours. There are global problems we face together – that's the nature of our interdependent world. It's a classic case of what economists call a Nash Equilibrium where no participant gains through unilateral action. Gains only come through co-operation.

And yet co-operation raises profound questions cutting across traditional assumptions about nation state sovereignty that is often thought to be unlimited, indivisible and accountable to no one but itself. The United Nations Charter says countries have a duty to co-operate, to uphold human rights and to treat minorities with respect. But the Charter also emphasises the importance of territorial integrity, the idea that countries have absolute control of their own destiny, and more significantly is adamant about the case for non-interference, which 'strengthens universal peace'.[5] This leads to a perceived contradiction, which is not easily resolved, between the go-it-alone camp and those countries seeking to collaborate.

The reality is that, globally, we rarely co-operate successfully. Perhaps we can change that. As Scott Barrett explains in his aptly titled book *Why Cooperate*, 'learning how one kind of global public good has been provided may suggest ways in which another can be provided'.[6] Getting co-operation right in one arena doesn't just prove the power of co-operation – it also offers a blueprint for how to surmount other global challenges, from climate change to pandemics and financial instability.

Of course, not every problem requires a global groundswell. Shared problems and common problems are not necessarily global problems. If two countries are squabbling over a border or seeking to reduce trade barriers, then that can be resolved between the two of them. But today we are seeing a disproportionate number of challenges with two outstanding features: the cause is global and any durable solution must also have an important global component.

But even when leaders acknowledge that a problem is more than just common or shared but is global in nature, there is often a reluctance to follow the logic to its natural conclusion: to seek out global solutions through co-operation.

Following the Global Financial Crisis, Jeffry Frieden, Michael Pettis, Dani Rodrik and Ernesto Zedillo itemised four barriers to co-operation: scepticism about the need for co-operation; domestic political pressures that force protectionist responses; a divergence of goals between countries; and the historically largely limited success of international efforts at co-operation. In the face of these obstacles, they suggest 'incremental rather than radical objectives', concluding that co-operative efforts between countries should be focused 'on where they are most required, and most likely to succeed'.[7]

This approach is similar to David Mitrany's functionalism theory of international relations. His thesis is simple, and the solution for countries elegant: 'In all societies there are both harmonies and disharmonies. It is largely within our choice which we pick out and further.'[8] Countries should co-operate where they can. They should harmonise efforts. Writing shortly after the Second World War, Mitrany recognised the limits of full co-operation with competing interests often getting in the way. But from the rubble of war, he believed: 'We must begin anew, therefore, with a clear sense that the national can be bound together into a world community only if we link them up by what unites, not by what divides.'[9]

To be clear, any action, including co-operation, comes with positive and negative externalities – that's a technical way of saying side effects or spillovers on someone else, some being positive and others negative. Gains and losses accrue to you, but there are also implications for other people or countries. But the side effects of co-operation are minimal as long as a country does not take a dogmatic view that surrendering a bit of autonomy for a better outcome is a betrayal of their national sovereignty. For example, had the world not shared information on the genetic makeup of the Covid virus, a vaccine would not have been developed as quickly. Not sharing evidence of Covid early enough, and the implicit failure to co-operate, meant the disease spread quickly and cost lives.

It is our belief that collective action on the international stage can offer many more benefits than drawbacks. That might not have been as resonant in the past when we were not as economically integrated, or socially interconnected, as now. But the reality of today's interdependence has made what was once aspirational now achievable. And when the facts change, as the oft-repeated line by Churchill and Keynes reminds us, we ought to change our minds.

So, our challenge in our interdependent world is two-fold. First, we cannot just assert that global problems need global solutions but must go a step further and persuade the sceptical. And if leaders can accept that point, the second issue

193

becomes how we co-operate to the best effect. Today, few would disagree that in this economically integrated, socially interconnected and geopolitically interdependent world, we are managing co-operation unco-operatively – or at best imperfectly. Like a grade-schooler's report card, the mark the world gets is 'NI': Needs Improvement.

Our Interdependent World

Ask ten people to define globalisation, and you'll get ten definitions.

International affairs and political science scholars Robert Keohane and Joseph Nye define globalisation as 'a state of the world involving networks of interdependence at multicontinental distance'.[10] The leading *Financial Times* commentator Martin Wolf views globalisation as the 'integration of economic activities, via markets. The driving forces are technological and policy changes – falling costs of transport and communications and greater reliance on market forces.'[11] Thomas Friedman once defined the world as 'flat' as globalisation had created increasingly level playing fields between countries and people.[12] We're defining globalisation as the world becoming a smaller place. This can happen through trade, travel, knowledge and communication, and linkages are constantly being formed and fused across distances near and far.

More important than any narrow or broad definition we can provide, think about what globalisation means in your life. When you last placed an online order, where did the product you purchased come from – and if your answer is an Amazon fulfilment centre, where was it before that? Think of Zoom calls you're on and the vast geographies represented by those on the call. Where was your car made? The answer isn't always obvious. Your Ford might have been made in Mexico. That Mercedes in Tuscaloosa County, Alabama. And that Volvo in China.

The sheer breadth and depth of globalisation can lead one to wonder to what extent is British Petroleum, or BP, British? Is Volkswagen German? All have headquarters on multiple continents. All have operations and assembly lines outside of their home country. And all depend on foreign transactions to reinforce their balance sheets.

Before modern globalisation, before container ships transported the majority of the world's goods, before jumbo jets made it possible to connect continents affordably, before the internet and email – before all of those advances that made the world a smaller place, countries were like lone islands in a vast ocean. There was a measure of independence, and it was easy to forget – or to believe you were insulated from – the wider world beyond the surrounding waters.

In Shakespeare's *Richard II*, John of Gaunt delivers a speech which reflects a deep sense of English patriotism. But it also offers a window into geopolitical thinking centuries ago as Shakespeare writes of the British Isles:

> This fortress built by Nature for herself
> Against infection and the hand of war,
> This happy breed of men, this little world,
> This precious stone set in the silver sea,
> Which serves it in the office of a wall,
> Or as a moat defensive to a house,
> Against the envy of less happier lands,
> This blessed plot, this earth, this realm,
> this England . . .[13]

When Shakespeare wrote these words about England – a 'precious stone set in the silver sea' – this wasn't merely meant to be a rousing speech in a play. It also reflected the dominant view of the era – that England was largely immune to the issues facing continental Europe and the wider world. Without question England engaged globally and was, as Shakespeare writes several lines later, 'Renowned for their deeds as far from home' and 'Dear for her reputation through the world'. But back then, the English Channel acting as a 'moat defensive' was enough to provide some degree of protection from 'infection and the hand of war'.

For centuries, that thinking held true for the UK and many other countries, islands or not. But that is not the case today.

All of the world's close to two hundred countries are linked by a high level of trade, travel and telecommunications with fibre optic cables spanning oceans transmitting messages instantaneously. We have narrowed physical distances from months and weeks to hours and minutes through jet travel, highways, and high-speed rail. And even if those physical connections are severed by a plane grounding or conflict, national economies are tethered by a globalisation of financial institutions, a globalisation of supply chains and a globalisation of services.

Interdependence is the only way to explain why an American mortgage crisis can spread within days to other advanced economies. A bank may be headquartered in New York, but its liabilities could be in Germany, its assets in Asia and its tech support in South America. Indeed, Adam Tooze's view that 'what drives global trade are not the relationships between national economies but multinational corporations coordinating far-flung "value chains"' is winning over more and more observers, especially in light of the supply chain breakdowns throughout the Covid crisis.[14]

And interdependence best explains why the United Nations Conference on Trade and Development Secretary-General, Rebeca Grynspan, in October 2022, called on the Federal Reserve and other major central banks to address the impact of interest rate rises on inflation. Grynspan spoke to the danger of each country acting on its own without any thought to the cumulative impact on the rest of the world and inadvertently 'hurting the most vulnerable, especially in developing countries and risk[ing] tipping the world into a global recession'.[15]

Ours is an era of unprecedented and ever-rising interdependence. Let's look at global trade, which in 2021 exceeded $28 trillion.[16] That's larger than the US economy, which stood at $25 trillion in GDP. Between 2011 and 2019, trade in services outpaced the trade in goods and accounted for 75 per cent of GDP in developed economies – that's up from 40 per cent in 1950.[17] As Richard Baldwin's examination of global trade data has shown, around 2018 the trade in goods as a share of GDP peaked.[18] Global trade in services, on the other hand, continues to climb and shows no signs of slowing down – a 'wake-up call', Baldwin notes, that the nature of globalisation has shifted. Even when physical supply chains are severed, the services trade continues to expand with the outsourcing of everything from call centres to accounting. Just like a cloud, 'The Cloud' knows no boundaries – unless we impose them. While server farms can move from one country to another, the user experience remains unchanged.

According to data compiled by Brookings, the non-profit public policy organisation based in Washington, DC, half of the US trade across North America and 37 per cent of trade with EU partners is in intermediate goods or parts, not finished products.[19] Rather than production we see 'co-production'. Components for Ford's popular Mach-E electric vehicle are sourced from around the world, but final assembly takes place in Northern Mexico at the Cuautitlán Izcalli plant before the car makes its way to a dealership in Dayton, Ohio. That's deep integration and interdependence.

So as much as today's global powers would like to think they are islands alone in an ocean – able to build bridges when they want and draw them up when they seek to isolate – these countries are, in fact, part of a greater interconnected whole. Maps showing tidy geographic boundaries fail to reveal today's most defining features from internet connections to air corridors.

'I am part of all that I have met,' wrote Lord Tennyson in his poem 'Ulysses'.[20] In an interdependent world, every country has met every other. Think of the digital handshakes taking place millions of times every second between banks and customers thousands of miles away. Think of the smoke from fires in one country choking the skies above your home. Think about a war in a distant land impacting food and fuel prices a world away. This is our permacrisis world.

The Weaponisation of Interdependence

John Maynard Keynes famously said, 'If you owe your bank a hundred pounds, you have a problem. But if you owe your bank a million pounds, it has.' Global interdependence has become so tightly intertwined that it is easy for this strength to become a vulnerability with interdependence increasingly becoming weaponised. As described by Henry Farrell and Abraham Newman, states with control over the flow of 'money, goods, and information travel are uniquely positioned to impose costs on others. If they have appropriate domestic institutions, they can weaponize networks to gather information or choke off economic and information flows, discover and exploit vulnerabilities, compel policy change, and deter unwanted actions.'[21]

Interdependence driven by globalisation, along with market forces that have encouraged monopolies and oligopolies, have brought a minefield of 'centralized network structures' all but impossible to challenge. Farrell and Newman cite Facebook/Meta in social media and advertising, Google in internet searches and Visa and Mastercard in global payments as dominant forces in their respective markets. As of September 2022, more than 3.71 billion people use one of Meta's family of applications – that's close to half the global population.[22] Three firms control two thirds of the multi-trillion-dollar cloud infrastructure market with Amazon Web Services alone enjoying a 34 per cent market share, Microsoft Azure at 21 per cent and Google Cloud at 11 per cent.[23] And while the Society for Worldwide Interbank Financial Telecommunication (SWIFT) is not a private sector entity like the other examples, it too enjoys market dominance with 44.8 million financial messages routed every day as of late 2022.[24] That bank wire you just made overseas to make a hotel deposit or loan someone funds – SWIFT made that possible.

Farrell and Newman rightly point out that the internet has long been viewed as a 'fundamentally liberal space characterized by open exchange and cooperation', but in today's highly interdependent world 'focal points of cooperation have become sites of control'.[25] This control can take various forms, from surveillance to the severing of ties.

In late 2022, the United States banned Nvidia from selling certain high-end artificial intelligence chips to China without prior authorisation from federal regulators. Then, in mid-2023, China turned around and banned certain Chinese companies from purchasing products made by US memory chipmaker Micron Technology due to 'serious network security risks'.[26] These types of targeted bans are becoming increasingly common.[27] We have seen a shift in central bank and payment systems policies as countries have moved to expel adversaries from the SWIFT global payments system as was the case with Russia following the invasion of Ukraine, or have frozen national reserves held in foreign banks as has happened to Iran and Afghanistan in the United States. And currency wars are brewing; just look at China's 2022 launch of a digital yuan, which is seen as a major move towards reducing the dollar's dominance in international trade. The ability for today's internet to be controlled by centralised actors has led to increasing talk of a decentralised Web 3.0 with peer-to-peer blockchain technology circumventing countries and monopolies.

Interdependence is being weaponised. European Union industrial policy now prevents European companies with annual turnover exceeding $520 million from being acquired by state-backed foreign firms.[28] Some countries have raised tariffs or broken with the WTO to advance their economy at the expense of others. Following global sanctions in response to its invasion of Ukraine, Russia closed its airspace to certain foreign carriers and countries. Finnair, seeking to capitalise on its geographic advantage with the shortest Europe to Asia non-stop flights, had spent more than a billion dollars to build a terminal for quick connections. With Russia's airspace closure, the airline suddenly saw its entire business model upended. A flight from Helsinki to Tokyo, which previously took nine hours, rose to an uncompetitive thirteen.[29]

Interdependence and the threat of weaponisation, whether perceived or actual, risks descending into a different kind of global arms race where what is at issue is not building armaments but opposing arguments. A Western-dominated internet may quickly come to see the rise of a competing decentralised unregulated internet – or splinternet – all at once lessening global vulnerabilities for states but increasing risks for humanity with trade, terror and trafficking easily financed. Or the world economy risks seeing a full and complete breakdown of and withdrawal from global supply chains that defined the era of hyper-globalisation in favour of reshoring, ally-shoring and near-shoring. Of great concern is that moves to rewire supply chains and trade away from China lead not just to de-risking but to a decoupling. And as we think about trading systems, let's not forget financial systems and how they could be exploited, not least by cyber-attacks – particularly if an adversary set their sights on an open system such as the one found in the US. There is much speculation that the dominance of the US dollar as the world's reserve currency could yield to fragmentation with competing currencies used as reserves, a scenario that appears plausible until a major economy not used to having their currency viewed as a trusted reserve defaults.

The role of the dollar will change if people fear they can't risk using it. Currencies, including the US dollar and international payments systems, should be sparingly used as weapons – especially when there are other weapons that can be more effective. For example, indicting President Putin for war crimes in Ukraine would not rebound in the same way as dollar weaponisation, or worse banning Russia from the international payments system, SWIFT. The ban does not seem to have had the desired short-term impact as the Russian economy, which was supposed to collapse by 10 per cent and stay down, for a time grew faster than Britain's. Forced to work around the dollar, Russia has done just that. It has sold gas to India and China, been paid in local currencies, converted to Saudi and Turkish currencies, and switched to roubles. What message does this send to China? It signals seismic shifts in our world – in global polarity, nationalism and globalisation. And it proves that working around the dollar is possible, perhaps presaging the erosion of dollar hegemony.

We can imagine a future where trade, technology capital

and resource wars are set to intensify. This does not guarantee a full fracturing of the global order. But it does mean that in a permacrisis world, the way we manage our interdependence must evolve and improve.

Three Seismic Shifts

Three historic shifts – one geopolitical, one economic and one ideological – are starting to define the new world order in this interdependent age. This is significant and means we have to rethink what we call the liberal rules-based order. In the same way that from 1945 to the 1970s tariffs and fixed currencies limited the spread of globalisation in advance of the era of hyper-globalisation that opened the world up to a free-for-all, now new tariffs and non-tariff barriers are once again defining the limits and extent of globalisation.

Shift 1: Unipolarity to multipolarity

First, geopolitics has shifted from a world defined by unipo-larity – America as the hegemon – to one that is becoming multipolar with additional centres of political gravity. While America is indispensable, indisputably first among equals and still effective at combining military, economic and soft power for some time to come, it cannot freely rely on command and control but instead will have to practise the power of persuasion.

In 1945, at the dawn of the superpower age with America as the global hegemon, the US accounted for 50 per cent of global GDP, a figure that fell by half by the 1970s.[30] By the 1970s, American power was based on an economic order in which national controls over trade, currency and financial movements kept hyper-globalisation at bay. Throughout the 1970s, as the end-product of high inflation, worsening trade deficits, as well as the growth of neoliberal thinking, a different kind of US superpower emerged with America ceding power not to another country but to market forces. While militarily hegemonic and still the industrial leader, America became temporarily dependent on rest of the world for its energy as well as for the world's savings to finance its debt. In 1985, a chief investment officer at Nomura Securities described Japan ploughing tens of billions of dollars into US Treasuries as 'potentially the biggest single flow of capital in world history'.[31] In other words, America was no longer a freestanding colossus but one that depended on the rest of the world doing well.

America could not opt out of an interdependent world; rather, it had to ensure the world worked in its interests. Despite growing economic imbalances, by the 1990s with the end of the Cold War, America was the indisputable military hegemon with unrivalled force projection, and an economic juggernaut too with the dollar reigning supreme. In this new era, America's military and financial superiority is not enough – during moments of internationalism – to arrest the advance of our multipolar world.

This growing multipolarity is time and again reflected by non-aligned countries weakening their commitment to one of the big powers. Consider India. During a March 2022 visit to India, China's Foreign Minister Wang Yi made the pitch: 'If China and India spoke with one voice, the whole world will listen.'[32] And yet India, in the words of Narendra Modi's Minister of External Affairs Subrahmanyam Jaishankar, is pursuing a 'multi-alignment approach'. Jaishankar writes in his book *The India Way*, 'This is a time for us to engage America, manage China, cultivate Europe, reassure Russia, bring Japan into play, draw neighbours in, extend the neighbourhood and expand traditional constituencies of support.'[33] Jaishankar wants India to play the big powers off against each other, and concludes, 'It is only a multipolar Asia that can lead to a multipolar world.'

India's embrace of multi-alignment recalls the spirit of that memorable aphorism from the animated superhero movie *The Incredibles* – 'When everyone is super, no one will be.' When a country is non-aligned, then it is multi-aligned. There's a strategic reason for this of course. The non-aligned movement of fifty years ago argued their case from what they saw as universally valid principles against colonialism and for a non-nuclear and more equal world. The new and growing list of multi-aligned countries are acting out of a narrow self-interest playing countries off against each other – principally China and America – in the hope it will lead to better trade deals, more favourable debt restructuring, other incentives born out of courtship, and enhanced global status. And this is as true of South Africa, Brazil, Argentina, Malaysia and many other smaller countries as it is of India.

We're seeing new opportunistic alliances with what are sometimes called 'swing states', 'hedgers' or 'fence sitters' using their control of resources, their access to capital or their strategic geographic position for maximum national advantage. Brazil's recently re-elected President Lula has advocated for a new 'pole' of power in South America bringing Brazil in closer alignment with Colombia, Argentina, Bolivia and Chile.[34] He is also proposing that the BRICS – Brazil, Russia, India, China and South Africa – create their own reserve currency and extend their membership, with Saudi Arabia, the UAE, Egypt and Algeria among nearly two dozen countries said to have expressed an interest in joining. Poles of power are shifting with Iran possibly joining the China-led Shanghai Cooperation Organisation and consorting with Russia to create an alternative to the SWIFT payments system, which both countries have been excluded from. In 2023, China negotiated a new peace between Saudi Arabia and Iran. China, Russia and South Africa have mounted joint naval exercises. And as we move from the oil age to a minerals-intensive age, countries like

Indonesia and Chile – who command substantial reserves of nickel and copper – are already practising resource nationalism seeking to use their enhanced economic bargaining power as leverage. This is made all the more significant because the proportion of rare earth minerals held by China, cobalt by the Democratic Republic of the Congo, copper by Chile and Peru, and nickel by Indonesia are in each case around a third of discovered resources.[35]

Share of global mineral reserves by country*
(in per cent)

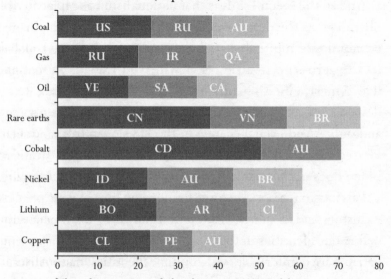

* Share of proven reserves of selected economies; 2020. For lithium, resorces, not reserves.

Source: Alberto Americo, Jesse Johal and Christian Upper, 'The energy transition and its macroeconomic effects', Bank for International Settlements, May 2023

Country codes:
AR Argentina, **AU** Australia, **BO** Bolivia, **BR** Brazil, **CA** Canada,
CD Congo (DRC), **CL** Chile, **CN** China, **ID** Indonesia, **IR** Iran, **PE** Peru
QA Qatar, **RU** Russia, **SA** Saudi Arabia, **US** United States of America
VE Venezuela, **VN** Vietnam

The end of a unipolar world has created a vacuum that has left everything in flux. But sometime in the next decade, as countries have to make real choices between America,

China and an increasingly multi-aligned world, the cement will set.

Shift 2: From neoliberalism to neonationalism

Political logic and economic logic are diverging. If for the last thirty years economics drove political decision-making, now politics is determining economic decisions with country after country weaponising their trade, technology, industry, supply chains and competition.[36]

And so the second shift is that nationalism has replaced neo-liberalism as the dominant ideology of the age. The win–win economics of mutually beneficial commerce is being replaced by the zero-sum rivalries of 'I win, you lose' as movements like 'America First', 'China First' and 'India First' threaten to descend into an 'us versus them' geopolitics of 'my country first and only'. And even a change in the US slogan from 'America First' under President Trump to 'Buy America' under President Biden does not fundamentally alter the nationalist messaging.

Patriotism is a positive force founded on love of your country, its history and its values, while accommodating the hyphens that define our identities in today's interdependent world. But while patriots are comfortable with multiple identities, nationalists are not. Nationalism is an ideology which promotes the idea of an 'us' and a 'them' in constant conflict and focuses on the sins of the outsider in an effort to breed resentment and whip up xeno-phobic responses. Nationalists traffic in absolutes – hostile to outsiders and demanding a single identity. In George Orwell's words, nationalism is 'inseparable from the desire for power'.[37] And this nationalist line in the sand makes it impossible to meet the challenge of our times: to balance the autonomy people desire with the international co-operation the world needs.

As has been the case throughout history, we are living through a period where patriotism is being weaponised in the form of an aggressive nationalism. That positive love for your country and pride in it has in many places morphed into a negative nationalism that has become an instrument of hate, identifying and even inventing enemies that don't exist and fuelling resentments that are more imaginary than real. Think of tensions between ethnic and religious communities within countries and also the ever-growing list of conflicts beyond the nationalist war between Ukraine and Russia. There are well-recorded tensions, for example, between China and Taiwan, India and China, Pakistan and India, Ethiopia and Eritrea, Sudan and South Sudan, Morocco and Tunisia; the proxy war between the Democratic Republic of the Congo and Rwanda; and the close to a dozen countries that left the Soviet bloc that have suffered ethnic conflicts with huge swathes of territory still subject to dispute.

There's defensive nationalism, which led to protectionism and was a feature of the world from 2016 to 2019 with trade barriers, import controls, border posts and a reluctance to co-operate. And then there's aggressive nationalism making a virtue of non-co-operation and unilateralism on the part of many states.

A symptom of this aggressive nationalism is protectionism metastasising into a deeper mercantilism – the use of all the power and resources of the state to pursue one's own interests at the cost of co-operation. And this 'us versus them' aggressive nationalism has become a corruption of patriotism with many leaders unafraid to give even the most economically irrational actions a shot. Bans on trade, including preventing the export of commodities and technology with countries deemed unfriendly or to protect local supplies, are rising. There are bans on labour through immigration controls, as well as more recent travel bans targeting specific groups of people. Countries have erected inward investment bans preventing one country from investing in another, either directly or by denying access to stock exchanges. And there are bans on outward investment preventing a country's own companies from investing in regimes considered unfriendly.

Without a healthy patriotism that recognises the benefits of co-operation, we will see the intensification of an aggressive nationalism. So, what we need is a patriotism free of nationalism – and that is a hard needle to thread.

Shift 3: Hyper-globalisation to a managed globalisation-lite

Our third shift, which is partly the result of a more fractured and fragmented world order, is the transition from a globalisation-heavy or hyper-globalised world to one that is a managed globalisation-lite defined by changing supply chains, near-shoring, friend-shoring and a new mercantilism with countries politically realigning towards their strongest trading partners.[38]

Globalisation-heavy was based not only on the free flow of capital, labour, energy and technology but also on low-cost capital, energy and labour. But in today's world, everywhere we look we see new restrictions on the free flow of labour, capital and technology through direct bans, indirect barriers and higher costs. And while most of the European Union, which is itself a free trade area, remains committed to the principles underlying free trade, equal treatment, reciprocity and the rule of law, American public opinion has always veered between openness and protectionism – internationalism and isolationism. After 1945, the US built the structure of global trading relationships championing international trade agreements. Now, America's trade surplus of the past has yielded to an even bigger deficit – a deficit which has been used as a talking point to reinforce 'America First' demagoguery.

It is not trade that is changing the way we do politics, but politics that is changing the way we do trade. Trade rose twice as fast as growth in the hyper-globalised era from 1990 to 2009, but increased economic integration through trade did not bring about the greater global harmony that some had hoped it would. In 1996, as the West rode high in the wake of the fall of the Soviet Union, Thomas Friedman called it the 'Golden Arches Theory of Conflict Prevention' – that no two countries with a McDonald's have fought a war with each other.[39] For the better part of three decades, that theory held true. But Russia's war in Ukraine, and the ramifications from it, have shattered the theory. It is perhaps a metaphor for our times that while McDonald's has reopened in Ukraine, the house that built the Big Mac – which was one of the first US corporations to enter Russia after the fall of the Berlin Wall – was among the 1,000 companies to exit the Russian market in 2022 and quickly replaced by the knock-off 'Vkusno i Tochka', or 'Tasty and That's It'.[40]

And what were once campaigns against globalisation and in particular free trade outside World Trade Organization Summits or in the American heartland are no longer confined to street protestors. The leaders inside the buildings where demonstrations are taking place feel something of the same unease – Hungary's Viktor Orbán, Britain's Boris Johnson, Turkey's Recep Tayyip Erdoğan and America's Donald Trump have all railed against the perceived harm an open world has caused their countries.

The idea that free trade made us free, and that 'rights and opportunities enjoyed by the citizens of Western countries could and should be universal' has become so radioactive that, according to Canada's anti-protectionist Finance Minister and Deputy Prime Minister Chrystia Freeland, 'it's impossible to utter these words without a shamefaced grimace'.[41]

Globalisation is still very much alive – albeit to a different degree and changing. Describing a world of slowing cross-border trade and investment, dwindling bank loans and shrinking supply chains, *The Economist* called the death of 'The Golden Age of

Globalisation' and labelled the new era we're in 'slowbalisation'.[42] In this new era, companies and countries are emphasising resilience above efficiency, with guaranteed supply – a policy of 'just in case' – taking priority over the lowest cost, the old policy of 'just in time'. Globalisation is facing an identity crisis. But rather than thinking of it in terms of 'fast' or 'slow', we prefer to think of a future defined by a globalisation-lite that will work best if globalisation is managed well and not badly.

Despite Covid and the war in Ukraine, globalisation has endured – although it is bloody, bruised and evolved. There are peaks and valleys – troughs and crests – but that's no different from any business cycle. With shifts in globalisation, planes aren't flying slower. The railways aren't throwing more red lights bringing trains to a halt. And digital traffic is, if anything, moving faster.

While globalisation lives, the era of hyper-globalisation has died. Today's security-focused globalisation-lite is like a dimmer switch that can be turned brighter or darker – heavier or lighter – by balancing the degree of integration countries need with the independence they desire. And the era of hyper-globalisation's bright light showed us what wasn't working in stark relief.

In the United States, the globalisation light has dimmed somewhat. In a recent speech, National Security Advisor Jake Sullivan contested the neoliberal view that all trade is good, that all growth is good and that both lead to prosperity and peace.[43] The bipartisan CHIPS and Science Act of 2022 is spending $50 billion to 'revitalise domestic manufacturing, create good-paying American jobs, strengthen American supply chains, and accelerate the industries of the future'.[44] Micron announced it would spend $100 billion to build a computer chip factory in New York, while Intel is dedicating a similar amount in Ohio.[45] According to the IMF, since the Covid outbreak, 'mentions in companies' earnings presentations of reshoring, onshoring, and near-shoring have increased almost tenfold'.[46] The 'China Plus One' strategy, where companies avoid investing only in China and seek to diversify businesses, is gaining acceptance. But if decoupling becomes a reality, this will only be a temporary response.

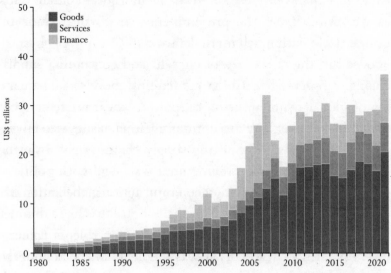

Global flows of goods, services and finance

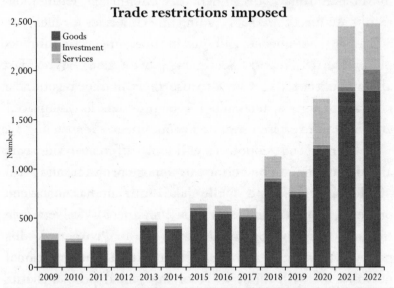

Trade restrictions imposed

Source: Kristalina Georgieva, 'Confronting Fragmentation Where It Matters Most: Trade, Debt, and Climate Action', IMF, 16 January 2023. Note: The figures show exports only.

It will take time, from the announcements of greater protectionism to the implementation of these measures, for reshoring, near-shoring and ally-shoring to shorten global supply chains. Free from protectionist restrictions on cross-border data flows, online trade in services will continue to expand because of advances in digital connectivity as we switch from the pre-eminence of physical trade to online trade with much more data and in turn fewer physical goods. But the sheer size of current and continuing supply chains is reflected in China controlling more than a quarter of global manufacturing output. As we have seen with Covid lockdowns, any disruption in China has severe downstream consequences. Shifting supply chains is not a vanity exercise but a major economic upheaval. And with political considerations now driving economic actions, the shifts are coming fast.

For thirty years, governments saw their role as freeing up – liberating – trade. That was the heart of the neoliberal movement. Today, governments are attempting, with mixed results, to direct markets trading off economics for security, efficiency for resilience, and 'just in time' for 'just in case'. As put by the US Treasury Secretary, Janet Yellen, 'We cannot allow countries like China to use their market position in key raw materials, technologies, or products to disrupt our economy or exercise unwanted geopolitical leverage.'[47]

Both trade and geopolitics will look different in the years ahead and come to be defined by a more protectionist form of globalisation. And while Jake Sullivan has advanced bilateral, regional and issue-based alliances – for example the Indo-Pacific Economic Framework for Prosperity – his policy is more sceptical about the role of the international network of institutions in resolving global problems that need global solutions.[48] And if we get that balance wrong, what the IMF calls 'runaway geoeconomic fragmentation' could lead to 'a new Cold War that could see the world fragment into rival economic blocs'.[49] And fragmentation comes at a cost. IMF data suggests this shift towards greater economic security could reduce global output between 0.2 per cent and 12 per cent depending on the degree of the shift over the coming years.[50] The European Central Bank has calculated the potential impact on inflation where, depending on the degree of wage flexibility in the countries where onshoring occurs, inflation could rise between 0.9 per cent and 4.8 per cent.[51]

That does not need to happen. A new Cold War bringing with it profound economic consequences can be avoided. Indeed, our challenge is to distinguish between what's essential to advance sustained economic growth and what's necessary to preserve countries' autonomy.

Crisis and Comeback

And what's the result of these seismic shifts?

As we write, global trade is anaemic when it should be surging as we emerge from the Covid crisis. WTO Director-General Ngozi Okonjo-Iweala in September 2022 called the global trade outlook 'not promising' due to a confluence of factors, from Russia's war in Ukraine to lingering supply chain bottlenecks, extreme weather events and China's 'Covid Zero' policy.[52] The World Bank warned the global economy was on a 'razor's edge' and at risk of falling into a major recession.[53] And the IMF not only forecasts global growth slowing from 3.4 per cent in 2022 to 2.8 per cent in 2023, but a minimum of five years of low global growth.[54]

Such are the challenges in our permacrisis world. And there's no single strand solution to this permacrisis. But before us are achievable changes to the existing global architecture that could make a world of difference, which we will unpack in the rest of this section.

12

GLOBALISATION-LITE: 'GREAT TASTE, LESS FILLING'

'Avoid the Moon Shot'

Perhaps the boldest, most optimistic expression of globalisation came with Boeing's 787.

Launched in 2004 with a targeted entry into service in 2008, the 'Dreamliner' promised to revolutionise travel. And this revolution wasn't meant to be through speed in the way that the supersonic Concorde halved travel times between New York and London. Or how the 747 made travel affordable and accessible by increasing the number of seats an airline could sell.

The game-changing promise of the 787 was the plane's skin. Up to this point, most airliners were made from aluminium alloy sheets fastened together with rivets. The 787 offered an entirely new approach through composite materials. For the first time, advanced composites would be the dominant material in a commercial airliner offering a 20 per cent reduction in weight, a 30 per cent reduction in maintenance costs, and a 50 per cent reduction in mechanical complexity.[1]

Taken together, these advancements pointed towards a goldilocks aeroplane – a machine that could efficiently and inexpensively transport between 200 and 300 people vast distances while burning very little fuel, costing even less to operate, and

215

bypassing congested hub airports such as Heathrow in favour of longer, less trafficked point-to-point travel.

With figures and promises like these, the plane could sell itself. And it did, becoming the fastest-selling widebody jet in history.[2] There's the obvious way the plane captured the spirit of globalisation by connecting vast distances that previously were unreachable without a layover or unaffordable to operate as a commercial flight – linking Addis Ababa and Rio de Janeiro, Amritsar and Birmingham, and Los Angeles and Lomé.[3]

But there was yet another revolution. The 787 wasn't just connecting the world, it was also built by the world. On the original jumbo jet, the 747, 5 per cent of components came from overseas. On the 787, overseas components were a record 30 per cent, and with domestic non-Boeing suppliers factored in that figure rose to 70 per cent.[4]

Safran in France manufactured landing gear.[5] Cabin lighting came from Diehl in Germany. Alenia in Italy manufactured portions on the horizontal stabiliser. In Japan, Mitsubishi made the wings, Kawasaki the forward fuselage, and Fuji the centre wing box. This was a risky gamble by Boeing to reduce costs, increase margins and spread risk. And it did not pay off.

Layering a new global supply chain with a groundbreaking aircraft design backfired. Boeing's management also took a new approach to managing suppliers. As detailed in the *Harvard Business Review*, 'rather than having the puzzle solved and asking the suppliers to provide a defined puzzle piece, they asked suppliers to create their own blueprints for parts. It should come as little surprise then, that as the components came back from far-flung suppliers, for the first plane ever made of composite materials . . . those parts didn't all fit together.'[6]

Entry into commercial service was pushed from 2008 to

2011 as delays compounded. At the plane's launch, analyst estimates for the 787's development stood at $8.5 billion.[7] By 2021, accounting for overruns and groundings, that figure was believed to be closer to $50 billion.[8] And Boeing at various points had to step in and bring component manufacturing in-house.

Globalisation didn't fail. Indeed, without globalisation the 787 would have never been possible. But both globalisation and Boeing needed to be managed well, and here there were breakdowns. You can't run globalisation by simply saying 'let's work together across oceans' and have haphazard integration. You have to manage globalisation in a co-ordinated way that extends far beyond simply ordering parts from around the world. And here, as is often the case, proper management did not happen.

Reflecting on the 787 fiasco in 2014, Boeing's then CEO Jim McNerney said, moving forwards, 'Our mind-set will be to avoid the moon shot.'[9] Instead, McNerney said, 'We want to be more like Apple', favouring incremental developments. In the time since, that is the path they have pursued with iterative updates to both the 737 and 777. Both models have struggled against newer products from Airbus, and Boeing's market share has suffered. As of 2023, Boeing has not launched a new clean-sheet aircraft since the 787.

A Kinder, Gentler, Managed Globalisation

The Economist holds the view that this new iteration of globalisation 'will be meaner and less stable than its predecessor'.[10] And that may well be the case, but only if it is poorly managed. As the era of hyper-globalisation draws to a close, in its wake we need to deliver a well-managed globalisation-lite.

There's a scene in the 2005 movie *Syriana* where an oil

executive navigating a merger shares the following insight: 'Stare at that liability hard enough and before long it'll turn into an asset.'[11] A well-managed globalisation delivering opportunity and not angst can be an asset, not a liability. The issue isn't whether we have globalisation or not, but rather whether it is managed well or badly.

Countries who reject hyper-globalisation now have the chance to frame globalisation as something that can be managed. Think back to the earlier example of Intel and Micron investing tens of billions of dollars to scale domestic chip manufacturing. America isn't walling itself off to globalisation. Rather, the US is choosing to change how it manages globalisation and foreign vulnerabilities by investing in itself – local economies, local workers and locally manufactured products. And with time, these investments made in the American heartland will radiate outward as those semiconductors reach foreign markets. But the best, most effective industrial policies will not cut America and other countries off from global supply chains. What we must do is manage globalisation in such a way that we get the balance right between the domestic autonomy people seek and the international co-operation people need.

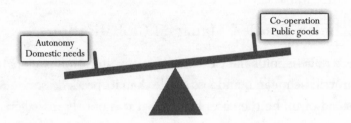

We need not wish away national strategies to improve competitiveness as if they are in conflict with globalisation. So as more of the world's countries develop their own industrial strategies and implement them – 100 countries contributing more than 90 per cent of global GDP now have such plans – it's an opportunity not just to better compete but to better connect with citizens who for too long have been left out and left behind.[12]

The shift to a globalisation-lite – a globalisation that remains open but has become more inclusive and, one hopes, better managed – is also a pathway to a more ecologically conscious and socially responsible economy. We rarely think about beggar-thy-neighbour policies through the lens of what we throw away – the single-use plastics, rotted tyres and decomposing garbage that are byproducts of human existence. There has long been a globalisation of trash with wealthier countries exporting their waste to less advanced economies. Not all of what we throw out winds up in a landfill across town. Every year billions of pounds of scrap and trash are sorted, boxed into containers and put on ships headed to countries around the world. EU waste is likely to wind up in Turkey, American trash in Malaysia and South Korean scrap in Vietnam.

But the trash tide has recently turned. China banned imports in 2018, Malaysia was next, Thailand stopped issuing licences and other countries are sending trash back.[13] This is an instance where countries throwing up barriers where there previously were none is, on balance, better for the world. Why? Wealthy countries should be forced to deal with their own rubbish instead of making it someone else's problem – even if there is a market for those messy goods. Such a shift forces the world's biggest polluters, countries like the US, to come face-to-face with their own waste and devise solutions.

This is better for our climate as global shipping contributes one billion tons of greenhouse gas emissions every year.[14] And it's better for the countries that formerly received the trash as their own environment and populations will now be spared. Having to rethink globalisation as it shifts from hyper to managed provides an opportunity for individuals and countries to become more cost-conscious – not just in a narrow financial sense but also in terms of costs to our environment.

And trash isn't the only unhealthy thing wealthy countries export to poorer ones. There's financial contagion as profligate spending in financial markets has caused global recessions. The West exports inflation through interest rate hikes and a historically high dollar. And then there's what we don't export, skills and education, as funding for these goods is a walled domestic garden that does not trickle down to what Paul Collier calls 'the bottom billion' – the world's poorest.

'Great Taste, Less Filling' was the famous slogan for Miller Lite beer. A managed globalisation-lite would retain what was good about hyper-globalisation with less of the baggage – that same great taste but far less filling. As the name implies, when managed well this new globalisation has the potential to move from punching bag to a pillar of national economic strength and stability.

Build Your Own World Order Adventure

Success in today's new global order means thinking through the kind of arrangements that will manage interdependence successfully, and by extension globalisation, maximising its inclusivity without destroying its openness. The issue is not retreating from the interdependence that defines our everyday lives. Our challenge is to manage interdependence to the benefit of the many and not the few.

In late 2022, with Russia's war in Ukraine still raging, missiles falling into NATO member Poland, and US–China relations coming out of the Bali G20 still firmly rooted in distrust, journalist and foreign policy expert James Traub asked a question: in the aftermath of a near-Third World War-level event, 'How would, or should, the world order be rebuilt?'[15] Traub puts parameters on the thought exercise, among them that we would live within a liberal rules-based order. The hypothetical exercise is a necessary one because seismic geopolitical shifts just as we're experiencing now have previously given birth to new and reformed institutions – from the United Nations to the World Bank. There are many proposed answers to Traub's question worthy of consideration. A global reordering and what it could achieve is one of the driving forces that led us to write this book.

First, there's the idea of an American-led free trade area. Bloomberg's John Micklethwait and columnist Adrian Wooldridge make the case that the answer to our current challenges isn't to 'abandon economic liberalism, but to redesign it'.[16] And they have a very specific redesign in mind – 'the free world comes together and creates another, more united, more interconnected and more sustainable one than ever before'.[17] Given the recent move away from economic integration and the advance of protectionist policies from heightened tariffs to near-shoring and reshoring – not to mention the opposition within America to trade deals that would require, for example, common agricultural standards – this proposal is likely to meet stiff resistance. But even if this American-led free trade area succeeded, it would likely develop without China. Thomas Friedman has a name for this – 'Chexit'.[18]

There's a second idea: a coalition of democracies. Where the American-led free trade area is largely apolitical, the coalition of democracies idea is based on values. As described by Adam Posen, this would look like 'a common market among democracies that is as broad and deep as possible – including for goods, services, and even labour opportunities'.[19] G. John Ikenberry and Anne-Marie Slaughter make the case for a 'Concert of Democracies' where liberal democracies 'commit themselves to a stringent set of obligations towards one another'.[20] This is somewhat similar to Traub's own idea for a 'Compact for Peace and Justice' open to countries agreeing to 'accept the ruling of international judicial bodies, reform the mercantilist and predatory aspects of its economy, moderate support for brutal dictators abroad, and so on'.[21]

Data is currently on the side of those making the case for a liberal coalition. The US and its allies account for more than half of global GDP – 60 per cent in all. So, the task before the Western world would be to 'deepen economic integration among like-minded nations; but leave the door open to autocracies if they become more flexible', and that by advancing free trade we could 'glue together the free world'.[22] And yet qualitatively the proposal runs into trouble. A system of alliances based on values and not interests is absolutist – you're either in or out. And for those countries yearning for a new global order befitting the multipolar era we're in, a Western-led anything will likely feel like the same wine in a different bottle. There's another problem – how democracy is defined varies, and if it suited America's interests to include a non-democracy such as Saudi Arabia, then they would.

We saw this definitional awkwardness on full display during President Biden's 2021 Summit for Democracy. It's no surprise North Korea and Myanmar weren't present. But there were some surprises on the 112-country guest list. Singapore and Bangladesh were not invited and could reasonably complain that countries with a loose relationship with democracy and the rule of law – for example the Philippines, Pakistan, Nigeria and the Democratic Republic of the Congo – were invited. The Biden Administration did not share their invitation criteria, and as analysis from Brookings observed, 'deciding who to include under the first criterion should be more science than art' based on treaties, constitutions and principles.[23]

Richard Haass and Charles Kupchan have a third idea – instead of free trade being the glue bringing the world together, or an ideologically rigid coalition of democracies, a new concert of powers can be the unifying force. Haass and Kupchan see the stabilising force of the Concert of Europe that came together between 1815 and 1914, where France, Russia, Austria, Prussia and the UK communicated and co-operated, as a worthwhile analogue for today's uncertain times. What sets the concert system apart from alternatives is that its two defining characteristics of 'political inclusivity and procedural informality' make it well suited for today's world of contrasts.[24] Under a concert system, gone are binding agreements replaced instead with a forum for dialogue where members can speak privately and candidly without the pressure so often tied to decision-making bodies. Dividing lines between democracies and autocracies also dissolve.

The Concert of Europe is said to have kept the peace for a century – longer than it might have otherwise lasted. But ultimately it couldn't avert the First World War. In Haass and Kupchan's 'Global Concert for the Twenty-First Century', they propose just six members – China, the European Union, India, Japan, Russia and the US – together representing more than 70 per cent of global GDP, a grouping that recalls the old G8 with China and India now added.[25] Together they would 'rely on dialogue to build consensus' and would be free to criticise counterparts where co-operation is not possible. But the two authors assume that the six powers will seek to 'preserve, not overturn, the territorial status quo', which is optimistic in light of China's activities in the Taiwan Strait and South China Sea, not to mention Russia's invasion of Ukraine.

A fourth proposal is for a G2 uniting the US and China recognising the dominance of these two great powers. The late Zbigniew Brzezinski, President Carter's National Security Advisor, put forward the idea of a G2 more closely linking the US and China – a concept echoed by C. Fred Bergsten at the Peterson Institute for International Economics. Brzezinski put it this way in 2009: 'The relationship between the US and China has to be a comprehensive partnership, paralleling our relations with Europe and Japan. Our top leaders should therefore meet informally on a regular schedule for personal in-depth discussions not just about our bilateral relations but about the world in general.'[26] He warned against a static relationship and that inevitably relations between the two countries will 'expand or narrow'. Since then, the case for an expansion has only grown.

Former US Treasury Secretary Hank Paulson has warned against a 'decoupling' between the US and China which would leave us 'with less competitive economies and a less stable and peaceful world'.[27] As Gordon identified in his book *Seven Ways to Change the World*, there are ten fault lines along which we could see a great fracture or decoupling: trade, currency, intellectual property, industrial policy, technological leadership, human rights, the Taiwan question, nuclear weapons, climate change and security challenges including cyberwarfare and supremacy in the Asia-Pacific.[28] This fracturing could lead to the Asian Monetary Fund competing with the IMF, the Asian Infrastructure Investment Bank competing with the World

Bank, the Chinese yuan competing with the US dollar as a global reserve currency, and differing internet standards. The G2 idea has a core deficiency in that it fails to take account of differences in values between the US and China as well as the political barriers to its creation and ability to act.

So where do these proposals leave us? A G2 is no doubt bound to enrage Japan, France, Germany, the EU and other major economies excluded from high-level discussions. An American-led free trade zone is also unlikely to work not just because Congress is against abandoning current policies protecting industries to give sufficient privileges to Europe or Asia, but also because such a zone would only extend to less than half the world. An economic version of the Coalition of Democracies proposal is destined to struggle because America is inconsistent in its own definition of democracy. While it penalises China for abusing human rights, it tolerates regimes like Saudi Arabia and Rwanda. This is hardly the basis for successful global governance, and the end result may be to expel members one-by-one for their failure to adhere to democratic norms within their own borders. The Concert system proposal is problematic as well. By excluding countries from its orbit, the Concert will never be global in nature and will reinforce the idea of an exclusive club-like ideological chasm between the West and East.

There is a draw towards the idea that states other than China and America can come together and use their power as swing states to manage the global economy. A related idea is that civil society – non-governmental organisations and business – could link arms to encircle the world and provide a measure of global governance. These ideas would also likely struggle. Why? Consider the Treaty on the Prohibition of Nuclear Weapons comprising a group of smaller countries. Conspicuously absent are nuclear powers, all but guaranteeing the failure to control nuclear weapons. So, these other options – from civil society coming together to small countries forming their own counter-vailing bloc – aren't a plausible way to think of managing the world.

Perhaps the biggest downside of all of these proposals is that they conjure up new exclusive clubs, and none of them extend across the wider world. While global institutions from the UN to the IMF may not be as impactful as they once were, they still are forces for good. Overlooking international institutions in any proposal is an admission of failure.

American-led Free Trade Area	✗
Coalition of Democracies	✗
Concert of Powers	✗
US–China G2	✗
Civil Society Leading	✗
Radically Reform and Strengthen Existing Institutions	✓

Which brings us to our sixth and primary option: rebuilding the global architecture by reforming international institutions and making the test of co-operation less about the internal arrangements of states and more about whether they are pre-pared to abide by internationally agreed rules of the game.

A New Multilateralism for a Multipolar World

Whether you're replacing a roof or building from the foun-dation up, construction requires permits. Overhauling the international architecture should be no different – there should be a set of standards ensuring all on the job site, in this case countries, are looking at the same set of blueprints and that renovated and renewed institutions will be built to last.

But before countries work together, they need to see if agreement is possible on the minimum baseline rules that will govern any reformed global order. As we have outlined, the case for internationally co-ordinated action cannot be assumed – it has to be made case-by-case and issue-by-issue ranging from resolving disputes without resorting to war, avoiding beggar-thy-neighbour policies, and addressing pandemics, pollution, migration and other threats both people and our planet face.

Any rules must address the autonomy upon which nation states depend for their legitimacy. And when deciding the scope for co-operation, we also have to take into account the world's different value systems, differing systems of government, and the different needs that arise for countries at different stages of development. Contrary to expectations at the end of the Cold War, there has been no universal convergence of ideology, interests and identities into a homogeneous global order.

There is, however, a way forward that achieves a proper balance between autonomy and co-operation, but it depends on us recognising that the independence of each country is constrained by the interdependence of all countries.

Go to Utah's Fishlake National Forest, and you'll find yourself surrounded by 107 acres filled with 47,000 quaking aspen trees. Each of these trees is unique in their own way, but they are all genetically linked with the same root network making the grove one of the world's largest living organisms.[29] Viewed through an international affairs lens, the world is a lot like that aspen grove.

The trees closest to us are our families, friends, neighbourhoods – our immediate surroundings. From there, we

227

fan outward in the grove to countries sharing similar values, systems of government and national missions. The most obvious example is the European Union which, over decades, has moved from being a customs union and then a common market to a single market and currency union. Although the EU is not a fiscal union, members are sufficiently well integrated to redistribute resources from richer to poorer states. The obligations attached to membership of the European Union are clearly more extensive and profound than what is required for affiliation to the United Nations or participation in the World Health Organization. Which brings us outward again in the grove to a set of rules under which countries do not transfer sovereignty, as happens in the European Union, but simply constrain it in areas where there is mutual benefit.

And farthest away in the grove, at the outermost reaches of the frontier, are those we share little in common with except a commitment to peaceful coexistence and non-interference by one country in the ways of life of another. While there will of course be matters that are of national importance to individual states about which no multilateral agreement is possible, there will also be matters of mutual interest where co-operation is desirable – in particular the avoidance of beggar-thy-neighbour policies and the delivery of global public goods.

Dani Rodrik and Stephen Walt have written of what they call a meta-regime, which would be 'a device for structuring a conversation around the issues where states agree and disagree, and facilitating either agreement or accommodation' as the basis of a reformed world order.[30]

The authors rightly identify four broad constructs to guide global action that include 'Minimising the Risk of Major War', 'Respecting Human Rights', 'Preserving Conditions for Sustained Human Existence' and 'Managing the Movement of

Goods, Capital, Information and People'.[31] These basic rules go part and parcel with our proposals for overhauling institutions – from the IMF to the World Bank, WTO, G20 and United Nations – and the need to better deliver global public goods. Rodrik and Walt say there is an inherent incompatibility between deep global integration, national sovereignty and democracy – their version of the trilemma – as if the only choice were between global government and self-government.

We believe it is possible to balance co-operation and autonomy without undermining any country's commitment to their own democratic values, and that is by reforming and restructuring international institutions. Without doubt, countries will agree to pooling and sharing power only after costs are weighed against gains. Because these institutions are unreformed and ill-equipped to meet the new needs of a world that is no longer unipolar, neoliberal or hyper-globalised, we must modernise them so they are fit for purpose and more effective – and that can and should be done to the benefit of all countries.

It is said of the British Constitution that it does not work in theory but it works, at least until recently, in practice. The same may now be said for international co-operation in a world with so many barriers – ideological, ethnic, economic or historical – which together prevent us from pronouncing an overall theory of how co-operation will work in future. However, co-operation can be made to work in practice if we focus issue by issue and institution by institution.

At the outset of the book, we acknowledged that the desirable is not always feasible, and overhauling the global order is where this gap is greatest. But it is not insurmountable.

We are not proposing to go back to the old multilateralism of the post-Cold War world. By placing resilience before efficiency, security concerns now often override the free flows of

229

trade that once characterised our world, and this is unlikely to change anytime soon. And so, we find ourselves in need of a new multilateralism defined by a set of renewed global institutions to deal with issues either not presently covered, or not covered well.

We have to get this right. The tensions between China and America are so great, it's not hard to imagine a total breakdown between the world's leading superpowers with no dialogue on trade, no information exchange on pandemics, no attempt at co-operation in famine prevention, and no burden-sharing for peacekeeping. That would be a world that is completely broken, and that could easily be our world.

Renewing these global institutions would open the door to the kind of multiplicative gains our world needs. Institutions that are able to fund our environmental targets and hold the world accountable. Institutions that help facilitate responsible global investments. And institutions that don't just react to crises but survey and spot the storm clouds on the horizon. Often the building of institutions happens only after a breakdown – a war or financial crisis. But today, given our tight interdependence, the work of rebuilding is not a choice but a necessity.

13

REBIRTH OF INTERNATIONAL INSTITUTIONS

Avoiding a Great Fracture

Reforming international institutions hinges on our willingness to co-operate.

In October 2015, President Xi Jinping made a State Visit to the United Kingdom. Gordon had previously met Xi during, and after, his time as Prime Minister. Far away from prying cameras, the two had a moment to speak candidly about an ever-changing world.

At the start of the conversation, Xi shared his concerns — worries surrounding two traps facing China. The first was the middle-income trap leaving the country in an economic no man's land. The second concern was more sobering: the Thucydides Trap.

'It was the rise of Athens, and the fear that this instilled in Sparta, that made war inevitable,' Thucydides wrote in his *History of the Peloponnesian War*. Peace preceded war with Sparta, but that peace was shattered by Sparta's view of an ascendant Athens challenging its place. War broke out and Sparta, at great cost, defeated Athens. But far more important to world history than the war's outcome is the fact that it happened in the first place.

The American political scientist Graham Allison coined the term 'Thucydides Trap' to describe 'the natural, inevitable discombobulation that occurs when a rising power threatens to displace a ruling power'.[1] Exploring this topic at length in his book *Destined for War*, Allison sees relations between China and the US in a precarious place:

> For seven decades since World War II, a rules-based framework led by Washington has defined world order, producing an era without war among great powers. Most people now think of this as normal. Historians call it a rare 'long peace'. Today, an increasingly powerful China is unraveling this order, throwing into question the peace generations have taken for granted.[2]

Questions exploring the durability of peace abound. Russia's invasion of Ukraine thrust Taiwan into the spotlight leading to renewed questions over how far the US would go to protect the island. The US and China regularly exchange barbs over technology with everything from semiconductors to social media in the crosshairs. And disagreements at global forums from the WTO to the UN lead to visible fissures in the relationship. With varying amounts of enthusiasm, America's allies and partners, such as the European Union, have labelled China not just a 'tough competitor' but a political adversary.[3]

But war, should relations deteriorate to that point, isn't the only risk. Already we are seeing a slide towards a 'one world, two systems' future with competing global institutions, competing alliances, competing plans to command resources, and divergent plans to confront our toughest challenges – from climate change to economic growth. As UN Secretary-General António Guterres has warned, 'Our world cannot afford a future where the two largest economies split the globe in a Great Fracture.'[4] So how can we order the world to avoid this Great Fracture?

One area is obvious. Although it has taken many years to get there, both the US and China now understand that pollution is an existential problem and cannot be solved without the two countries – which are responsible for close to half of global emissions – working together. It's a critical issue where both powers have expressed a desire to co-operate, but at the same time it is not so politically charged that progress is unimaginable. Pollution is just the first issue of many where we need mechanisms for co-operation. And if the two countries are successful in working together in this area, it could open the door to deeper collaborations.

We have to get the guardrails right. Both the US and China should recognise there is an inherent danger to their competition and conflict. But once this is agreed, former Secretary of State Henry Kissinger sees pathways for collaboration appearing with new 'mechanisms by which they can talk to each other in the early phases of crises to see how they could be limited or avoided all together, and how to deal in common with some issues, of which climate control is the most outstanding example'.[5]

During the Cold War, Washington and Moscow talked to avoid nuclear war. Washington and Beijing now need to talk to avoid any number of apocalyptic outcomes – from an accidental conflict to climate catastrophes. While better communication is necessary, it is not sufficient. By creating what China calls a 'safety net', the US and China can lessen the likelihood of disaster, but we are not blind to the reality that risks remain.

And there are two ways of looking at avenues for co-operation: through a bilateral or global lens. At the bilateral level, China and the US can and should aim to reach agreement on issues where they have both spoken of co-operation such as pandemic prevention or climate change mitigation. And at a global level, the two countries should work together *through* international institutions so that these bodies are not just stronger but also more effective. It is by co-ordinating action through stronger, not weaker, international institutions that we will achieve the most.

A fault line that can be mended is how the US and China view and work with post-war international institutions. The G20, United Nations, WTO, IMF and World Bank were designed to support national aims and national public goods. Now our challenge is to reform these institutions so they look beyond borders and deliver global public goods (GPGs) – goods which benefit all countries and individuals.[6] These goods can be enjoyed by everyone without diminishing benefits to anyone. Preserving a rainforest isn't just a national public good but a global public good. The same goes for vaccine development and improved health outcomes. The delivery of global public goods by definition should not lead to rivalries but rather mutual benefits. All of these institutions are in need of reform, and they can only be reformed through co-operation as they are power-sharing bodies.

Reforming the World Trade Organization

How do we get the balance right in the organisation of international commerce between the desire for autonomy and the need for co-operation? Today, there is no international authority explicitly charged with formulating rules on investment, data, the movement of labour and restrictions on international transfers and payments. There are none outside the rich economies club – the Organisation for Economic Co-operation and Development (OECD) – that is setting global rules on taxation, where, despite various initiatives including a new global agreement for a minimum tax on corporate profits and pressure for a UN-led tax convention, limited progress has been made in curtailing tax havens, which undermine the very idea of an inclusive globalisation.

Historically, world trade deals have been the one success of multiculturalism in commerce. The WTO's role has arisen from a basic agreement among its member states to desist from protectionism and mercantilism, whether it be by removing tariff barriers, enforcing intellectual property rights or rejecting other beggar-thy-neighbour policies from industrial subsidies to currency devaluation. Between 1948 and 1995, in the absence of the International Trade Organization that was rejected by the US Congress, GATT – simply a General Agreement on Tariffs and Trade – worked to provide a level playing field by minimising the chances that domestic producers were favoured over foreign competitors. This professedly temporary compromise relied on diplomacy, bargaining and voluntary agreements to resolve disputes. While ensuring tariffs fell to historically low rates, the GATT did not interfere with the social and economic arrangements of its member states. But when the WTO was created with new legally enforceable rules, the balance between autonomy and co-operation shifted.

If the 2009 G20 Summit was a high point in international co-operation in favour of free trade, that spirit did not spill over to the WTO. Since 1993, when the Uruguay Round brought the last multilateral trade agreement, no new world trade agreement has been possible. In today's more integrated and interdependent economy, we can't even get the kind of world trade deals we had in the less integrated economy of the last century. And that's because of nationalism as countries are not prepared to accept they'll be overruled by the WTO.

Not surprisingly, we haven't seen a stagnation in trade cooperation but a regression. All told, some 443 Covid-related trade measures were introduced in recent years with dozens still in effect.[7] The Ukraine war dealt a further blow to international trade, not to mention the very nature of onshoring, near-shoring and ally-shoring, which represents a clear move away from a global trade ethic. And now America and China are increasingly drifting away from the WTO. This is hardly surprising as a growing body of experts have argued that the gains from trade are uneven both between countries and between citizens within countries. Public opinion in advanced economies attributes the loss of manufacturing jobs in developed economies to the opening up of trade rather than to the opening up of technology, and developing countries are frustrated by the promise of well-paid manufacturing jobs that never materialised. They feel that well-paid jobs in advanced economies have been replaced by low-paid jobs in poorer countries and complain that if half the world has advanced, half the population of the developed economies has stagnated.

All this has overshadowed the achievements of the WTO under Director-General Ngozi Okonjo-Iweala whose successful arbitration ended restrictions on food for humanitarian agencies, guaranteed vaccines would be more available to poor countries, ended most fishery subsidies and pushed ahead with a forward-looking agenda covering digital trade and climate change.[8]

But trade agreements have yet to fully recognise just how much the world economy has changed in recent decades. When China joined the WTO in 2001, it accounted for less than 5 per cent of global trade; today its share is more than triple that.[9] Over that same period, the US share has dropped from 11 per cent of global trade to 8 per cent trailing China. During that time, American complaints about unfair competition have escalated. The latest view from the US Trade Representative, Katherine Tai, offered harsh words for China: 'China has not moved to embrace the market-oriented principles on which the WTO and its rules are based, despite the representations that it made when it joined twenty years ago. China has instead retained and expanded its state-led, non-market approach to the economy and trade.'[10] The Peterson Institute for International Economics found that between 2002 and 2018, 'US officials have challenged Chinese practices twenty-three times in the WTO; the win–loss record is 20–0, with three cases pending'.[11] That's a win–loss record any sports team would kill to have.

Some would argue that neither the GATT nor the WTO was designed to cope with the rise of a country like China, which today is classified as a developing economy but is no longer of the same status as low-income countries. Others suggest that universally applicable rules cannot hold when we are dealing with very different ideologies and radically different political systems. This conflict has contributed to a somewhat obstruc- tionist American approach at the WTO, at times blocking appointments to the appellate body due to frustration that WTO judges have the right to overrule member states as, in the words of the Office of the US Trade Representative, 'the WTO has no authority to second-guess the ability of a WTO Member to respond to a wide-range of threats to its security'.[12] This raises a more fundamental question: whether a rules-based and judge-based system can ever offer countries the autonomy they desire. Because no one has yet agreed on any workable reform, the entire WTO system is stalled.

In part, the WTO's troubles arise because the unipolar era is over. Throughout much of the post-war period, not unlike the IMF and World Bank, the WTO was widely regarded as a 'club for members with similar political views'.[13] And to the extent there's a 'club', the US is the ringleader.

If you can't thrive in the club, then start a parallel one with people of like-minded views and interests — which in turn protects your autonomy. And that is what is happening globally with the regionalisation of trade bodies. The Regional Comprehensive Economic Partnership (RCEP), composed of 15 member states throughout the Asia-Pacific and led by China, is the largest trade body in the world, accounting for nearly 30 per cent of global GDP.[14] The body has few rules members have to follow, although its strength has been somewhat hampered by India's decision not to join.

China has also sought to join the 11-member Comprehensive and Progressive Agreement for Trans-Pacific Partnership (CPTPP), the successor to the Trans-Pacific Partnership the US conceived but then abandoned. An important step towards avoiding a one world, two systems future could come from a joint US–China ascension of the CPTPP. This wouldn't be to the benefit of just the two countries but the entire Pacific Rim. The WTO must work within and alongside these regional trade bodies as it now makes no sense to circumvent them.

Not surprisingly, China also wants to see change at the WTO. Xi Jinping has called for 'reform of the World Trade Organization and the international financial and monetary system in a way that boosts global economic growth and protects the development rights, interests and opportunities of developing countries'.[15] That's code for leadership positions within these institutions and greater voting shares in some of them. China feels its rise as a global powerhouse has not been met with rising respect across global institutions – quite the opposite as it is perceived by the United States to continually be a threat.

So how do we get the autonomy–co-operation balance right at the WTO? While other major reforms are needed, including 'updating the WTO's subsidy rulebook to address level playing field concerns in agriculture, industry and services and the growing digital economy', overshadowing this is a reformed and functional dispute settlement system.[16] Countries like the US, as suggested by the WTO's former legal affairs officer, should explore reforming dispute resolution by making it faster and more transparent by 'putting more issues into the mix . . . such an approach can be an effective way to resolve differences, as there are more opportunities for tradeoffs'.[17] And that requires more flexibility, more use of arbitration, and it may mean more time at negotiation tables and fewer courtroom edicts. There's already progress on this front with Director-General Okonjo-Iweala aiming for a 2024 overhaul of the dispute system.

For the WTO to remain relevant, all parties will need to recommit to basic principles that encourage them to work through the organisation and not around it. So, alongside an updated dispute resolution process and defining country status, active members should have their trade representatives come together to outline a reimagined WTO 2.0.[18] An over-hauled WTO must take account of the current geopolitical landscape and trends towards reshoring and ally-shoring, as well as the likely expansion of regional trade agreements. Accusations that the WTO is blinkered, focusing narrowly on the interests of wealthy members at the expense of poorer countries, can be put to rest with a more holistic approach that resets the balance between autonomy and co-operation by protecting labour and trading rights, especially in poorer countries.

And most of all, as Dani Rodrik suggests, the WTO will have no choice but to live with, if not embrace, a 'diversity in economic models'.[19] It makes practical sense for the WTO and member countries to reject a narrow 'my way or the highway' approach. Industrial policy is back on the agenda everywhere, and at least some important aspects of the economic models employed by China and other rising economies are the very same tools the Western world used to get where they are today. Of course, regional trade agreements will be more extensive than the thin agreements that encompass the entire world, but we should try to ensure decisions on trade are less a 'them versus us' issue and more about 'them and us' and jointly finding a way to co-operate in defining the rules of competition.

A Reimagined G20

As explored in the prior chapter, talk of a US–China G2 should serve as a wake-up call to an outdated G20. As is the case in the private sector, a lack of change opens the door for 'disruptions' – that oft-used term to describe everything from talkative pupils to the emergence of Uber and Lyft challenging taxis.

As G20 summits come and go, the group has shown its limitations in addressing global public goods either on a country-by-country basis or through multilateral institutions such as the World Bank. G20 members have failed to consistently propose co-ordinated measures to address topical issues from inflation to surging energy prices. And when proposals are introduced, such as 2009's 'Multilateral Action Process' to co-ordinate a global push for non-inflationary growth, they don't go anywhere. And the G20, as implied in the name, is now too exclusive a club for an interconnected world where the decisions of the few impact the many.

The US, China and Europe, as the dominant members within the G20, should lead on a reform programme to increase the G20's ability to take collective action that makes a difference. As a starting point, the G20 lacks a secretariat – a consistent home base of operations. Other multilateral institutions have secretariats with the United Nations in New York City, the WHO and WTO in Geneva, and NATO in Brussels. Under the G20's current structure, instead of having a permanent head-quarters co-ordinating action, the annual G20 Chair establishes a temporary secretariat for their term usually based in the chair country's capital. Representatives of G20 members, known as sherpas, work through the temporary secretariat in what is an inefficient and ineffective system that limits transparency and co-ordinated action.

The G20 should have a permanent base. And rather than power being concentrated in the hands of sherpas, it should be spread across functional issue areas with teams of experts as is the case at the World Bank, IMF and UN. Countries have offices, the offices are composed of experts, and these experts help drive policies. The G20 lacks such a structure. And while bureaucracy is often thought of as a bad word, there are positive reasons why the profession has endured for millennia.

There's also an ongoing question surrounding the relation-ship between the G20 and the IMF. The distinction should be drawn that the G20 is a meeting of political leaders, while the IMF is run by administrators of an economic system. While the IMF is focused on stability, best practices, tech-nical assistance and surveillance, the G20 has a far broader mandate. We could think of an expanded G20 with its own constituency system as a forum where political leaders set out the strategy that international civil servants at the World Bank, IMF and WTO implement.

What is more, the G20 desperately needs a consistent agenda that is not dictated by the whims of chairs but the needs of the broader group. The current system where the presidency rotates annually is ineffective and leads to frenetic and unfocused communiques often skewed towards the issues appealing to the host country rather than the challenges impacting the wider group. Expanding the duration of the presidential term and making it a co-presidency with more than one state sharing the post simultaneously before a rotation occurs would result in more representative, and thoughtful, communiques.

G20 countries represent around 85 per cent of world GDP, 75 per cent of international trade and about two thirds of the world population.[20] And yet major economies in Africa such as Egypt and Nigeria, and in Asia with Singapore and Vietnam, are not permanent members. While the chair can invite guest countries to participate in the summit, this is not an inclusive process as it mainly reflects the chair's interests. And despite the G20's stated goal of securing 'economic growth and prosperity', the world's poorest countries most in need of assistance are altogether unrepresented, as America has now recognised with its support for greater African representation.

An enhanced G20 that finally includes more comprehensive developing-country coverage would at last achieve the representation, and thus the legitimacy, it needs to be effective as the premier decision-making forum for the global economy. That could be achieved by extending the membership; by 2050, 11 of the biggest 20 economies will be Asian countries and will need to be included. And by then, Africa will account for 25 per cent of the world's population and won't be satisfied with one member seat out of 20. So, the best way forwards might be a constituency system where countries are formed into geographical groups and, on a revolving basis, choose one country to be their annual representative. Far too many countries are excluded from the G20 decision-making table, so it's time to build a more representative one.

A Nimbler United Nations

The United Nations presents a particular challenge when it comes to reform efforts precisely because of the manner in which it was created relying on consensus. Indeed, the search for consensus can lead to the discovery of impasse. Dag Hammarskjöld, an early Secretary-General, famously alluded to this challenge: 'Everything will be all right – you know when? When people, just people, stop thinking of the United Nations as a weird Picasso abstraction and see it as a drawing they made themselves.'[21] If the UN is an abstraction, at least to some, then it's time for a reinterpretation and rethinking.

The United Nations should not be dismissed or disregarded. Over 80 years, the UN has played a central role in peacekeeping, reducing poverty and setting ambitious global targets such as the Sustainable Development Goals which, while a work in progress, are moving the world towards a better future. If the UN did not exist, a natural impulse would be to create such an assembly of nations. The body has presided over failures as well, from underfunding those global goals to slowly reacting to atrocities and genocide. Through it all, the UN's relevance endures. Kevin Rudd, as Chair of the Independent Commission on Multilateralism, wrote a 2016 report detailing pathways for UN reform noting that one of the many reasons the UN matters is that it 'cannot readily be replaced' and is capable of reinventing itself.[22]

The top item on many reform lists is the Security Council, the UN's principal organ tasked with international peace and security. Not unlike the G20, the Security Council is an exclusive club of five permanent members – China, France, Russia, the UK and the US – with ten rotating members. UN Peacekeepers deployed by the Security Council have helped keep the peace in hotspots around the world, from the Sinai Peninsula to the former Yugoslavia. But despite being the most powerful and influential UN body, the Security Council is plagued by two long-recognised structural flaws: a limited membership and *liberum veto* where all it takes is one 'no' vote to obstruct a proposal. It is weak by design. As was the case in 2022, when the Security Council took up a resolution to demand Russia cease its war on Ukraine. Russia promptly vetoed the proposal.

Writing in 2006, G. John Ikenberry and Anne-Marie Slaughter pitched a suite of reforms for the United Nations. Their vision was for a 'representative and effective' Security Council with an expanded membership paired with an abolition of one-country veto power making swift crisis response possible.[23] Back then they were talking about the responsibility to protect, the need to confront genocide in Darfur, nuclear weapons in Iran, and simmering tensions between Israel and Hezbollah. Times have changed, but the issues have not. They have only multiplied. From the civil war in Syria to genocide in Myanmar and Russia's invasion of Ukraine, an empowered and emboldened Security Council certainly would not have hurt our chances at resolving these crises.

Expanding Security Council membership is, over time, an achievable goal. The world has changed a great deal since the five permanent members were originally selected in 1945. France and the United Kingdom have seen their economic power steadily diminish, while India, Brazil, Indonesia,

Nigeria, South Africa and Egypt have emerged as major economic and regional powers all keen for permanent Security Council representation that would make resolutions more inclusive and representative, which might lessen the perception of a Western-centric power structure. Expanding the membership would also likely help to address the first challenge facing the council, veto power, by removing the requirement for unanimity on issues surrounding human rights and acts of aggression, and it would allow a renewed emphasis on the responsibility to protect citizens from abuses beyond genocide.

The challenges don't end there. Unsurprisingly, the UN has its own budget woes. Member countries are assessed based on national income and population – the US pays billions to Botswana's millions, as well as funds independently directed to various UN organs, from the World Health Organization to the World Food Programme. But member countries don't always pay what they can afford – or are supposed to pay. Under President Trump, the US suspended funding the UN Population Fund and reduced funding for the UN Programme on HIV/AIDS and the WHO.[24] As political winds shift in member countries, contributions fluctuate even though the UN's costs only increase.

To make matters worse, assessments only cover a limited portion of the UN's budget – the gap must be filled by voluntary contributions from member countries and other donors. In the United States, it is common around the holidays to see children with UNICEF charity boxes collecting loose change for school drives. As Kevin Rudd identified in his report, the UN has a budget process 'unlike any other corporate institution in the world' – a process that begins two years and three months before the beginning of that year, an 11-stage decision-making process, and an 8,000-plus-page proposal.[25] This must be addressed. The days of a begging bowl being circulated must come to an end with a dedicated funding stream. The UN's global role cannot be quashed by budget woes. Financial innovations and greater burden-sharing, measures long called for by Secretary-General Guterres, can help to address budget shortfalls.

Aliens Incoming

Areas of co-operation are evident. The need is there. All that is missing is political will.

So, will the US and China come together to confront a big issue? Years after the 1985 Geneva Summit, Premier Mikhail Gorbachev would recount a memorable conversation with President Reagan. During a conference break, Reagan asked him if Russia would cease hostilities and come to America's aid in the event of an alien invasion.[26] Gorbachev said, 'No doubt about it,' and Reagan said the US would do the same for Russia. While that scenario never came to pass, the spirit of the dialogue made clear that some issues are big enough to thaw the coldest of tensions.

Similar to how Reagan and Gorbachev agreed to cease hostilities in the event of an alien invasion, could the world's two pre-eminent powers today, the US and China, set aside their differences to help the world? They could, but only time will tell if they do.

By seizing on areas of agreement, and trying to work around areas of disagreement, progress can be made. This is what Joseph Nye calls 'Peace in Parts'.[27] Progress in one arena can spill over into another and help to build an enduring peace, or at the very least lessen the likelihood of conflict. Small steps can turn into big co-operative leaps that don't just benefit the US and China, but the wider world.

14

FINANCING OUR FUTURE

Well and Good

If you want to learn about the history of the Hawaiian Islands, James Michener's novel *Hawaii* is a good place to start. Telling the story of the islands from their volcanic birth on through to becoming a part of the US, it's a sweeping history rife with colourful lessons and rich detail.

The economic power structures of the Hawaiian Islands we know today were, in many ways, shaped by missionaries who became the island's 'founding families'. Michener famously captured the mood of this period, writing:

> In later years, it would become fashionable to say of the missionaries, 'They came to the islands to do good, and they did right well.' Others made jest of the missionary slogan, 'They came to a nation in darkness; they left it in light,' by pointing out: 'Of course they left Hawaii lighter. They stole every goddamned thing that wasn't nailed down.'[1]

It's an interesting lesson – the tenuous relationship between what it means to do 'good' and 'well'. How paternalistic, hierarchical structures can damage and destroy cultures and societies. How the helping hand is often the helping oneself hand. How market forces are always at play.

247

The international institutions born after the Second World War, institutions that defined the *Pax Americana* following the fall of the Soviet Union, did a tremendous amount of good by reducing poverty, fighting disease and helping economies grow. But talk to the people on the receiving end of those interventions, and time and again one hears a different story – a story of painful structural reforms as conditions for economic lifelines and of aid coalescing around donor darlings leaving far too many countries orphans.

To meet and master our toughest challenges in the years ahead – and do a bit of good along the way – the world's international financial institutions must be overhauled.

Meet the Bretton Woods Sisters

Both the World Bank and the International Monetary Fund were born out of the 1944 Bretton Woods Conference. Originally known as the International Bank for Reconstruction and Development (IBRD), the Bank was tasked with helping post-war Europe rebuild. Only in the 1960s did the Bank make the big shift from reconstruction to development when it set up the International Development Association (IDA) to provide highly concessional loans, or credits, to the poorest countries, helping to provide the funding for heavy infrastructure projects from power stations to roads as well as fighting poverty, ill-health and illiteracy. World Bank aid played a role in lifting hundreds of millions out of poverty, as was the case in China.

The International Monetary Fund was set up to perform a different role serving as a lender of last resort for countries in crisis, with its goal as a facilitator of global macroeconomic co-operation substantially watered down from the original ambitions of its British architect, John Maynard Keynes.

While the World Bank and the IMF have different roles, it is important to talk about them together. The two institutions are the two truly global economic institutions that share a past, and that will be true of the future as well. The question is what kind of future.

For 80 years, the World Bank and IMF haven't always been the saviours that countries have wanted through emergency loans or development initiatives. Even in the best of financial times, take 1960, the lending arm of the World Bank was only able to support loans equal to a little over 1 per cent of GDP in middle-income countries. Structural adjustment programmes have, at times, mandated borrower countries adopt austerity and free market policies of deregulation and privatisation, selling off state-owned enterprises.

Now the country-led model cannot cope with global problems that require global solutions through the delivery of global public goods that address everything from climate change to pandemics. As noted by Treasury Secretary Janet Yellen, 'our existing multilateral development finance architecture was not designed to address these types of cross-border challenges'.[2]

Too often we see countries pursuing their own narrow interests through the World Bank and other development banks. There's nothing wrong with self-interest, but we run into problems when we think about externalities – how one country's spending comes with side effects for another country and the wider world. Tackling global public goods demands a global lending model the World Bank can lead. And in a more interdependent and integrated world, the IMF needs to adopt a complementary role – surveillance of the global economy.

Can America and Germany, which have both called for reform of the World Bank, and China, which is seeking to moderate Western leadership of the IMF and the World Bank, agree on a restructuring that reshapes these institutions for new times and gives them a new relevance?

The need is profound and urgent. After decades of impressive progress, the World Bank's primary objective of poverty reduction has stalled. Today, roughly 650 million people – 8 per cent of the world's population – still live in extreme poverty surviving on less than $2.15 a day, the current international poverty line set by the World Bank, and few think that figure will be substantially reduced by 2030, the deadline set by the international community for abolishing extreme poverty.[3] And if we bump the threshold up to $6.85 per day, the watermark used for upper-middle-income countries, close to half of the global population lives below that level. But while post-Covid needs are now greater, low-income and lower middle-income countries are less well placed to spare their populations from poverty and to sustain quality education, healthcare and employment opportunities. Total gross debt in developing countries reached 42 per cent of gross national income in 2020 denying them the fiscal space needed to spend on anti-poverty programmes.[4]

The World Bank has a second objective beyond the abolition of extreme poverty 'on a livable planet' – an objective which is still beyond its reach – and that is to raise the income share of the bottom 40 per cent of the world.[5] While this can measure the extent to which economic growth is inclusive, overall growth rate matters too. The more that poor countries diverge from their wealthier counterparts, the more difficult it is to raise the incomes of the less well off.

Not only are extreme poverty on the rise and within-country inequalities widening, but problems ranging from pollution to pandemics require us to deliver global public goods. In turn, the World Bank must embrace an expanded mission – financing global public goods. And all global priorities face a steep financing mountain to climb. As of 2022, health accounts for only 15 per cent of World Bank annual financing, while education is under 5 per cent. That's less than 20 per cent of Bank spending going towards two of the most pressing global public goods.

The World Bank is still the single largest source of development financing and is uniquely placed to help deliver the Sustainable Development Goals with an enhanced global public goods framework. But set against the needs that have to be met, the available resources appear inadequate. When it comes to the cost of financing the Sustainable Development Goals and global public goods, the bill tops $4 trillion annually.[6]

When we look beyond domestic sources of finance to international aid as a whole, official development assistance is stuck at around $180 billion a year – a fraction of the $4 trillion needed. And while other financing for development such as hard loans provided by the World Bank surged to $150 billion during the Covid crisis, it was just $115 billion pre-crisis. In real per capita terms, support for middle-income countries is already below the levels seen in the 1980s.

Despite its tremendous potential to do good, today World Bank lending is shrinking as a share of the world economy. In 1960, the Bank's main division, IBRD, had loans outstanding worth over 1 per cent of middle-income country GDP. Today they are half that. In the ten years from 1995, financing for development from the World Bank to low- and lower middle-income countries averaged $19 billion a year, or 1.1 per cent of the national income of those countries. But in the ten years to 2019, financing for development averaged $47 billion a year or 0.7 per cent of the GDP in those countries. Even as the population of Africa doubles by 2050, the World Bank estimates support for low-income countries through IDA will more than halve.

Various initiatives have attempted to combine in-country support with the delivery of global public goods. Most recently, the Bridgetown Initiative led by Barbados Prime Minister Mia Mottley demanded action from both the public and private sectors, including the development of carbon markets and natural disaster clauses in sovereign, development bank and private sector debt contracts as part of a wider set of initiatives on debt restructuring. But the main burden to deliver our global public goods falls on the IMF and the World Bank.

Over at the IMF – where to her credit Managing Director Kristalina Georgieva has made resilience, sustainability and health priorities – the Fund should offer better-designed loans to countries in payments crisis, and there are growing calls for a Mitigation Trust Fund financed by new money to ensure countries in need will not have their development goals derailed by the threat of default. But the World Bank should be the tip of the spear in this work, expanding its lending by boosting its capital base and being more innovative in the way it uses existing resources and leverages guarantees, as well as making developing countries eligible for more concessionary lending.

A Renewed and Recapitalised World Bank

Taken together, the World Bank has $268 billion in equity that supports $470 billion in its stock of financing – from hard and soft loans to developing countries, to investments including equity and loans to support the private sector, and guarantees against political risk.

Former US Treasury Secretary Larry Summers identifies overhauling the World Bank as the Biden Administration's 'greatest opportunity for a key foreign-policy achievement', and that the Bank could become 'a major vehicle for crisis response, post-conflict reconstruction, and, most importantly, for support-ing the huge investments necessary for sustainable and healthy global development'.[7] That'll come at a price. The World Bank has incredible potential to be the world's global public goods bank, further reinforcing its development mandate, and such a shift will require a comprehensive set of reforms under its new president, Ajay Banga. Fortunately, President Banga recognises this. Writing in the *Financial Times* shortly after his nomination, Banga identified climate change, migration and pandemics as stark reminders that the World Bank 'must now evolve to tackle challenges that its founders couldn't imagine' and the central role the private sector will play in this work.[8]

President Banga is right. The World Bank has to be the proactive catalyst for mobilising funds. In 2015, a report from the IMF and World Bank titled 'From Billions to Trillions: Transforming Development Finance' envisaged the need for 'a paradigm shift' in development finance 'to catalyse and lever-age' the development aid budget.[9] Embracing a broad financing model with clusters for global issues such as health, education and the environment would force the World Bank and donor countries to move away from a country-by-country atomistic approach and towards a model guided by a broader strategy and a more holistic view of development.

The World Bank has to be the platform upon which we mobilise private finance. But today there is no incentive, as there should be, for World Bank officials to account for mo-bilising private funds to back up the use of public funds. This could include co-financing with the private sector, de-risking potential investments through subordinated loans and guaran-tees, and improving in-country capacity for public investments.

And therein lies the Bank's real challenge – crowding in the funding necessary to address these global public goods. But for that to happen, funding must be mobilised not only from the private sector but also member countries. We need to grow the World Bank's capital base and balance sheet so it doesn't just lecture others about addressing global public goods but puts up money to get the job done. Funding our global goals and addressing global public goods means we need to find money where we don't think there is any. We need to squeeze all of the funding we can out of the limited pools that exist.

So, let's start by looking at lending by the World Bank's premier facility for middle-income countries: IBRD. While it reached a peak of more than $30 billion during the Covid crisis, it averaged $21 billion between 2011–20. That's not enough when we consider the trillions needed to achieve the Sustainable Development Goals.[10]

And that's not the only problem. The funding pool is so small, and the process so bureaucratic that the average loan takes more than two years to fund. When you're a country in the emergency room, that's a long time to wait for surgery, hence why countries turn to the IMF as a lender of last resort. By comparison, the IMF cuts cheques at light speed but with greater conditionality and some stigma. But there's another problem with those IBRD loans – they're loans with interest, not grants.

Just like how rising interest rates force home buyers out of the market, the same has happened with finance ministers who then choose not to invest in public goods. Low-income countries are able to benefit from the International Development Association (IDA), the World Bank's funding window for the world's poorest countries, which offers loans at a 1.25 per cent rate. But once countries graduate to lower middle-income status, their lender generally becomes IBRD – not IDA – and with the shift come higher interest rates and less favourable terms. As a result, countries graduating from cheap IDA financing to IBRD market terms see lending for human development fall by 60 per cent.[11] A given country's desire to spend on climate change mitigation or education declines.

The current structure of World Bank lending punishes countries who move up the economic ladder but still want to invest in development. Think of the IBRD and IDA windows as lemonade stands – the IDA stand is offering you a much better deal.

The solution has been long-acknowledged – expanding the capital base which will in turn allow the Bank to lend more. That will require the Bank to pursue a General Capital Increase where shareholders cough up more money. The Centre for Global Development estimates that a $32 billion increase in the same proportion could provide just under $50 billion annually to 2030. In our work to run up the funding numbers to address both human capital and climate change together, that's a start.

But the World Bank could further expand its lending power by more strongly leveraging International Development Association equity and thus be in a better position to offer more help to low-income countries. The IDA arm does not work like a traditional bank utilising leverage but rather functions more like a grant-awarding and lending fund. And many of these loans are coming due with IDA standing to benefit from, and able to borrow more on the strength of, future repayments on long-term loans awarded decades ago. All told, IDA equity has a conservative value in excess of $180 billion, and so leveraging IDA could provide an additional $100 billion in capital the World Bank could deploy.

There's another option before the World Bank, and that is merging its low-income country fund, IDA, with the IBRD fund catering to wealthier countries.

Which brings us to leverage – an underutilised and powerful tool that, when used properly, will not endanger the AAA rating of the World Bank. When you carry a balance on a credit card or take out student loans, that's leverage. The challenge in international development is that the spending limit on the funding credit card has historically been very low. The five times leverage IBRD can unlock is good, but not great. That's the old development financing architecture.

A merger between IDA and IBRD would quadruple the capital from $50 billion in IBRD to just under $200 billion with the addition of around $180 billion in equity from IDA. Further discounting the IDA equity by 25 per cent for credit risk would still leave $100 billion in equity from which IBRD could make $500 billion in loans to middle-income countries. Add that $500 million to perhaps as much as $100 billion from a General Capital Increase, and that $600 billion does not get us close enough to the SDG funding gap. Policymakers must look elsewhere. Let's explore what could become a new finance model.

In the second half of 2023, we are finally seeing the emergence of International Financing Facilities (IFF). The Asian Development Bank announced a new climate fund built around guarantees from the US and eight other countries, and will soon apply the same model to financing education.[12] In their report advocating a tripling of annual multilateral investment by 2030, India's G20 working group, co-chaired by Larry Summers, has advocated a similar guarantee-based facility that would raise $30–40 billion, echoing a 2022 G20 report on global health. A similar proposal is being examined by Mia Mottley's path-breaking Bridgetown 2.0 initiative. And under the fresh thinking of Ajay Banga, the World Bank has announced a new portfolio fund converting guarantees volunteered by shareholders into new investments worth $30 billion.[13] All of these programmes are based on the intelligent use of guarantees, and all reflect growing support for the IFF model.

The Power of IFF

Getting to great demands new thinking, and the International Financing Facility framework offers just that. What sets the IFF apart is that it uses guarantees provided by shareholders, and this in turn frees up multilateral development bank capital for other lending. Leverage, the amount you can borrow, is always tied to credit risk. Similar to how wealthy individuals often have good credit scores, developed lender countries tend to have very good credit ratings allowing them to borrow and lend at minimal costs.

Instead of taking in $1 of capital, the IFF consists of $0.15 in paid-in capital and $0.85 in guarantees. Therein lies the power of IFF. Then the IFF can go to a multilateral development bank such as the World Bank and leverage the portfolio further, drawing on the bank's AAA credit rating so $1 becomes $4. All told, through a small amount of paid-in capital and strong guarantee backing, that initial 15 cents can get leveraged to $4. A 27-times leverage multiplier on low-risk, paid-in capital for a development loan is unprecedented as compared with 5 times at IBRD.

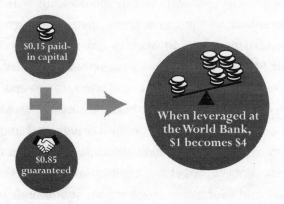

257

This is a window of opportunity the world cannot afford to miss. Multiple International Finance Facilities could be set up for any number of specific causes. With 130 million people experiencing acute hunger, 260 million children out of school, and one in three people lacking access to safe drinking water, the need for development assistance is there.[14] In practice, a group of countries seeking to make an impact on a specific issue could make their contributions backed by guarantees, co-ordinate through the multilateral development banks, and then deploy the funds to ensure children are schooled, drinking water is accessible, or hunger is eradicated.

Let's meet unmet needs through unused – and underused – resources.

IMF as an Early Warning and Crisis Prevention Agency

Let's not forget about the other Bretton Woods Sister. Without question, the IMF must continue to fulfil the primary job it assumed in the post-Bretton Woods world: that of crisis manager, providing emergency liquidity for countries experiencing financial shocks. The progressive leadership of Kristalina Georgieva has been good for the IMF, but in the future it will have to do even more. During the Covid crisis, the IMF pledged to put its $1 trillion balance sheet to work to save the world economy. In fact, only $267 billion of new financing was approved.

No one would dispute that crisis management and crisis prevention go hand-in-hand. And yet the complaint against the IMF is that too often in its interaction with countries facing exchange rate volatility, capital flight and national balance-sheet vulnerabilities, it does not get the balance right between respecting national autonomy and delivering co-operative solutions. On the one hand, it is criticised for invading individual countries' independence, which makes it unpopular and even illegitimate in the eyes of debtor countries. On the other hand, it is criticised for doing too little in areas where it could act with greater legitimacy.

In the wake of the 1997 Asian Financial Crisis, Gordon, as Chair of the G7 Finance Ministers, visited all the main Asian economies and saw a clear pattern. In country after country, it was evident that the IMF overreached, overriding not just national politicians but long-established national institutions by insisting that its agenda for liberalisation was the only route to credibility and prosperity. These interventions fared so badly that they gave rise to a demand for an Asian Monetary Fund, made China-led agreements advancing currency swaps more attractive to the continent than turning to the IMF, and led Asian countries to believe they had to amass far bigger currency reserves than were necessary. In the words of the respected central banker Paul Tucker, the IMF 'appeared as an instrument or organ of supranational governance rather than an agent of international co-operation'.[15]

The IMF's crisis prevention mission should lead it to be more ambitious. Gordon was Chair of the committee overseeing the body until the spring of 2007, and in this role he introduced a new report that would monitor and identify risks to the global economy. But this form of surveillance was in its infancy, and not once did the report explicitly warn of financial turbulence because of excessive risk-taking and overleveraged financial institutions. Fatefully, the IMF missed the early warning signs in advance of the Global Financial Crisis.

After an agreement between the German central bank, the UK and the US, a Financial Stability Forum was set up in 1999 in the wake of the Asian Financial Crisis to provide economic surveillance services alongside the Bank for International Settlements. The Forum was then upgraded into a Board following the Global

Financial Crisis-focused 2009 London G20. And yet here we are more than a decade on and the surveillance radar remains imperfect as evidenced by the financial crises and accidents that continue to rock our world. It's clear that the Financial Stability Board has to be strengthened yet again, and the IMF should step in by embracing in full the vacant role of a global economic surveillance and early warning organisation – identifying risks and threats and forecasting potential impacts to the global economy.

There's a practical benefit to this focus on best practices: countries would be better positioned for oncoming shocks and less likely to have to seek out emergency loans or hold huge reserves to service debts. And there is a good reason why proper surveillance is more needed than ever.

Today, the IMF risks missing an even more worrisome storm cloud on the horizon: a global shadow banking crisis. Shadow banks, or non-bank financial intermediaries (NBFIs), operate outside the jurisdiction of financial authorities like the Federal Reserve and instead operate in the 'shadows' with depositor funds unprotected and balance sheets mostly escaping supervision and regulation. The bets that shadow banks make with depositor funds go largely unregulated. And a stress test of some of these non-banks, specifically liability-driven investment funds, only assumed a 1 per cent rise in interest rates – far below the actual rate. Even then, many struggled.

Unlike the largest regulated banks, these institutions are not subjected to the same kind of stress tests to make sure they can continue to operate in the face of economic slowdowns, and do so without posing a risk to global financial and economic wellbeing. A 2021 report from the Financial Stability Board estimates that NBFIs account for roughly 50 per cent of global financial assets worth more than $200 trillion dollars.[16] This is one graveyard the world can't afford to whistle past. Alongside the Bank for

International Settlements and the Financial Stability Board, the IMF should take the lead in sounding the alarm.

The historical roots of the IMF's surveillance mission can be traced back to the organisation's infancy following the Second World War. Before an emergency loan was made, and throughout the lending period, the IMF would continuously monitor the balance of payments. Back then, the IMF conducted this surveillance privately without saying much publicly. Today, in an interconnected world, the IMF must be open and transparent about what it sees. While a country's books may not be open, tightly bound global interdependence has changed the game with incomplete information threatening not just one country – but everyone.

Asymmetric information has been the cause of, or the contributing factor to, multiple crises. In the run-up to the Global Financial Crisis, different stakeholders with different degrees of information on bad debt, problematic leverage and terrible market bets capitalised on the lack of information held by the counterparty. Ahead of 9/11, US intelligence agencies were infamously siloed and didn't share knowledge that could have averted disaster. We have to make do with the information we have, but humanity is better off when knowledge is shared.

Surveillance is a powerful tool when used properly. So, the IMF should 'stretch its analytic boundaries' to survey and forecast the adverse impacts of climate change, pandemics and new trade barriers.[17] There's nothing to stop the IMF from doing this.

From reducing poverty to vaccinating the globe against deadly diseases, the global public goods the World Bank needs to fund must be backstopped by the IMF telling the story of what happens if we fail to finance these investments.

Risk-modelling isn't just good for the bottom line, but also the bottom up, helping countries to plan and prepare for challenges ahead. A 2016 report from the Center for Global

Development identified the potential for 'upgraded disease surveillance and pandemic prevention and management' as an area with positive spillover effects benefitting multiple countries.[18] With the advantage of hindsight, it's easy to imagine how this surveillance could have helped the world mitigate the Covid pandemic. And a new report identifies a 28 per cent risk of a new pandemic within the next decade.[19] The power of surveillance doesn't just hold true for pandemics, but also other global public goods such as climate change. Indeed, climate surveillance has been added to the responsibilities of central banks and should be an area of focus for the IMF.

First introduced in 2009 at the G20 in London as the Mutual Assessment Process (MAP) to prepare a co-ordinated global growth plan, the IMF should resume this work seeking to co-ordinate a global push for non-inflationary growth. Back then the world was reeling from the Global Financial Crisis, and many of those same challenges – from low growth to high inequality now layered with inflation – persist today. A renewed Mutual Assessment Process could encourage and bring about a more ambitious global growth plan.

Today, the IMF's status as the world's pre-eminent lender of last resort, and its capacity to set the right terms, is under threat – principally from China. Perhaps as an outgrowth of China's Belt and Road Initiative investing hundreds of billions of dollars in infrastructure projects in developing countries, an initiative that directly challenges the World Bank, China has now diversified into emergency lending. Since 2017, Pakistan, Sri Lanka and Argentina have together received more than $32 billion in emergency loans.[20] IMF loans are conditional and come with painful adjustments. By comparison, Chinese emergency loans have tended to be more akin to a spoonful of sugar without the medicine. With the backdrop of the war in

Ukraine and the subsequent collapse of the Russian rouble due to sanctions, there has been a flight to safety in currencies. The United States, of course, has been a beneficiary with countries moving large portions of their reserves from local currencies into dollars reinforcing the greenback's status as a global reserve currency. But China has sought to expand interest in the Renminbi in currency swaps as an effort to move towards a more fully fledged reserve currency.

Through it all, China has stated its readiness and willingness to co-operate at the IMF. If the IMF is going to truly fulfil its role reporting on the imbalances and opportunities in the world economy, then the voting structure and representation must reflect the world – and that's to China's benefit. But even if the China question is resolved, the IMF will continue to see its lending business challenged by others, only strengthening the case for expanding its surveillance role.

US leadership is necessary but not sufficient to reform the World Bank and IMF. Any meaningful changes will only come through persuasion and co-operation with the rest of the world, including China. And the need for collaborative change is immediate, not just for global peace and prosperity – but for developing countries counting on support from the world's international financial institutions.

The end of the easy money decade isn't just hitting the world's wealthiest companies, but the world's poorest countries struggling to repay loans and avoid default. Early 2023 data from the IMF has 25 per cent of emerging markets at risk of default, 15 per cent of low-income countries already in debt distress and another 45 per cent at high risk.[21] To help lessen the likelihood of catastrophic defaults, the IMF – together with the World Bank and G20 – is leading in the creation of a global sovereign debt roundtable. Such a gathering must go beyond bringing borrowers together with public sector lenders and acknowledge the dramatic change in patterns of low-income country lending. Consider this: as of 2021, more than $100 billion, or 57 per cent of all debt held by the world's poorest countries, is owed to China.[22] With astounding speed, China is replacing advanced economies and international institutions as the main source of debt. There's a flip side to this: China is increasingly burdened by previously agreed commitments to more than a hundred recipient countries. But we are already seeing that there is a limit to China's lending generosity as growth slows at home.

Doing Good

The world knows how to come together and deliver relief and results.

When Covid struck, countries across the world cut interest rates and switched on printing presses to churn out money and keep economies moving. When firestorms rip across a continent, countries share resources to stop the flames. And when a major hurricane tears through an island nation, the international community bands together to deliver relief. Just because a crisis lacks the shock and awe of a pandemic, fire or flood does not mean it is any less severe. Indeed, the most insidious crises are often the silent ones not marked by devastating imagery but the creeping march of time as pipes rot, polluting drinking water, or as generations of children grow up without schooling deprived of the hope that can only come with an education.

But we have it within our power to do something – to do good. Too often development funding has been used as an emergency band-aid to combat the consequences of low levels of growth and high levels of poverty. We now have the opportunity for aid to combat the causes of low growth and poverty by rethinking the design of international institutions and recentring them around global public goods.

15

ACHIEVING OUR GLOBAL GOALS

The Man Who Saved a Billion Lives

'The battle to feed all of humanity is over.'[1] Those are the opening words of Paul Ehrlich's 1968 book *The Population Bomb*. Having stretched food supplies and the wider environment to, and then past, the breaking point, Ehrlich saw a world where humanity was on death row. Increased food production would only produce a 'stay of execution'. Ehrlich argued the clock was ticking, hundreds of millions would starve, and dramatic population control measures – from taxing families having children to mass sterilisations – were urgently needed. 'At this late date,' Ehrlich concluded, 'nothing can prevent a substantial increase in the world death rate.' What Ehrlich didn't account for was Dr Norman Borlaug.

Around the time of the book's publication, Dr Borlaug was in the fields of Pakistan. An agronomist, Borlaug had developed a high-yielding and disease-resistant variety of wheat. It was a semi-dwarf strain, avoiding the common issue wheat faces – mature wheat would collapse under the weight of its grain and could not be harvested. Wheat losses due to collapsing stalks, disease and low yields left growing populations in poor countries starving. What Borlaug called the 'population monster' needed to be fed, and he had found a way to do just that.[2]

India produced 9.8 million tons of wheat in 1964.[3] Five years

266

later using Borlaug's semi-dwarf variant, wheat production rose to 18 million tons. In Pakistan, between 1964 and 1969, wheat yields skyrocketed from 4 million to 7 million tons. In a 1968 speech, William Gaud, then Administrator for the US Agency for International Development, had a name for the scale of the breakthroughs: 'These and other developments in the field of agriculture contain the makings of a new revolution. It is not a violent Red Revolution like that of the Soviets, nor is it a White Revolution like that of the Shah of Iran. I call it the Green Revolution.'[4]

The private sector through the Ford and Rockefeller Foundations, individuals with the knowledge and know-how like Borlaug, and governments such as the United States and Mexico came together to address the population monster. Where Ehrlich saw an invincible Goliath, a band of optimists saw a global problem that could be managed.

Today, semi-dwarf wheat accounts for 99 per cent of global acreage. It's what's in your cereal and bread, assuming you're not gluten-free. For Borlaug's research, he was awarded the 1970 Nobel Peace Prize and has widely been regarded as the 'person who saved a billion lives'. In his Nobel lecture accepting the prize, Borlaug quoted a fellow laureate, Lord John Boyd Orr – the first director-general of the Food and Agriculture Organization – who said, 'You can't build peace on empty stomachs.'[5]

Half a century on, those words are just as powerful – and just as relevant. We can't build peace when the world is filled with abject poverty. We can't build peace when our environment and fellow species are being eradicated. And we can't build peace when we fail to finance the goals we seek to achieve.

What Borlaug and the world achieved with the Green Revolution is a reminder that the combination of innovation

267

and co-operation is an unstoppable force that can overcome the greatest of odds. The Green Revolution wasn't just a revolution in agriculture. It was also a revolution in global co-operation. A revolution in knowledge-sharing. And a revolution in positive-sum thinking. We need that same kind of revolution now.

Burden-sharing

Having restructured international institutions such as the World Bank and the IMF and unlocked new funding from countries, we must now fix our eyes on a different prize – new and additional resources that can be secured to deliver the Sustainable Development Goals from the investment market.

Promises made to deliver overseas aid should be honoured. But even if all aid promises were met, it could not bridge the ever-widening funding gap, nor will $500 billion of global philanthropy or $700 billion of remittances, important as they are.[6]

Shifting only 1.1 per cent of global financial assets towards SDG financing needs in developing countries would be sufficient to fill the $4 trillion annual funding gap needed to achieve our global goals.[7] Some of the world's $85 trillion pool of professionally managed money, and a similar amount in pensions and insurance funds, could be marshalled through specialised SDG-linked funds: green bonds, impact-linked bonds and loans, and – for maximum anti-poverty results – outcomes partnerships funded by social impact bonds. While that's all desirable, it's not likely to happen anytime soon if governments do not provide the right policy incentives to attract private finance at scale and make this shift possible.

The philanthropist, venture capitalist and impact investor Ronald Cohen estimates that most of the funds needed to achieve

268

the SDGs could be raised if companies representing just 20 per cent of the $100 trillion invested in the global stock market measured their impacts that relate to the SDGs, and if green and sustainability-linked bonds and loans, which already account for $2.5 trillion of the $80 trillion bond market, reached 10 per cent. Just look at oil and gas companies. Their profits more than doubled from $1.5 trillion in recent years to $4 trillion in 2022 and remain near record levels. These firms, and the countries in which they are based – mainly across the Middle East – should pay a substantial levy towards climate mitigation and adaptation as well as investments in human capital.[8] And then there's the innovative plan put forward at COP26 in Glasgow by Mark Carney, the former Governor of the Bank of England, where four out of every $10 managed globally would go towards addressing climate change, amounting to $130 trillion.[9]

Working with international financial institutions, new tools that can take in private funding can and should be deployed to close funding gaps. There's 'socially responsible investment' where private capital can deliver a market return while supporting development with grant financing from donors tied to guaranteed outcomes. There's 'impact investing' where donors choose a social impact and not just financial returns, so we do good and do well at the same time. There's 'conditional funding' with performance targets – strings – attached to grant financing, debt swaps and outcomes. And there's 'catalytic funding', which offers untapped potential to leverage up additional resources beyond grants and loans for donor country guarantees. All of these innovative private sector financing tools can and should be layered on top of World Bank reforms.

Of these four models, catalytic funding shows the most promise. Catalytic funding has seen big advances with public agencies partnering with private capital markets to build from donor pledges. Such an approach is used at Gavi, the vaccine alliance, through the International Finance Facility for Immunization (IFFIm), which has raised $8 billion for vaccinations globally and is a model for what we can do in health and climate to make aid go further and work better.

Whichever funding model we choose, it is clear costs must be shared between international financial institutions, governments and the private sector. We need our international institutions to provide a stronger platform so innovative finance can do more. And whether aid comes from private, bilateral or multilateral channels, we also need a commitment from the world's richest and most powerful countries to fair burden-sharing. Such an agreement on burden-sharing is the key to generating predictable and sustainable resources upon which innovative financing can be built and our global health goals achieved. The United States and China can jointly claim the moral high ground by being first-movers.

For everything from UN humanitarian aid to the oft-discussed but never-delivered $100 billion climate fund for developing countries, we must bring an end to the days of passing around a begging bowl. Countries that belong to the UN Security Council, that sit on the boards of the IMF and World Bank and count themselves among the world's wealthiest nations, should have a great financial responsibility.

When in 1966 the world sought to eliminate smallpox, a burden-sharing agreement was possible. Surely we know so much more a quarter into the twenty-first century about what can be done as well as what is needed. New agreements on burden-sharing and enhanced multilateral bank finance can be the basis for generating predictable and sustained resources upon which innovative financing can take us across the finish line in our race against poverty, disease and ill health.

Investing in Public Health

Our failure to fund global public goods extends to health.

Development assistance for health increased from $40.4 billion in 2019 to $54.8 billion in 2020 in large part due to the Covid response.[10] But this uptick cannot hide the dire state of global health – the current and future financing gaps between what we invest today, and what we need to invest tomorrow, to sustainably fight disease, promote wellbeing and prepare for pandemics. Global health spending per capita highlights this chasm.

In 2019, US health spending reached $11,345 per capita compared to $94 in Venezuela or $7 in Somalia.[11] While 2020 saw a global spending uptick, one year of additional support does not a trend make. Indeed, *The Lancet* found that from 2012 to 2019, health development assistance plateaued at an annualised rate of 1.2 per cent.[12] Even before the surge in inflation, that's an amount below the global inflation rate, all but ensuring currency depreciation negates any additional funding.

It's no surprise that a majority of the world's poorest countries are not on track to meet their health targets by the 2030 Sustainable Development Goal deadline. That means more mothers will die in childbirth. Communicable diseases will go unchecked. The health workforce won't receive needed funding. And malnutrition will continue to dampen future generations' prospects.

There are different avenues that can increase global health financing. International financial institutions from the World Bank to the IMF need to increase their funding for global health. In the wake of the September 11 attacks in the United States, all travellers found a new tax on their plane tickets – the '9/11 Security Tax'. This funds airport security and staffing to keep air travel safe, and few complained. In 2006, France led the way with an airline tax to pay for global health with a focus on combating AIDS, tuberculosis and malaria. Now, let's use this same logic and think bigger. Drawing on lessons learned during the Covid crisis, countries like the United States with the means to help fund global health should consider taxation to close funding gaps. Aid has to be the platform for mobilising not billions but trillions for global health, and private investment and capital markets can also work to the benefit of developing countries.

Burdens must be shared. Disease anywhere carries the threat of disease everywhere, and no one is safe until everyone is safe. The US, Europe and China, taking the lead, can do more than just write cheques. They can go a step further, not just sharing their experiences with communicable diseases and outbreaks, but also standing together and being prepared to lend to countries lacking the means to respond to health crises. Bill Gates explores urgent funding needs at length in *How to Prevent the Next Pandemic*.[13] The lesson in both his text and ours is clear. Without the needed funding and support for the one international organisation that can bring people together on global health – the World Health Organization – humanity will struggle to stop future pandemics.

Financing an Education for All

Young people are destined to be the greatest long-term losers from today's biggest crises: war in Ukraine, floods in Pakistan, famine and climate-induced droughts in Africa, and the recent explosion in the numbers of refugees and displaced children.

Long after the immediate crises disappear from the headlines, the damage from a missed education as a result of the above will last a lifetime, depriving children of the skills they need for the jobs of tomorrow. And this won't just set back their lives but also their country's fortunes. No country can ever truly be rich if it is education poor.

Indefensible gaps in multilateral aid result in the international community doing the least to educate the young people who need it the most. Ukraine and Pakistan – not to mention countries like Jordan, Lebanon, Bangladesh and India, which are all refugee transit hubs – have one trait in common: they are lower middle-income countries. Already burdened by the costs of delivering food, healthcare and a safety net, their own domestic resources are insufficient to fund new schools and teachers. And yet, despite the fact that lower middle-income countries contain the biggest number of out-of-school children, they are deprived of the international financial support for education that they need on terms they can afford.

Global education is trapped between a humanitarian system that struggles to focus on basic needs – food, shelter and healthcare – and an underfunded development aid system that has, in recent years, reduced the share of education aid to less than 10 per cent.

Annual spending on education by the World Bank's facility for middle-income countries – the International Bank for Reconstruction and Development – amounts to little more than $1 per pupil. That's not enough to pay for one textbook for an entire class, let alone cover the cost of teachers' salaries or the construction of new schools. And that $1 the World Bank can provide comes in the form of loans – not grants – with the interest rate above 4 per cent with IBRD financing.

Indeed, only 6 per cent of IBRD's current lending power is taken up by education, compared with IDA which commits nearly double that – 11 per cent. This is tragic in so many ways, especially in light of the dividends lost. Education's return on investment is seen in better employment levels, higher productivity, greater gender equality and improved health, particularly among mothers. All told, for every $1 spent on education, countries realise $12 in benefits.

Ukraine, whose economy is collapsing by 35 per cent according to the IMF, is still considered a lower middle-income country, which means it cannot access favourable lending terms for its educational reconstruction. While Pakistan is eligible to borrow from both IDA and IBRD, it cannot afford to draw on a facility charging more than low IDA interest rates, and so with a national income of little more than $1,500 per head and the cost of educating a child taking up a substantial part of that, 25 million were out of school even before the 2022 floods destroyed thousands of schools.

When we look at where needs are greatest, and where loans are the most favourable, the two don't overlap. An estimated 41 per cent of the close to 90 million forcibly displaced people are below 18 years of age. And low- and middle-income countries host 83 per cent of the world's refugees.

Aid should be increased, and so must the domestic mobilisation of resources – including through better use of public spending and tax reform – so education can receive its fair share. But the international community must go a step further to incentivise more domestic spending, and that begins with making assistance for low- and lower middle-income countries a priority. The solution comes in the form of the IFF model introduced earlier – specifically an International Finance Facility for Education (IFFEd).

As discussed, the parameters developed for IFFEd – that have been reviewed and assured by credit-rating agencies – would require commitments from donors of 15 per cent in cash and

85 per cent in guarantees for every $1 of equity supplied before development banks such as the World Bank leverage funds. Every 15 cents of cash as paid-in capital to an IFF financing vehicle could produce up to $4 in loans for financing development. All told, this new facility could raise and then deploy, depending on the level of commitment, between $10 and $15 billion over the next two years. That takes us above and then beyond needed funding levels to achieve the fourth Sustainable Development Goal of a quality and inclusive education for all of the world's children.

This is an investment worth making. To not deliver on the promise of an education for all means to write off an entire generation of dreamers who have yet to move the world in unimaginable ways. We need to develop their talents and potential, and that is done through an education.

Opportunity in Africa

If history repeated itself, then today Africa – like India – would be at the centre of the next phase of modernisation and industrialisation. At a time when labour in the rest of the world is in short supply, Africa – with an average age of 19 – has a pool of young workers.

If low-income countries across Africa are to develop and enter middle-income status, we must turn regular talk of a Marshall Plan for Africa into a practical agenda for action that deals with the multiple interlocking emergencies the continent faces – food and energy shortages, drought and floods and high levels of debt. As we write, a quarter of Africa's total population, more than 300 million people, are facing food shortages, with 12 per cent of sub-Saharan Africa's population in acute need. Problems extend far beyond poverty and political turmoil. The future is perilous too. With a fertility rate twice the global average, Africa has to prepare to feed a population that in the coming decades will be larger than China and India. Taken together, it's no small wonder that, for the first time in decades, Africa's Human Development Index has registered a decline.

Africa needs investment to grow, and today's debt problem reflects the continent's desperate search for capital and its failure to secure it on sustainable terms. Gordon was involved in negotiating 2005's historic debt write-off after which there was a promise of higher levels of aid and help to reform domestic tax systems. But with Western governments reluctant to continue lending, Africa looked elsewhere – taking on both private sector and Chinese debt – an approach that is now backfiring with debts coming due. Indeed, development assistance through the World Bank has never been enough to achieve the investment Africa needs, and at its peak in 2017, Chinese lending in Africa was larger than that of the World Bank.

Consider Ghana, one of Africa's most educated and best-governed countries, not to mention a major cocoa and gold producer. The country has so much going for it, and yet Ghanaian debt has grown to 78 per cent of GDP – although not as high as the UK's debt-to-GDP ratio – with debt interest payments now consuming close to 60 per cent of government revenue. And Ghana is far from ranking atop the list of most indebted countries. The challenge countries like Ghana face, to draw on Carmen Reinhart's framing in a recent study on Chinese lending, is not a short-term liquidity problem but rather a long-term solvency problem, and without debt restructuring, poverty will stalk the continent for decades to come.[14]

An educated workforce is the best hope to secure Africa's future. Only through education can agriculture be made more efficient, can a service and IT sector grow, and can manufacturing take hold. Before Covid-19, nearly half the ten-year-olds in the world's low- and middle-income countries could not read. Now that figure is closer to 70 per cent and, according to Brookings, school fees still discourage learning with 84 per cent of respondents in a recent survey of individuals in sub-Saharan Africa reporting being either 'somewhat worried' or 'very worried' about paying for education-related expenses.[15] The appeals for humanitarian aid to crisis-affected countries raise less than 7 per cent of what is needed to close the education gap. Health presents the same troubling picture, with only four out of 36 African countries – Rwanda, Ghana, Gabon and Burundi – having health insurance coverage above 20 per cent.[16]

We can, and should, build on what works. Brokered by the African Union and established in 2018, the African Continental Free Trade Area covers much of the continent and has the potential to double intercontinental trade, grow incomes by 9 per cent, and create 18 million new jobs – particularly if it focuses on developing food and fertilizer production in countries able to service the whole of Africa.[17] And the willingness to embrace new technologies, as has been witnessed with rising investment and government backing in Rwanda, Senegal, Côte d'Ivoire and Kenya, can buck the trend of lacklustre growth and achieve growth rates twice the continent's average. But Africa cannot move forwards without international support, and it is in our interests to prevent further divergence between the rest of the world and Africa.

Many Hands, Light Work

Working together, we can prove the power of co-operation and remind the world that even as countries battle over trade, immigration and currency issues, we can reach out across oceans and fight the best kind of war – a war against poverty, illiteracy, ill-health and famine.

There's a story about Olof Palme, Prime Minister of Sweden from 1982 to 1986, and his meeting with President Ronald Reagan. Before the meeting, President Reagan asked his staff if Palme was a communist. No, the president was told, he's an anti-communist. To which Reagan replied: 'I don't care what kind of communist he is.' Later asked by Reagan if he was the kind of leader who wants to abolish the rich, Palme replied, 'I'm the person who wants to abolish the poor.'

We are moral enough to understand that it's not anti-wealth to say the wealthy should help the poor. It's not wrong to ask the comfortable to do more to help those who go without comfort. And it's not bad business to invest in those businesses who put people over profits. We are enlightened enough to know that when the strong help the weak it makes us all stronger.

CONCLUSION

Embracing Imperfections

When pottery breaks, the next stop is usually the trash can. For more sentimental pieces, from Chinese porcelain to elementary school art projects, super glue might be called upon. But even then, the piece is never the same. We like things perfect.

The ancient Japanese art of *kintsugi* calls for a different approach. Dating back more than 500 years, broken pottery isn't thrown out but rather saved and celebrated through innovative artistry. In the *kintsugi* method, roughly translating 'to join with gold' or 'golden joinery', powdered gold is used to fuse broken pieces together. Gold veins fan out like highways criss-crossing the porcelain. There's no attempt to pass off a once-broken piece as undamaged; the imperfections are there hiding in plain sight.

Indeed, imperfections are celebrated. The piece has lived and survived, its story borne out in gold relief. All at once, *kintsugi* both preserves and reinvents the pottery.

Ours is a broken world – a permacrisis world rocked by shocks leading to increasingly low growth, high economic uncertainty, climate emergencies and greater divisions between countries and within them. But the magnitude of those challenges should not deter us from trying to build a better world.

279

There are many fine people all over the world so engaged, in projects great and small. Our aim has been to point out interventions that can get us out of this permacrisis rut – interventions that can help fuse a broken world back together.

Shocked

As we've written through 2022 and 2023, it seems we've only slipped deeper into a permacrisis. Global summits have come and gone – G7s and G20 meetings, World Bank and International Monetary Fund gatherings, UN General Assemblies, COPs – and yet countries cannot sufficiently agree on a realistic implementation plan for globally co-ordinated action to deal with the halving of global growth, inflation, or challenges facing the global order from addressing the climate crisis to the shift towards a multipolar world.

Countries that created international institutions to deliver co-operation are behaving unco-operatively, even though it is obvious that many of their problems can only be solved co-operatively. At the very moment the world needs to come together, it is being pulled apart by nationalism and its byproducts, from conflicts to rising protectionism.

All this is taking place in what is an inherently interdependent, integrated and interconnected world where, as we have demonstrated, global problems need global solutions. Solutions can and should begin with new models for growth, economic management and a renovated global order. And these solutions don't live within one discipline – narrowly achieved through economics or international relations alone – but rather are multidisciplinary.

There are moments where the world seems to get a bit of relief – where things appear less broken – but the reality is closer to a never-ending game of Whac-A-Mole where challenges don't just go away but shift and, too often, reappear.

Lumber prices fall, but egg prices skyrocket. Inflation tapers in one country only to surge in another. The economy seems to stabilise only for a bank to suddenly fail. A labour deal is reached only to have a new breakthrough in automation threaten the industry. A house swept away in a recent storm is rebuilt, only to be consumed by a fire during a drought. Agreements for climate change funding are reached, only to have the action that must follow run dry.

The world isn't becoming any simpler – any less challenging. What the world desperately needs is a vision of a well-managed globalisation. For there's nothing inevitably permanent about a permacrisis. We have it within our power to fix a fractured world.

The Stakes

There are realities we must come to terms with – and boldly address.

First, after decades of growing wealth throughout the post-war era, which saw billions of people lifted out of poverty, we can no longer guarantee prosperity – and poverty is likely to rise on the current course. This is not just about income uncertainty due to slow growth but a far more insidious blend of slow growth and cost-of-living pressures making policy responses more difficult. Growing levels of sovereign debt, a tightening labour supply, the changing nature of globalisation, the climate crisis and heightened geopolitical tensions are all mixing together to pressure global growth, both actual and potential.

These shifts aren't going to hit developing countries in isolation but the wider, wealthier world too. Emerging economies that have been 'catching up', defined among other things by populations entering the middle class, are now at risk of falling behind. The world's least developed countries seeking to climb the economic ladder leading to greater prosperity won't make it as far as they once would. Fragile economies will crumble. And the wealthiest countries will find it impossible to quantitatively ease their way to growth.

A new gap is developing between the global north and south. Divergence and fragmentation rather than convergence and co-operation are the order of the day. Without new models for both growth and national economic management, growth will be too low to ensure improving living standards and a greater prosperity that is inclusive and consistent with our planet's realities. Children and grandchildren will be worse off than their parents. But new models can bring new prosperity, higher productivity, and both better and more sustainable pathways to development.

Second, we have to better prepare for shocks at a time when both our human and financial resilience has been run down. Shocks are not the exception. They are becoming the norm, not just more frequent but also more violent. Countries have used up much of their fiscal and monetary policy ammunition after a decade of easy money policies, contributing to record inflation and planting the seeds for banking and financial instability. So, when the next crash comes, the solution to our challenges won't come from flooding the system with handouts and printing more money. And efforts to provide relief through interest rate cuts could backfire, only serving to fuel inflationary pressures.

Resilience goes far beyond dollars and cents, pounds and pence. Let's not forget about human resilience. Our resilience, as individuals and collectively as a society, is being tested. A climate emergency increasingly characterised by hotter, wetter and dryer conditions is not just a manifestation of our planet being pushed to an ecological breaking point, but humanity as well. This threatens a decade of despair characterised by insecurity and anxiety causing millions to lose hope. We, of course, have both the means and the knowledge to change this trajectory, but the action we've taken so far has been incomplete, unco-ordinated and halting.

Shocks will continue to come, that's for certain. Our ability to respond to them is not. Planning and preparing today are the only way to successfully confront tomorrow's disruptions and disasters.

Third, in large part because of the variety of challenges we're facing, ours is a world of many possible outcomes – and of multiple equilibria where one bad outcome makes a worse one more probable. If the world was once cyclical and mean-reverting where the effects of shocks were temporary, that world is now long gone.

In our world of multiple equilibria, bad situations feed off of one another. A flood won't just claim lives and destroy property, it'll consume livelihoods, worsening inequality and making flood insurance even harder to obtain. A pandemic forcing economies to shut down won't just see wages shrink and unemployment increase, but also scores of young people shut out of a proper education. It's a corrupted Newton's Third Law where every shock has an aligned and amplified reaction.

As a result, we need to strengthen our ability to think laterally across many possible outcomes. We can't just fight the fire before us. We have to think about protecting all the foliage around us. And that, to return to the second point, means clearing brush and building resilience. And if we don't do that, we run the risk of losing control of our collective destiny. Inaction is akin to buying a lottery ticket for future generations – our kids and grandkids – and hoping that decades from now they'll have winning numbers. The odds aren't good.

And fourth, if we stay the present course, this is a world where beggar-thy-neighbour policies become even more tempting and frequent, seemingly offering to help one country while hurting others. Already, we don't co-operate nearly enough, and we fail to recognise that by giving up a little autonomy we can get back a lot. And on the infrequent occasions we do co-operate, we don't co-ordinate and sustain our action for maximum impact.

Much of the world agrees inflation is bad, yet what have we done to collectively overcome it through better supply chain management? Much of the world agrees Russia's war in Ukraine is unconscionable, but have we gone far enough in designing a way out? All of the world wanted to bring an end to the pandemic – a virus that will only be vanquished when everyone everywhere is vaccinated, eliminating pathways for problematic variants – and yet vaccines did not trickle down fast enough to the world's poorest.

By not co-operating, not only do we lose out on the benefits of joint action, but we find ourselves slipping closer to a world of greater nationalism and protectionism. Security in all its forms – national security, economic security, energy and food security, personal safety and, in the aftermath of a global pandemic, health security – is being used as an excuse for isolation.

We are not confronted by a false choice between going it alone or co-operating. We can – and must – balance the autonomy we desire with the co-operation the world urgently needs.

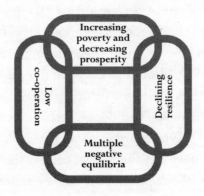

Escaping the Permacrisis

In aviation, accidents are rarely explained by a single point of failure. Rather, investigators widen their view to include accident chains – a series of events leading to disaster.

The deadliest aviation accident in history took place in 1977 when a KLM 747 on takeoff collided with a taxiing Pan Am 747 at Tenerife Airport. Neither plane was supposed to be at Tenerife that day, but a bombing at the nearby Las Palmas Airport forced many aircraft – including the two planes destined for disaster – to divert. A smaller airport not equipped for a massive influx in jet traffic, Tenerife quickly reached capacity, forcing planes to park on taxiways. Further complicating matters was a thick fog obscuring visibility and making it difficult for crews to navigate the unfamiliar airport, and controllers to monitor ground traffic. Delays made crews impatient, and the eager-to-depart KLM began its take-off roll without clearance – down a runway the Pan Am jet was taxiing on. Radio transmissions to the tower were garbled, and by the time the two planes saw each other a collision was unavoidable.

Had Las Palmas Airport not been bombed, forcing diversions, the accident chain would have been broken and disaster averted. Had the weather been clear, both planes would have always been in visual contact. Had the Pan Am plane turned off the runway sooner during its taxi, there would have been nothing for the KLM jet to crash into. And had the KLM pilots not deviated from instructions and instead patiently waited for take-off, 583 lives would have been saved.

That is the accident chain. And if a single point on the chain is removed, the links all fail and an accident can be avoided. Make no mistake, there are still negative links on this chain – from bad luck to poor decisions – but one smart choice can change the course. And that is our collective challenge: to take a world facing an increasing number of shocks and break a ceaseless cycle leading to greater disasters and division.

Permacrisis Antidote: Growth

Declining global productivity, the growing ranks of the elderly, a shrinking labour pool, rising in-country inequality, the changing nature of globalisation through onshoring and reshoring, and increasing global shocks – all of these things represent significant changes and substantial headwinds to growth. If that is all there is to the story, a reasonable prediction would be for an extended period of supply-constrained growth, muted productivity and persistent inflation. Fortunately, that is not all there is to the story. A new model for growth can give a new purpose to growth: prosperity for countries, companies and citizens. And this new model for growth must take into consideration the link between security and sustainability – everything from food and energy security to economic and health security. Our goal of inclusive, sustainable and secure growth means the actions we take must deliver a *more* inclusive, *more* sustainable and *more* secure world. That's easier said than done, but we have no choice but to try.

TURBOCHARGING PRODUCTIVITY THROUGH TECHNOLOGY: Scientific and technological transformations – from 3-nanometre semiconductors to AI-empowered chatbots – are being enabled by the arrival of powerful technologies and tools. Applications of these and other technologies have the potential to produce a surge in productivity. In fact, they already have in the tradable sector of the economy from manufactured goods like smartphones to tradable services such as finance and consulting. But meaningfully boosting productivity means reaching the non-tradable side of the economy, which accounts for 80 per cent of employment and two thirds of output – think government, education, healthcare, traditional retail, hospitality. Technology improving efficiencies in this non-tradable sector is the bigger prize. And what's more, this will also create opportunities for inclusive growth patterns by expanding the range of services available to remote or low access populations that do not live in urban environments.

AUGMENTATION, NOT FULL AUTOMATION: Technologies, especially AI, can advance to the point where they produce a productivity surge in large sectors that have thus far been resistant to advancement. Teachers will not and should not be replaced, and their effectiveness can be augmented through the use of digital tools. Video conferencing can help with instruction outside of school hours, and advanced programs can detect patterns in learning where a student may be struggling. Sensors in hospitals and care facilities can spot when patients are uneasy on their feet and likely to need a hand. And in retail, advanced software can provide added insights to inventories and procurement processes to reduce overstock items eventually sold at a loss. In all of these scenarios and many others, technology should be a tool for empowerment, not replacement. In that regard, we are striving for augmented intelligence, not a human-less artificial intelligence.

FIXING SUPPLY CONSTRAINTS: Ours is a supply-constrained world, and that's unlikely to change anytime soon. Central banks, policymakers and indeed markets initially viewed these pressures as transitory based on a belief that pandemic-induced supply-side imbalances and blockages would diminish and the post-pandemic surge in demand would subside. While shipping and lumber costs have fallen, the overall picture is yet to recover fully due to the presence of secular features – everything from fragmented globalisation and the energy transition to ageing and a shrinking global labour force – preventing a reversion to the mean marked by low inflation and ample liquidity. Our challenge is to raise supply elasticity, better enabling producers to react to changes in demand, and in parallel lower supply constraints to growth. Increasing the global labour supply by improving domestic labour force participation and tapping into overlooked markets eager to be brought into the global economy, especially across Africa, can ease supply-side constraints.

Permacrisis Antidote: Economic Management

'Give me a word – any word – and I show you how the root of that word is Greek.' With a Windex bottle in hand, that's one of the early lessons Gus Portokalos teaches his on-screen daughter in *My Big Fat Greek Wedding*. And if Gus were writing this section, he would point out the word 'economy' comes from the Greek word *oikonomia* roughly translating to 'household management'.[1] We can do a much better job managing the global household's financial books.

REIMAGINING ECONOMIC MANAGEMENT: These days, the term 'economic management' resembles a contradiction in terms. With inflation lingering, recessions looming, banks failing and households suffering, where's the successful management? Policymakers and central bankers need to be open to new perspectives, the kind of perspectives that make groupthink less of a threat and protracted mischaracterisations, such as the 'transitory' inflation call, less likely.

Greater cognitive diversity within the ranks of economic decision makers isn't just an important value statement but also a goal that will lead to better policy. There must be co-ordination and accountability – not just within governments but across them, also facilitating the emergence of more effective public–private partnerships. One positive step to surmount infrastructure and innovation hurdles would be the rise of more domestic infrastructure banks complementing regional and multilateral institutions, spurring private sector activity, spreading risk and sharing expertise. Moreover, the National Economic Council (NEC) and Treasury Borrowing Advisory Committee (TBAC) models provide general frameworks for wider adoption and 'safe zones' where governments can collaborate and co-ordinate better. The Bank of England's example of including independent outsiders on key policymaking committees should be followed. And, most visibly, there needs to be improved leadership. Acknowledging policy missteps and making 'we got it wrong' part of economists' vocabulary will help to restore confidence and build trust with those feeling the brunt of policy decisions.

RETHINKING ECONOMIC FRAMEWORKS: New management can go a step further and rethink outdated economic frameworks – frameworks that undermine reaction function and see a constant tug of war between fiscal and monetary policy. First, central banks must undertake a fundamental revamp of the monetary framework – a blueprint rooted in the quantitative easing, easy money era of the past and not the supply-constrained, new normal era of the present. Second, walled policymaking gardens such as America's Federal Open Market Committee must be expanded to include qualified outside appointees, including market experts and behavioural scientists. Financial volatility storm clouds born out of monetary policy – such as the 2023 banking crisis – would be easier to spot if we had more eyes on the horizon, as would problems among non-bank financial institutions. Having a diversity of thinkers isn't an end unto itself; it also helps manage risk. And third, the Federal Reserve must take the lead – preferably in sync with other central banks and possibly through the G20 – in carefully and gradually revising its inflation target from an unrealistic 2 per cent to what is likely to be a more appropriate 3 per cent for years to come.

The Fed, not to mention other central banks, will find it all but impossible to meet their aims of price and financial stability, together with maximum employment, without revised frameworks and greater cognitive diversity suited for today's world. Central bankers need to stop acting like Rip Van Winkle, as if they have just awoken from a decades-long slumber and assumed the cyclical, mean-reverting, low-inflation, easy money era endures. That Rip Van Winkle world is over.

PEOPLE AND THE PLANET – NOT JUST PROFITS: Economic policy is continually looking at the challenges beside us and not the ones looming in front of us. We have stretched balance sheets to unprecedented levels with trillions of dollars of debt and liquidity sloshing about in the global system in the wake of the Global Financial Crisis and Covid. Despite – or rather because of – the way we have thrown so much money at the problems before us, inequality has grown just as the impact of every dollar printed has diminished. It's time to build economic resilience – a product of the proposals just covered – which will in turn leave the world better prepared for more frequent and violent external shocks. And the cost of sustainability must be calculated in fiscal policy. We know the price tag of a more sustainable economy – that's a more than $4 trillion annual bill. But everything from GDP projections to inflation expectations must factor in the costs of inaction on a range of challenges from increasing climate catastrophes to the surging costs of global debt. The cost of inaction is far greater than action, and this reality must shape how the world spends.

Permacrisis Antidote: Renovated Global Order

No one would argue that climate change or war are problems confined to narrow national boundaries. Financial contagion spreads quickly from one economy to another – a liquidity crisis in one banking sector can scuttle global markets. A different kind of contagion – this time viruses – easily spreads between countries as germs hitch a ride on planes, trains and automobiles traversing the globe. Ours is an interconnected, interdependent world. And global problems demand global solutions.

A WELL-MANAGED GLOBALISATION-LITE: Globalisation must be better managed so we get the balance right between the domestic autonomy people seek and the international co-operation they need. Self-sufficiency strategies and the use of finance for nationalist ends have been the reflex response of many governments to their perceived vulnerability to global flows of finance. But if we are to head off deep insularity and retain the openness which is essential for a better guarantee of trade, growth, investment and prosperity, we need a mindset shift.

We need to first recognise what it really means when we no longer think of ourselves just as a set of national economic islands sufficient unto ourselves but rather part of a global system that has to be made to work. Every country has neighbours and allies that are often strong trading partners. But beyond those are other countries to whom we are still connected, albeit in less intense ways. We must find a way forwards that is not 'us versus them' but 'us plus them'. Instead of a destructive, adversarial nationalism, what we need is a patriotism free of nationalism, able to all at once embrace one's own country and be comfortable with multiple identities.

REBIRTH OF INTERNATIONAL INSTITUTIONS: Globalisation delivered an open economy, but not an inclusive one. Until we deliver openness together with inclusivity, globalisation will fail. Our best chance of making that happen is working through international institutions and overhauling these post-war structures for today's multipolar world.

China and the United States can take the lead driving action as their interests align, a collaboration that would hedge against a 'one world, two systems' future. The World Bank can and should expand its mandate to take on global public goods, a mission which will necessitate an expanded capital base. The IMF must broaden its scope beyond lender of last resort and better perform the all-critical function of global surveillance body. Both institutions must shed the feudal practice of reserving their leadership positions for certain nationalities. The G20 should have a durable secretariat that ensures better continuity as the presidency rotates from country to country. And the WTO and UN Security Council should be reformed to less resemble a Western-led club and instead a truly global coalition. Such a renovation can spur co-operation, ease debt crises gripping the poorest countries, help the emergence of innovative solutions to our climate crisis, and unlock vital humanitarian aid.

INNOVATIVE FINANCING: Budgets are statements reflecting our values, and global spending to turn global public bads into global public goods – from climate change to public health and education – is woefully short. Where we need trillions we instead pledge billions, only to then spend millions. Our task and challenge is to better leverage public capital through tools such as the innovative International Finance Facility model, as well as mobilise private capital sitting on the sidelines through risk-tranching partnerships. If we are to achieve the Sustainable Development Goals, policymakers must convince investors to not just develop growth-enhancing innovations, but to crowd in capital and share in the responsibility to fund more in the spectrum from the clean energy transition to an education for all.

It Can Be Done

Permacrisis was the 2022 word of the year. As we write in 2023, it's hard not to wonder what the 2024 word will be. Comeback? Co-operation? Resurgence? All of these are better, more hopeful words. Not fancy portmanteaus, but words that suggest real benefits for real people. Words that lend hope to a world in need of reinvigorated growth, strengthened economic management and a renewed global order. Words picked not for their rhetorical flourishes, but for the global flourishing they reflect.

Taken together, the reforms and actions we have proposed are bolt cutters that can break the cycle of declining prosperity and resilience, multiple equilibria and low co-operation. They can restore the much-needed stabilising anchors of high and sustainable growth, credible domestic economic management and win–win global policy co-ordination.

Innovative financing won't just increase prosperity but will improve human resilience. Better economic management won't just help us fight the next economic shock, it will also move us closer towards our global goals, calling for a more inclusive and equitable world. And harnessing technology, alongside more human resources, to improve productivity and relax supply-side constraints won't just help to keep inflation at bay by lowering costs, but it will also fuel growth in the advanced countries and serve as a powerful tool that developing countries can harness to move up the economic ladder.

And here's the really good part: the measures we have proposed provide the initial momentum that will make other challenges with a higher degree of difficulty more addressable over time. So, to those who say that escaping a permacrisis isn't possible, history proves otherwise.

Faced with the destruction of the ozone layer, the world came together and universally ratified the Montreal Protocol phasing out harmful substances – an action that didn't just save, but ultimately restored, the ozone. The physics research taking place at CERN by thousands of scientists from more than a hundred countries has helped us better understand the first moments of the universe and contributed to the launch of the World Wide Web. And if we cast our eyes up to the heavens, the International Space Station has brought friends and foes together behind a common mission of scientific research and cosmic exploration. Examples of co-operation are all around us.

The single greatest answer to a permacrisis world is a world of co-operation, at home and internationally. Co-operation is the very thing that will make it possible to restore growth, improve economic management, avoid more climate calamities, lower inequality and reimagine the global order. And co-operation is within our reach.

We're at a turning point.

We began this book asking you to imagine what a changed world might look like.

To imagine a society where growth delivers prosperity, all while moving us closer to a more sustainably balanced world.

To imagine a world where policymakers don't careen from economic crisis to crisis, but rather proactively prevent crises and better manage the future to the benefit of the many and not the few.

And to imagine a global order arranged along lines of addition and multiplication, not division and subtraction.

It's easy to imagine this world, and possible to deliver it. The only thing stopping us is us. We have it within our power to escape this permacrisis.

ACKNOWLEDGEMENTS

Permacrisis is written in one voice. But we each have our own thank yous, and we'd like to acknowledge those who made this project possible.

GORDON: Masood Ahmed and the Center for Global Development team, former Save the Children UK Managing Director Kevin Watkins, and Justin van Fleet at Theirworld and the Global Business Coalition for Education helped shape my thinking. Ronald Cohen, Asad Jamal, Nicholas Vaughan, Pedro Alba and the Berggruen Institute were of immense help.

The University of Southern California, especially the Center for the Political Future, provided support, and I am grateful to my longtime friend Robert Shrum, as well as Professor Steven Lamy and Dean Amber Miller. At the Office of Gordon and Sarah Brown, I'd like to thank Mary Bailey, Peter Tompkins, Ross Christie, Carmel Nolan, Eddie Barnes and Henry Stannard.

Most of all, I am grateful to my family – Sarah, John and Fraser – for their love and support.

MOHAMED: I owe so much to my family, and I am blessed to have Anna, Georgia, Samia and our beloved dog Bosa in my life. No words can express the depth of my appreciation and love.

Over the past three years, I have called Queens' College at the University of Cambridge my home. The students, staff and Fellows have been a source of strength and creativity. Returning to Queens' also serves as a reminder of all those who have guided my journey in economics, finance and policy. My early teachers and colleagues at the Universities of Cambridge and Oxford, the ongoing interactions at the Wharton School and the Lauder Institute at the University of Pennsylvania, my fifteen years working at the International Monetary Fund, and the fourteen years at PIMCO – I am grateful to my colleagues and friends.

My late parents were firm believers in the transformative power of education and made tremendous sacrifices to provide me and my siblings with the opportunity to benefit from enriching academic and intellectual experiences. Their love, vision, wisdom and dedication made this possible.

MIKE: I want to thank my family: my wife Giuliana, my five children – Graham, Catherine, Marya, Alessandro and Chiara – and my brothers Randy and Alan for their love and support. They give meaning to life, research and writing.

I owe a debt to my teachers, especially my thesis advisors – Ken Arrow, Tom Schelling, Richard Zeckhauser – for their wisdom and friendship. Dave Brady, my colleague and friend at Stanford, helped me understand and appreciate the importance of politics and political economy. Roberto Zagha, the secretary to the Commission on Growth and Development that I co-chaired with Danny Leipziger, guided me in development economics. My special thanks to Bill Ford, Fred Hu and Mark Wolfson for their insights into the economic and financial global system. James Manyika at Google and Professor Fei-Fei Li at Stanford tutored me in modern digital technology, especially AI.

My parents gave me and my brothers love and support, sometimes at considerable sacrifice. They endowed us with the belief that anything is possible, and the confidence to go forwards without fear – a priceless gift.

COLLECTIVELY: Our friendship got us talking. Jonny Geller at Curtis Brown got us writing. And Simon & Schuster brought those words to life. For this support from so many, we are sincerely grateful.

NOTES

INTRODUCTION – PERMACRISIS: THE 2022 WORD OF THE YEAR

1 'The Collins Word of the Year 2022 Is . . .', Collins Dictionary, accessed 28 November 2022 – https://bit.ly/3GQMfj9

2 Jon Henley, 'Hunger stones, wrecks and bones: Europe's drought brings past to surface', *Guardian*, 19 August 2022 – https://bit.ly/3EE2Gws

3 'The Cost of Sequencing a Human Genome', National Human Genome Research Institute, accessed 12 August 2022 – https://bit.ly/2JHdHlK.

4 Garrett Hardin, 'The Tragedy of the Commons', *Science*, 162:3859 (13 December 1968), 1243–1248 – http://www.jstor.org/stable/1724745

5 Michael Spence, 'Some Thoughts on the Washington Consensus and Subsequent Global Development Experience', *Journal of Economic Perspectives*, 35:3 (2021), 67–82.

6 Mohamed A. El-Erian, 'Jay Powell is focusing too much on the present', *Financial Times*, 27 August 2022 – https://on.ft.com/3RnwuTa

7 Pierre-Olivier Gourinchas, 'A more fragmented world will need the IMF more, not less', International Monetary Fund, June 2022 – https://bit.ly/3DbonRz

1. TAILWINDS TO GROWTH

1 Todd Matthews, 'Costco CEO Craig Jelinek on Shareholders, Costco.com, and Hot Dogs', *425 Business*, 18 April 2018 – https://bit.ly/3QlFqcn

2 Ibid.

3 Nicolas Vega, '"Lightning just struck me": Why Costco's CFO says the price of the $1.50 hot dog and soda combo is "forever"', CNBC, 26 September 2022 – https://cnb.cx/3ZeV2SK

4 'GDP based on PPP, share of world', International Monetary Fund, accessed 4 January 2023 – https://bit.ly/2OC7TxK

5 'International Yearbook of Industrial Statistics: Edition 2022', United Nations Industrial Development Organization, 2022 – https://bit.ly/3GovdNo

6 'GDP per capita (current US$) – China', World Bank, accessed 27 December 2022 – https://bit.ly/3jyoHDe

7 Mark J. Perry, 'Chart of the Day (century?): Price Changes 1997 to 2017', American Enterprise Institute, 2 February 2018 – https://bit.ly/2lJB6d1

8 Randy Alfred, 'March 25, 1954: RCA TVs Get the Color for Money', *Wired*, 25 March 2008 – https://bit.ly/3i1GsNE

9 'Urban Development', World Bank, accessed 5 January 2023 – https://bit.ly/3GIH6ZY

10 'Digital Technology and Inclusive Growth: Luohan Academy Report 2019 Executive Summary', Luohan Academy, 2019 – https://bit.ly/3WUMgrB

11 Frank Swain, 'The device that reverses CO2 emissions', BBC, 11 March 2021 – https://bbc.in/3Qdx7Pu

12 'Net Zero by 2050', International Energy Agency, May 2021 – https://bit.ly/3IsugjV

13 Michael Spence, 'Is It Time to Give Up on 1.5°C?', Project Syndicate, 23 December 2022 – https://bit.ly/3GEln5p

14 'For a livable climate: Net-zero commitments must be backed by credible action', United Nations, accessed 4 January 2023 – https://bit.ly/3CnWVTj

15 'Climate Change 2022: Mitigation of Climate Change', Intergovernmental Panel on Climate Change, 2022 – https://bit.ly/46nAECs

16 Steve Lohr, 'Universities and Tech Giants Back National Cloud Computing Project', *New York Times*, 30 June 2020 – https://nyti.ms/3vUvZH8

17 Benjamin Weiser, 'Here's What Happens When Your Lawyer Uses ChatGPT', *New York Times*, 27 May 2023 – https://www.nyti.ms/3CJwWpd

18 John Markoff, 'How Many Computers to Identify a Cat? 16,000', *New York Times*, 25 June 2012 – https://nyti.ms/2IsBAOP

19 Fei-Fei Li et. al., *ImageNet*, accessed 11 January 2023 – https://image-net.org/about.php

20 'Number of smartphone subscriptions worldwide from 2016 to 2021, with forecasts from 2022 to 2027', Statista, accessed 4 January 2023 – https://bit.ly/3QfDrGg

21 Michael Spence, 'Lessons from Digital India', Project Syndicate, 25 November 2021 – https://bit.ly/3qal3lP

2. HEADWINDS TO GROWTH

1 Christian Martinez, 'Why your favorite Girl Scout cookie is in short supply in Southern California', *Los Angeles Times*, 28 February 2022 – https://lat.ms/3VrGwnQ

2 Kenneth Hall, 'Modern luxury vehicles claimed to feature more software than a fighter jet', Motor Authority, 5 February 2009 – https://bit.ly/3VrbFrd

3 Ondrej Burkacky, Stephanie Lingemann and Klaus Pototzky, 'Coping with the auto-semiconductor shortage: Strategies for success', McKinsey and Company, 27 May 2021 – https://mck.co/3jmwve3

4 Emma Roth, 'Ford to ship and sell Explorer SUVs with missing chips', *The Verge*, 13 March 2022 – https://bit.ly/3Z5SSFh

5 Sean O'Kane, 'GM drops wireless charging from some SUVs due to chip shortage', *The Verge*, 13 July 2021 – https://bit.ly/3FSFpHU

6 Annabelle Timsit, 'Elon Musk says Tesla's car factories are "gigantic money furnaces"', *Washington Post*, 23 June 2022 – https://wapo.st/3WwcnF6

7 Michael Wayland, 'Ford's supply chain problems include blue oval badges for F-Series pickups', CNBC, 23 September 2022 – https://cnb.cx/3Gnj72r

8 'Hurricane', *Station Eleven*, created by Patrick Somerville, season 1, episode 3, 2021, Viacom CBS.

9 'Global container freight rate index from January 2019 to November 2022', Statista, accessed 27 December 2022 – https://bit.ly/3Wqu6xO

10 Fareed Zakaria, 'The Rise of the Rest', *Newsweek*, 12 May 2008 – https://bit.ly/2EzZnZR

11 Paulo Afonso B. Duarte et al., eds, *The Palgrave Handbook of Globalization with Chinese Characteristics*, Singapore: Palgrave Macmillan, 2023.

12 Nicole Maestas, Kathleen J. Mullen and David Powell, 'The Effect of Population Aging on Economic Growth, the Labor Force and Productivity', National Bureau of Economic Research, July 2016 – https://bit.ly/3PXKT8O

13 'Janus Henderson Sovereign Debt Index Edition 2', Janus Henderson Investors, April 2002 – https://bit.ly/3I445Qx

14 Tom Rees, 'Want a Pay Raise? Work Five Days a Week in the Office', Bloomberg, 27 January 2023 – https://bloom.bg/3l28UAs

15 Jose Maria Barrero, Nicholas Bloom and Steven J. Davis, 'Long Social Distancing', National Bureau of Economic Research, October 2022 – http://www.nber.org/papers/w30568

16 Spencer Kwon, Yueran Ma and Kaspar Zimmermann, '100 Years of Rising Corporate Concentration', *Business Concentration*, accessed 3 January 2023 – https://businessconcentration.com/

17 'The US productivity slowdown: an economy-wide and industry-level analysis', US Bureau of Labor Statistics, April 2021 – https://bit.ly/3IpkkHU

18 Mohamed A. El-Erian, 'Fragmented Globalization', Project Syndicate, 8 March 2023 – https://bit.ly/3M1pxrm

19 'Low income', World Bank, accessed 31 January 2023 – https://bit.ly/4ofF2AD

20 For a discussion of the growth and development experiences of the post-war years, see Michael Spence, *The Next Convergence: The Future of Economic Growth in a Multispeed World*, Farrar, Straus and Giroux, 2011.
21 'Population growth 2012–2021', World Data, accessed 31 January 2023 – https://bit.ly/3YdFnC8
22 '2022 Ibrahim Index of African Governance', Mo Ibrahim Foundation, January 2023 – https://bit.ly/3jrodSx

3. SUSTAINABILITY AND SECURITY

1 Toby Luckhurst, 'Iceland's Okjokull glacier commemorated with plaque', BBC, 18 August 2019 – https://bbc.in/2THcXjy
2 Ban Ki-moon, 'Remarks at Summit for the Adoption of the Post-2015 Development Agenda', United Nations, 25 September 2015 – https://bit.ly/3HX6mwP
3 'The Millennium Development Goal Report: 2015', United Nations, 2015 – https://bit.ly/2uJRuv3
4 Ibid.
5 John Kenneth Galbraith and Andrea D. Williams, eds, *The Essential Galbraith*, Boston: Mariner, 2001.
6 Lydia Saad, 'Global Warming Concern at Three-Decade High in US', Gallup, 14 March 2017 – https://bit.ly/3BV3Gfl
7 'Devastating floods in Pakistan', UNICEF, accessed 26 December 2022 – https://uni.cf/3hQaggn
8 'GDP growth (annual %) – China', World Bank, accessed 26 December 2022 – https://bit.ly/3BYZfA4
9 'FACTBOX: China's Economic Development since 2002', Embassy of the People's Republic of China, 24 September 2012 – https://bit.ly/3WIu6sv
10 'China's share of global economy rises to over 18%: Official', State Council Information Office: People's Republic of China, 12 May 2022 – https://bit.ly/3WMVt4D
11 Rupa Duttagupta and Ceyla Pazarbasioglu, 'Miles to Go', International Monetary Fund, Summer 2021 – https://bit.ly/3Gjohwt
12 'Global Financial Stability Report', International Monetary Fund, October 2022 – https://bit.ly/3WOsnSJ
13 'Ending Poverty', United Nations, accessed 26 December 2022 – https://bit.ly/3PTrAgR
14 Homi Kharas and Meagan Dooley, 'The evolution of global poverty, 1990–2030', Brookings, 2 February 2022 – https://bit.ly/3JuRaXF
15 'Yes, Global Inequality Has Fallen. No, We Shouldn't Be Complacent', World Bank, 23 October 2019 – https://bit.ly/2BAU363

16 'Newborn Mortality', World Health Organization, 28 January 2022 – https://bit.ly/3I7HSRs

17 'GHE: Life expectancy and health life expectancy', World Health Organization, accessed 26 December 2022 – https://bit.ly/3FX1zsq

18 'Poliomyelitis (polio)', World Health Organization, accessed 26 December 2022 – https://bit.ly/3FS7QWx

19 'Drinking water', UNICEF, accessed 26 December 2022 – https://bit.ly/3jpRmo5

20 'Literacy rate, adult total (% of people ages 15 and above)', World Bank, accessed 26 December 2022 – https://bit.ly/2stQLzO

21 'The Education Commission: Creating a Learning Generation 2021 Impact Report', International Commission on Financing Global Education Opportunity, 2021 – https://bit.ly/3GjisyY

22 'Inequality – Bridging the Divide', United Nations, accessed 27 December 2022 – https://bit.ly/3C3uDoa

23 Lucas Chancel (lead author) with Thomas Piketty, Emmanuel Saez and Gabriel Zucman, 'World Inequality Report 2022', World Inequality Lab, 2022 – https://bit.ly/3YQeghu

24 Dianne Feinstein, 'Women in Politics and Business', United States Senator for California Dianne Feinstein, 22 March 2006 – https://bit.ly/3I31xC4

25 Chancel et al., op. cit.

26 Ibid.

27 Hannah Ritchie and Max Roser, 'CO2 Emissions', Our World In Data, accessed 27 December 2022 – https://bit.ly/3Vqv6AD

28 Kathryn Tso, 'How much is a ton of carbon dioxide?' MIT Climate Portal, 2 December 2020 – https://bit.ly/3VtNgRQ

29 'The evidence is clear: the time for action is now. We can halve emissions by 2030', IPCC, 4 April 2022 – https://bit.ly/3C32VRr

30 Michael Spence, 'Is It Time to Give Up on 1.5°C?', Project Syndicate, 23 December 2022 – https://bit.ly/3FhCwks

4. PRODUCTIVITY AND GROWTH

1 'Basics of Space Flight', NASA, accessed 5 January 2023 – https://go.nasa.gov/3vJoeUB

2 'About Us', Kenya Space Agency, accessed 5 January 2023 – https://bit.ly/3ZgHVAs

3 'The Uhuru Satellite', NASA, 24 September 2020 – https://go.nasa.gov/3Gc7xFW

4 'New satellite market forecast anticipates 1,700 satellites to be launched on average per year by 2030 as new entrants and incumbents increase

their investment in space', Euroconsult, 8 December 2021 – https://bit.ly/3IsdVMb

5 'Is Marsabit County Kenya's Next Spaceport Hub?', Kenya Space Agency, 18 November 2021 – https://bit.ly/3VJalA9

6 Ben Payton, 'Chinese and American interests vie for Kenyan spaceport', *African Business*, 16 August 2022 – https://bit.ly/3IpQNOk

7 'African Space Strategy: For Social, Political and Economic Integration', African Union, 2019 – https://bit.ly/3Zblj4u

8 'Nigeria and Rwanda: First African Nations Sign the Artemis Accords', US Department of State, 13 December 2022 – https://bit.ly/3QeEzKt

9 Albert Haque, Arnold Milstein & Li Fei-Fei, 'Illuminating the dark spaces of healthcare with ambient intelligence', *Nature* 585 (2020), 193–202 – https://doi.org/10.1038/s41586-020-2669-y

10 Oleg Bestsennyy and Greg Gilbert, 'Telehealth: A quarter-trillion-dollar post-COVID-19 reality?', McKinsey and Company, 9 July 2021 – https://mck.co/3GKfd43

5. CHANGING THE GROWTH EQUATION

1 Dashka Slater, 'Who Made That Charcoal Briquette?' *New York Times*, 26 September 2014 – https://nyti.ms/3GhEIrV

2 'Ford Motor Company Iron Mountain Plant Sawmill and Power House, circa 1920', The Henry Ford, accessed 3 January 2023 – https://bit.ly/3IogT4i

3 Slater, op. cit.

4 '1924 Ford Motor Company Institutional Message Advertising Campaign, "For the People and Posterity"', The Henry Ford, accessed 3 January 2022 – https://bit.ly/3D3PnFz

5 Erik Brynjolfsson, Danielle Li and Lindsey R. Raymond, 'Generative AI at Work', National Bureau of Economic Research, April 2023 – http://www.nber.org/papers/w31161

6 James M. Manyika, ed., *Dædalus* 151: 2 (2022) – https://bit.ly/3pXQa7N

7 'The American Upskilling Study: Empowering Workers for the Jobs of Tomorrow', Gallup, 2021 – https://bit.ly/3UWEbAP

8 Sara Ruberg, 'KLM Bans Checked Bags on Connections Through Amsterdam', *Wall Street Journal*, 21 July 2022 – https://on.wsj.com/3X9cTZF

9 Geneva Abdul, 'British Airways suspends Heathrow short-haul ticket sales', *Guardian*, 1 August 2022 – https://bit.ly/3ZiqcZp

10 'The Growth Report: Strategies for Sustained Growth and Inclusive Development', Commission on Growth and Development, 2008 – https://bit.ly/400vtVP

6. HOW QUICKLY THE WORLD CAN CHANGE

1 Adam Fisher, 'Sam Bankman-Fried Has a Savior Complex – And Maybe You Should Too', Sequoia Capital, 22 September 2022 – https://bit.ly/3h9pZqj

2 Cecile Vannucci, 'Sam Bankman-Fried Says He Has "Close to Nothing" Left After $26 Billion Wipeout', Bloomberg, 30 November 2022 – https://bloom.bg/3uxi1dQ

3 Joanna Ossinger, 'Crypto World Hits $3 Trillion Market Cap as Ether, Bitcoin Gain', Bloomberg, 8 November 2021 – https://bloom.bg/3iQHlZt

4 Fisher, op. cit.

5 Herbert Stein, 'A Symposium of the 40th Anniversary of the Joint Economic Committee, Hearings Before the Joint Economic Committee, Congress of the United States, Ninety-ninth Congress, First Session; Panel Discussion: The Macroeconomics of Growth, Full Employment, and Price Stability', p. 262 – https://bit.ly/3Dff9Xk

6 Hannah Miller and Olga Kharif, 'Sam Bankman-Fried Turns $2 Trillion Crypto Rout Into Buying Opportunity', Bloomberg, 19 July 2022 – https://bloom.bg/3Hm9bqI

7 Kadhim Shubber and Bryce Elder, 'Revealed: the Alameda venture capital portfolio', *Financial Times*, 6 December 2022 – https://on.ft.com/3HgZ5aO

8 Jesse Pound, 'Dimon calls crypto a "complete sideshow" and says tokens are "pet rocks"', CNBC, 6 December 2022 – https://cnb.cx/3VLWIRG

9 Kalley Huang, 'Why Did FTX Collapse? Here's What to Know', *New York Times*, 10 November 2022 – https://nyti.ms/3BmQcc1

10 Matt Egan, 'Bankrupt crypto exchange FTX may have over 1 million creditors as "dozens" of regulators probe collapse', CNN, 15 November 2022 – https://cnn.it/3UKECoW

11 John Kenneth Galbraith, *The Great Crash*, Boston: Houghton Mifflin, 1995.

12 Jesse Pound, 'A full recap of the Fed's market-moving decision and Powell's press conference', CNBC, 3 November 2021 – https://cnb.cx/3BmwBs

13 Namrata Narain and Kunal Sangani, 'The market impact of the Fed press conference', Centre for Economic Policy Research, 21 March 2023 – https://bit.ly/40wpuI5

7. THE GOOD OF ECONOMIC MANAGEMENT

1 John Weinberg, 'The Great Recession and Its Aftermath', Federal Reserve History, 22 November 2013 – https://bit.ly/3Bn9LRu

2 'The Causes and Effects of the Lehman Brothers Bankruptcy: Hearing

before the Committee on Oversight and Government Reform',
6 October 2008, US Government Printing Office – https://bit.
ly/3uEeomd

3 Richard Baldwin, 'The great trade collapse: What caused it and what
does it mean?', Centre for Economic Policy Research, 27 November
2009 – https://bit.ly/3VJCHLG

4 Patrick Wintour and Larry Elliott, 'G20: Gordon Brown brokers
massive financial aid deal for global economy', Guardian, 2 April 2009 –
https://bit.ly/3UOXc8e

5 'Speech by Mario Draghi, President of the European Central Bank at the
Global Investment Conference in London', European Central Bank, 26
July 2012 – https://bit.ly/3YakmZD

6 'The Treaty of Rome', European Commission, 25 March 1957 – https://
bit.ly/3Fi3yYe

7 'Credit and Liquidity Programs and the Balance Sheet', Federal Reserve,
accessed 11 December 2022 – https://bit.ly/3Bt9jB3

8 'Annual consolidated balance sheet of the Eurosystem', European
Central Bank, accessed 11 December 2022 – https://bit.ly/3BqOtlO

9 Fred Imbert and Thomas Franck, 'Dow plunges 10% amid coronavirus
fears for its worst day since the 1987 market crash', CNBC, 11 March
2020 – https://cnb.cx/3iYk8VC

10 Pippa Stevens, Yun Li and Fred Imbert, 'Stock market live Monday:
Dow drops 13%, Trump says recession possible, trading halted at open',
CNBC, 16 March 2020 – https://cnb.cx/3W6lDPF

11 Jesse Pound, 'Watch the full interview with Bill Ackman on the
coronavirus threat to economy – "shut it down now"', CNBC, 18 March
2020 – https://cnb.cx/3PxKqu5

12 Maggie Fitzgerald, Pippa Stevens and Fred Imbert, 'Stock market live
Wednesday: Dow drops 1,300, trading halted again, Ackman says shut
down country', CNBC, 18 March 2020 – https://cnb.cx/3iTytT7

13 Nick Timiraos, 'March 2020: How the Fed Averted Economic Disaster',
Wall Street Journal, 18 February 2022 – https://on.wsj.com/3BmXNHh

14 Ibid.

15 'Federal Reserve issues FOMC statement', Federal Reserve, 23 March
2020 – https://bit.ly/3uFkin9

16 William Watts, 'The stock market hit its COVID low 2 years ago today.
Here's how its performance since then stacks up', MarketWatch, 23 March
2022 – https://on.mktw.net/3W6AJ7U

17 Heather Stewart, '"Whatever it takes": chancellor announces £350bn aid
for UK businesses', Guardian, 17 March 2020 – https://bit.ly/4ochhZu

18 Timiraos, op. cit.

19 Mohamed remembers his older daughter's surprise when she, like a

hundred million others, received another cheque from the US Treasury even though she had worked and gotten paid throughout the pandemic.

20 'Credit and Liquidity Programs and the Balance Sheet', Federal Reserve, accessed 11 December 2022 – https://bit.ly/3Bt9jB3

21 'Annual consolidated balance sheet of the Eurosystem', European Central Bank, accessed 11 December 2022 – https://bit.ly/3BqOtlO

22 Mohamed A. El-Erian, *The Only Game in Town: Central Banks, Instability, and Avoiding the Next Collapse*, New York: Penguin Random House, 2016.

23 Andrew Ross Sorkin, 'Looking Back at Wall Street's Behavior in 2009', interview by Jeffrey Brown, PBS, 28 December 2009 – https://to.pbs.org/3lxcKlw

8. THE BAD AND THE UGLY OF ECONOMIC MANAGEMENT

1 Michael S. Barr, 'Review of the Federal Reserve's Supervision and Regulation of Silicon Valley Bank', Board of Governors of the Federal Reserve System, 28 April 2023 – https://bit.ly/3Ljpipx

2 Laura Noonan, 'European regulators criticise US "incompetence" over Silicon Valley Bank collapse', *Financial Times*, 15 March 2023 – https://on.ft.com/3yHq8GO

3 Sam Jones and Oliver Ralph, 'Swiss regulator defends $17bn wipeout of AT1 bonds in Credit Suisse deal', *Financial Times*, 23 March 2023 – https://on.ft.com/42Erv6H

4 Jim Tankersley, Jeanna Smialek and Emily Flitter, 'Fed Blocked Mention of Regulatory Flaws in Silicon Valley Bank Rescue', *New York Times*, 16 March 2023 – https://nyti.ms/3yLHn9W

5 Barr, op. cit.

6 Karl Russell and Christine Zhang, '3 Failed Banks This Year Were Bigger Than 25 That Crumbled in 2008', *New York Times*, 1 May 2023 – https://nyti.ms/3Lp2ULh

7 Edward Luce, 'The world is starting to hate the Fed', *Financial Times*, 12 October 2022 – https://on.ft.com/3VGh27Q

8 'The Fed That Failed', *The Economist*, 23 April 2022 – https://econ.st/3HL95Zg

9 'Annual Message to the Congress on the State of The Union, speaking copy, 11 January 1962', JFK Library, accessed 11 December 2022 – https://bit.ly/3VN98Jd

9. THREE STEPS TO IMPROVE ECONOMIC MANAGEMENT

1 Ulysses S. Grant, *The Personal Memoirs of Ulysses S. Grant*, New York: Cosimo Classics, 2006.
2 Ron Chernow, *Grant*, New York: Penguin Books, 2017.
3 Ibid.
4 Atul Gawande, *The Checklist Manifesto*, New York: Metropolitan Books, 2009.
5 Mohamed A. El-Erian, 'Navigating the New Normal in Industrial Countries', Per Jacobsson Foundation Lecture, International Monetary Fund, 10 October 2010 – https://bit.ly/3PqexFF
6 Christine Lagarde labeled it 'the new medicore' in 2015 when she was the Managing Director of the International Monetary Fund – https://bit.ly/3pevaJR
7 Mohamed A. El-Erian, 'Another Annus Horribilis for the Fed, Project Syndicate, 19 December 2022 – https://bit.ly/3Pu3NpH
8 Rufus E. Miles, 'The Origin and Meaning of Miles' Law', *Public Administration Review* 38:5 (1978), 399–403 – https://doi.org/10.2307/975497
9 Larry Elliott and Rowena Mason, 'Kwarteng accused of reckless mini-budget for the rich as pound plummets', *Guardian*, 23 September 2022 – https://bit.ly/3FOenCS
10 Cathy Newman, 'Economy was potentially hours away from meltdown, says Bank of England governor', Channel 4 News, 3 November 2022 – https://bit.ly/3WbHmpj
11 Harry Taylor and Andrew Sparrow, 'Liz Truss apologises for going "too far and too fast" with economic changes – as it happened', *Guardian*, 17 October 2022 – https://bit.ly/3VUyRPV

10. A BETTER WAY

1 'Trade and Logistics', Los Angeles County Economic Development Corporation, accessed 13 December 2022 – https://bit.ly/3UXxgHN
2 Fox Chu, Sven Gailus, Lisa Liu and Liumin Ni, 'The future of automated ports', McKinsey, 4 December 2018 – https://mck.co/3hmi5tZ
3 'High road training partnership: project overview', California Workforce Development Board, June 2019 – https://bit.ly/3FRtcEL
4 Jeremy Hunt, 'Speech at Bloomberg', 27 January 2023 – https://bit.ly/3JuRuFR
5 Benoit B. Mandelbrot and James R. Wallis, 'Noah, Joseph, and Operational

Hydrology', *Water Resources Research* 4:5 (1968), 909–18 – https://doi.org/10.1029/WR004i005p00909

6 '2020 Statement on Longer-Run Goals and Monetary Policy Strategy', Federal Reserve, 27 August 2020 – https://bit.ly/3VoBqi1

7 James Bullard, 'The Fed's New Monetary Policy Framework One Year Later', Federal Reserve Bank of St Louis, 12 August 2021 – https://bit.ly/3PqJO9k

8 'Guide to changes in the 2020 Statement on Longer-Run Goals and Monetary Policy Strategy', Federal Reserve, 27 August 2020 – https://bit.ly/3FvkqK

9 Mohamed A. El-Erian, 'Next year's unpleasant choices facing the Fed', *Financial Times*, 11 December 2021 – https://on.ft.com/44b6KiU

10 'Personal Saving Rate', St Louis Fed, accessed 14 December 2022 – https://bit.ly/3UTREcB

11 Richard H. Thaler and Cass R. Sunstein, *Nudge*, New York: Penguin Books, 2009.

12 Jan Strupczewski, 'EU to subsidise household fuel prices surging amid Ukraine crisis', Reuters, 15 March 2022 – https://reut.rs/3USogUg

13 Cass Sunstein and Lucia Reisch, eds, *The Economics of Nudge*, London: Routledge, Critical Concepts of Economics Vol. 4, 2017.

14 'Tokyo encourages residents to wear turtlenecks to save energy', *Japan Times*, 19 November 2022 – https://bit.ly/3FwWbvR

11. THE NEW ABNORMAL

1 Atthar Mirza et al., 'How the *Ever Given* was freed from the Suez Canal: A visual analysis', *Washington Post*, 2 April 2021 – https://wapo.st/3RiDvVk

2 Anna Cooban, 'Ikea furniture is still stuck on the *Ever Given* alongside $550,000 worth of wearable blankets, 2 months after the ship was freed from the Suez Canal', *Business Insider*, 16 June 2021 – https://bit.ly/3TLD1ci

3 Luke O'Reilly, 'UK experiences garden gnome shortage due to Suez Canal blockage and lockdown', *Evening Standard*, 16 April 2021 – https://bit.ly/3cOEzBt

4 Alex Christian, 'The untold story of the big boat that broke the world', *Wired*, 22 June 2021 – https://bit.ly/3U9IwAP

5 'United Nations Charter', United Nations – https://bit.ly/3NpL1g5

6 Scott Barrett, *Why Cooperate: The Incentive to Supply Global Public Goods*, New York: Oxford University Press, 2007.

7 J. Frieden, M. Pettis, D. Rodrik and E. Zedillo, 'After the Fall: The Future of Global Cooperation', *Geneva Reports on the World Economy* 14 (2012). Copy at https://tinyurl.com/ybmcm8yq

8 David Mitrany, 'The Functional Approach to World Organization', *International Affairs* 24:3 (1948), 350–63.

9 Ibid.

10 Robert O. Keohane and Joseph S. Nye, 'Globalization: What's New? What's Not? (And So What?)', *Foreign Policy* 118 (2000), 104–19 – https://doi.org/10.2307/1149673

11 Martin Wolf, *Why Globalization Works*, New Haven: Yale University Press, 2004, p.19.

12 Thomas Friedman, *The World is Flat*, New York: Farrar, Straus and Giroux, 2005.

13 William Shakespeare, *Richard II*, Folger Shakespeare Library, 2016, Lines 725–32.

14 Adam Tooze, *Crashed: How a Decade of Financial Crises Changed the World*, Penguin Books, New York, 2019, p.8.

15 Paul Hannon, 'U.N. Calls On Fed, Other Central Banks to Halt Interest-Rate Increases', *Wall Street Journal*, 3 October 2022 – https://on.wsj.com/3ygm28u

16 'Global trade hits record high of $28.5 trillion in 2021, but likely to be subdued in 2022', United Nations Conference on Trade and Development, 17 February 2022 – https://bit.ly/3VZNAth

17 'Executive Summary – World Trade Report 2019: The future of services trade', World Trade Organization, 2019 – https://bit.ly/311aNxh

18 Richard Baldwin, 'The peak globalisation myth: Part 4 – Services trade did not peak', Center for Economic Policy Research, 3 September 2022 – https://bit.ly/3TRWuHD

19 Elaine Dezenski and John C. Austin, 'Rebuilding America's economy and foreign policy with "ally-shoring"', Brookings, 8 June 2021 – https://brook.gs/3X5ZNwV

20 Alfred, Lord Tennyson, 'Ulysses' – https://bit.ly/3Ru5CAw

21 Henry Farrell and Abraham L. Newman, 'Weaponized Interdependence: How Global Economic Networks Shape State Coercion', *International Security* 44:1 (2019), 42–79 – https://doi.org/10.1162/isec_a_00351

22 'Meta Reports Third Quarter 2022 Results', Meta, 26 October 2022 – https://bit.ly/3ENgeWK

23 Ron Miller, 'As overall cloud infrastructure market growth dips to 24%, AWS reports slowdown', *TechCrunch*, 28 October 2022 – https://tcrn.ch/3ARgUJq

24 'SWIFT FIN Traffic & Figures', SWIFT, accessed 29 October 2022 – https://bit.ly/3UccLXv

25 Farrell and Newman, op. cit.

26 'China fails Micron's products in security review, bars some purchases', Reuters, 22 May 2023 – https://bit.ly/43ELvWr

27 Debby Wu, Ian King and Vlad Savov, 'US Deals Heavy Blow to China

Tech Ambitions With Nvidia Chip Ban', Bloomberg, 2 September 2022 – https://bloom.bg/3UTYVdA

28 Foo Yun Chee, 'EU agrees to curb takeovers by state-backed foreign firms', Reuters, 30 June 2022 – https://reut.rs/3XkoH9f

29 Taylor Rains, 'Airlines are flying up to 40% longer routes to avoid Russia, with one handing out "diplomas" to passengers flying over the North Pole', Insider, 23 March 2022 – https://bit.ly/3AXjUUF

30 'A short history of America's economy since World War II,' Wilson Center, 23 January 2014 – https://bit.ly/3AzUJaJ

31 Peter T. Kilborn, 'Japan Invests Huge Sums Abroad, Much Of It In U.S. Treasury Bonds', *New York Times*, 11 March 1985 – https://nyti.ms/3OeoZo7

32 Aparajit Chakraborty, 'India sees enhanced strategic cooperation with China, Russia, experts say', *China Daily*, 8 April 2022 – https://bit.ly/3TUzXcl

33 Subrahmanyam Jaishankar, *The India Way: Strategies for an Uncertain World*, New York: HarperCollins, 2020.

34 David Adler and Guillaume Long, 'Lula's foreign policy? Encouraging a multipolar world', *Guardian*, 1 January 2023 – https://bit.ly/3X8AWbF

35 Rodrigo Castillo and Caitlin Purdy, 'China's Role in Supplying Critical Minerals for the Global Energy Transition', Leveraging Transparency to Reduce Corruption, July 2022 – https://bit.ly/3NIhD77

36 Gordon Brown, 'Nationalism is the ideology of our age. No wonder the world is in crisis', *Guardian*, 15 November 2022 – https://bit.ly/3Nx8tbL

37 George Orwell, 'Notes on Nationalism', The Orwell Foundation, accessed 18 October 2022 – https://bit.ly/2PJaq52

38 Benny Kleinman, Ernest Liu and Stephen J. Redding, 'International Friends and Enemies' (July 2020), NBER Working Paper No. w27587. Available at SSRN – https://ssrn.com/abstract=3661079

39 Thomas Friedman, 'Foreign Affairs Big Mac I', *New York Times*, 8 December 1996 – https://nyti.ms/448LYkk

40 Elliot Smith, 'Russia faces "economic oblivion" despite claims of short-term resilience, economists say', CNBC, 2 August 2022 – https://cnb.cx/3sSmKWF

41 Chrystia Freeland, 'How democracies can shape a changed global economy', speech at the Brookings Institution, Washington, DC, 11 October 2022 – https://brook.gs/3gXs9cn

42 'The steam has gone out of globalisation', *The Economist*, 24 January 2019 – https://econ.st/2FQwomj

43 Jake Sullivan, 'Remarks by National Security Advisor Jake Sullivan on Renewing American Economic Leadership at the Brookings Institution', White House, 27 April 2023 – https://bit.ly/3HPgKG6

44 'Fact Sheet: CHIPS and Science Act Will Lower Costs, Create Jobs, Strengthen Supply Chains, and Counter China', White House, 9 August 2022 – https://bit.ly/3CAHVC8

45 Lauren Feiner, 'Micron to spend up to $100 billion to build a computer chip factory in New York', CNBC, 4 October 2022 – https://cnb.cx/3SYcMOh

46 Kristalina Georgieva, 'Confronting Fragmentation Where It Matters Most: Trade, Debt, and Climate Action', IMF, 16 January 2023 – https://bit.ly/3XyzTkY

47 'Remarks by Secretary of the Treasury Janet L. Yellen at LG Sciencepark', US Department of the Treasury, 19 July 2022 – https://bit.ly/3EhX78A

48 Jake Sullivan, 'Remarks by National Security Advisor Jake Sullivan on Renewing American Economic Leadership at the Brookings Institution', White House, 27 April 2023 – https://bit.ly/3HPgKG6

49 Georgieva, op. cit.

50 Ibid.

51 Maria Grazia Attinasi and Mirco Balatti, 'Globalisation and its implications for inflation in advanced economies', European Central Bank, April 2021 – https://bit.ly/44Dz3rj

52 Bryce Baschuk and Cagan Koc, 'WTO Chief Calls the Outlook for Global Trade "Not Promising"', Bloomberg, 6 September 2022 – https://bloom.bg/3y5mHtx

53 'Sharp Slowdown in Growth Could be Widespread, Increasing Risks to Global Economy | World Bank Expert Answers', World Bank, 10 January 2023 – https://bit.ly/3XxxuqP

54 Pierre-Olivier Gourinchas, 'Global Economic Recovery Endures but the Road Is Getting Rocky', IMF Blog, 11 April 2023 – https://bit.ly/3AOz3Hy

12. GLOBALISATION-LITE: 'GREAT TASTE, LESS FILLING'

1 Justin Hale, 'Boeing 787: from the ground up', *Aero Magazine – the Boeing Company*, 4th Quarter, 2006 – https://bit.ly/3RBlzVv

2 Chris Sloan, 'Ten years on, is the Boeing 787 Dreamliner still more dream than nightmare?', CNN Travel, 28 October 2021 – https://cnn.it/3e9c81R

3 'Opening New Routes', Boeing 787 Dreamliner commercial, Boeing, accessed 4 October 2022 – https://bit.ly/2IXusbF

4 Steve Denning, 'What Went Wrong at Boeing?', *Forbes*, 21 January 2013 – https://bit.ly/3Eh7Rnt

5 Bill Rigby and Tim Hepher, 'FACTBOX: Global supply chain for Boeing's 787', Reuters, 8 September 2008 – https://reut.rs/3yfejrt

6 James Allworth, 'The 787's Problems Run Deeper Than Outsourcing', *Harvard Business Review*, 30 January 2013 – https://bit.ly/3e3AHgK

7 'A Rocky Path for the 787 Dreamliner', *New York Times*, accessed 4 October 2022 – https://nyti.ms/3RGaNgC

8 Sloan, op. cit.

9 Doug Cameron, 'Boeing CEO Wants Incremental Innovation, Not "Moon Shots"', *Wall Street Journal*, 21 May 2014 – https://on.wsj.com/3e9AOaA

10 'The steam has gone out of globalisation', *The Economist*, 24 January 2019 – https://econ.st/2FQwomj

11 *Syriana*, Stephen Gaghan, Warner Brothers Pictures, 2005.

12 'The structure of the world's supply chains is changing', *The Economist*, 16 June 2022 – https://econ.st/3SZSeoN

13 Ann Koh and Anuradha Raghu, 'The World's 2-Billion-Ton Trash Problem Just Got More Alarming', Bloomberg, 11 July 2019 – https://bloom.bg/2JwWnOI

14 José María Figueres, 'Here's how we can reduce shipping industry emissions', World Economic Forum, 23 October 2020 – https://bit.ly/3RKeL7Q

15 James Traub, 'The U.N. (as We Know It) Won't Survive Russia's War in Ukraine', Foreign Policy, 4 November 2022 – https://bit.ly/3EejM49

16 John Micklethwait and Adrian Wooldridge, 'Putin and Xi Exposed the Great Illusion of Capitalism', Bloomberg, 23 March 2022 – https://bloom.bg/3X6B4sA

17 Ibid.

18 Thomas L. Friedman, 'How China Lost America', *New York Times*, 1 November 2022 – https://nyti.ms/3GkBjtZ

19 Adam S. Posen, 'The End of Globalization?', *Foreign Affairs*, 17 March 2022 – https://fam.ag/3AiP3l8

20 G. John Ikenberry and Anne-Marie Slaughter, 'A bigger Security Council, with power to act', *New York Times*, 26 September 2006 – https://nyti.ms/3Am5lKa

21 Traub, op. cit.

22 Ibid.

23 Ted Piccone, 'The awkward guests: Parsing the Summit for Democracy invitation list', Brookings, 7 December 2021 – https://brook.gs/3XU7sPw

24 Richard N. Haass and Charles A. Kupchan, 'The New Concert of Powers', *Foreign Affairs*, 23 March 2021 – https://fam.ag/3GkXb8G

25 Ibid.

26 Zbigniew Brzezinski, 'The Group of Two that could change the world', *Financial Times*, 13 January 2009 – https://on.ft.com/3zzpKuQ

27 Henry M. Paulson, 'Remarks by Henry M. Paulson, Jr., on the Delusions

of Decoupling', Paulson Institute, 21 November 2019 – https://bit.ly/3g6eIHo

28 Gordon Brown, *Seven Ways to Change the World*, London: Simon and Schuster, 2021.

29 Brigit Katz, 'Pando, One of the World's Largest Organisms, Is Dying', *Smithsonian Magazine*, October 2018 – https://bit.ly/3BQLNgK

30 Dani Rodrik and Stephen Walt, 'How to Construct a New Global Order', Harvard Kennedy School, 24 May 2021 – https://bit.ly/3VjzEcp

31 Ibid.

13. REBIRTH OF INTERNATIONAL INSTITUTIONS

1 Graham Allison, *Destined for War: Can America and China Escape Thucydides's Trap?*, Boston: Mariner Books, 2017, xvi.

2 Allison, viii.

3 Sabine Siebold and Philip Blenkinsop, 'EU should treat China more as a competitor, says diplomat chief', Reuters, 17 October 2022 – https://reut.rs/3UvSHj8

4 António Guterres, 'Address to the Opening of the General Debate of the 75th Session of the General Assembly', United Nations, 22 September 2020 – https://bit.ly/3CtaAI2

5 Henry Kissinger, 'Lessons From History Series: A Conversation With Henry Kissinger', Council on Foreign Relations interview by Richard Haass, 30 September 2022 – https://on.cfr.org/3G2I7fK

6 Gordon Brown and Daniel Susskind, 'International cooperation during the COVID-19 pandemic', *Oxford Review of Economic Policy* 36:S1 (2020), S64–S76.

7 'Report shows increase in trade restrictions amidst economic uncertainty, multiple crises', World Trade Organization, 6 December 2022 – https://bit.ly/3llCSzV

8 Kristalina Georgieva, 'Confronting Fragmentation Where It Matters Most: Trade, Debt, and Climate Action', IMF, 16 January 2023 – https://bit.ly/3XyzTkY

9 Alessandro Nicita and Carlos Razo, 'China: The rise of a trade titan', United Nations Conference on Trade and Development, 27 April 2021 – https://bit.ly/3SUEwnC

10 'USTR Releases Annual Report on China's WTO Compliance', Office of the United States Trade Representative, 16 February 2022 – https://bit.ly/3CsoQAW

11 Jeffrey J. Schott and Euijin Jung, 'In US-China Trade Disputes, the WTO Usually Sides with the United States', Peterson Institute for International Economics, 12 March 2019 – https://bit.ly/3VnzfpZ

12 'Statement from USTR Spokesperson Adam Hodge', Office of the United States Trade Representative, 9 December 2022 – https://bit.ly/3JvmEO7

13 Ngaire Woods, 'The End of Multilateralism?' In: *Europe's Transformations: Essays in honour of Loukas Tsoukalis*, edited by Helen Wallace, George Pagoulatos and Nikos Koutsiaras, Oxford: Oxford University Press, 2021.

14 Tobias Sytsma, 'RCEP Forms the World's Largest Trading Bloc. What Does This Mean for Global Trade?', Rand Corporation, 9 December 2020 – https://bit.ly/3ONUjmW

15 Xi Jinping, 'Let the Torch of Multilateralism Light up Humanity's Way Forward', Ministry of Foreign Affairs for the People's Republic of China. Speech delivered at the World Economic Forum Virtual Event of the Davos Agenda, 25 January 2021 – https://bit.ly/3MoSBXQ

16 Ngozi Okonjo-Iweala, 'National Foreign Trade Council: Strengthening the WTO and the global trading system', speech at the World Trade Organization, 27 April 2022 – https://bit.ly/3OfKhMM

17 Simon Lester, 'Ending the WTO Dispute Settlement Crisis: Where to from here?', International Institute for Sustainable Development, 2 March 2022 – https://bit.ly/3XeB8X8

18 Marianne Schneider-Petsinger, 'Reforming the World Trade Organization: Prospects for transatlantic cooperation and the global trade system', US and the Americas Programme, Chatham House, September 2020 – https://bit.ly/3Ti3zAy

19 Dani Rodrik, 'The WTO has become dysfunctional', *Financial Times*, 5 August 2018 – https://on.ft.com/2OKntnq

20 'About the G20', G20, accessed 14 July 2023 – https://bit.ly/3qXbKtk

21 'Dag Hammarskjöld Remembered: A Collection of Personal Memories', Dag Hammarskjöld Foundation, accessed 22 November 2022 – https://bit.ly/3GzWybn

22 Kevin Rudd, 'UN 2030: Rebuilding Order in a Fragmenting World', Independent Commission on Multilateralism, August 2016 – https://bit.ly/3EUDpiZ

23 G. John Ikenberry and Anne-Marie Slaughter, 'A bigger Security Council, with power to act', *New York Times*, 26 September 2006 – https://nyti.ms/3Am5lKa

24 'Funding the United Nations: How Much Does the U.S. Pay?', Council on Foreign Relations, 4 April 2022 – https://on.cfr.org/3Xozu5f

25 Rudd, op. cit.

26 Danny Lewis, 'Reagan and Gorbachev Agreed to Pause the Cold War in Case of an Alien Invasion', *Smithsonian Magazine*, 25 November 2015 – https://bit.ly/3Wk3UVY

27 Joseph S. Nye, *Peace in Parts*, Lanham: University Press of America, 1987.

14. FINANCING OUR FUTURE

1 James A. Michener, *Hawaii*, New York: Random House Publishing Group, 2013, p.415.
2 Janet Yellen, 'Joint IMFC and Development Committee Statement by Secretary of the Treasury Janet L. Yellen', U.S. Department of the Treasury, 13 October 2022 – https://bit.ly/3yTokuN
3 Marta Schoch et al., 'Half of the global population lives on less than US$6.85 per person per day', World Bank Blogs, 8 December 2022 – https://bit.ly/3HjWCdZ
4 Vitor Gaspar, Paulo Medas and Roberto Perrelli, 'Global Debt Reaches a Record $226 Trillion', IMF Blog, 15 December 2021 – https://bit.ly/3kVaJis
5 David Lawder, 'World Bank's new chief wants "better bank" before pushing for bigger bank', Reuters, 15 June 2023 – https://reut.rs/44251wS
6 'CEOs Explore Solutions to Bridge Annual USD 4.3 Trillion SDG Financing Gap', International Institute for Sustainable Development, 19 October 2022 – https://bit.ly/3OrwNMm
7 Lawrence H. Summers, 'A New Chance for the World Bank', Project Syndicate, 10 October 2022 – https://bit.ly/3rLNZS6
8 Ajay Banga, 'What the World Bank needs to do now', *Financial Times*, 16 March 2023 – https://on.ft.com/3ZZheAx
9 'From Billions to Trillions: Transforming Development Finance: Post-2015 Financing for Development: Multilateral Development Finance', 2 April 2015 – https://bit.ly/3pbSdVG
10 Charles Kenny, 'If We Want the World Bank to Solve Global Challenges, It Has to Be Bigger – but Also More Cuddly', Center for Global Development, 26 August 2022 – https://bit.ly/3pbSdVG
11 Roberta Gatti and Aakash Mohpal, 'Investing in Human Capital: What Can We Learn from the World Bank's Portfolio Data?' Policy Research Working Paper, No. 8716, World Bank, 2019 – https://bit.ly/3rAFPyY
12 'Q&A: Innovative Finance Facility for Climate in Asia and the Pacific (IF-CAP)', Asian Development Bank, 2 May 2023 – https://bit.ly/3pZZacE
13 'World Bank Announces New Steps to Add Billions in Financial Capacity', World Bank, 17 July 2023 – https://bit.ly/3DvRgL3
14 'Take Action for the Sustainable Development Goals', United Nations, accessed 27 October 2022 – https://bit.ly/3SKDXfd
15 Paul Tucker, *Global Discord: Values and Power in a Fractured World Order*, Princeton: Princeton University Press, 2022.
16 'Global Monitoring Report on Non-Bank Financial Intermediation', Financial Stability Board Report, 16 December 2021 – https://bit.ly/3UPSUhH

17 Mark Plant, Ronan Palmer and Dileimy Orozco, 'The IMF's Surveillance Role and Climate Change', Center for Global Development, 11 January 2022 – https://bit.ly/3CLoENt

18 Mantek Singh Ahluwalia et al., 'Multilateral Development Banking for This Century's Development Challenges', Center for Global Development, 2016 – https://bit.ly/3MMSR3l

19 'World Has 28% Risk of New Covid-Like Pandemic Within 10 Years', Bloomberg, 13 April 2023 – https://bloom.bg/3NmsH7Z

20 James Kynge and Jonathan Wheatley, 'China emerges as IMF competitor with emergency loans to at-risk nations', *Financial Times*, 10 September 2022 – https://on.ft.com/3Jt6p3n

21 Kristalina Georgieva, 'Confronting Fragmentation Where It Matters Most: Trade, Debt, and Climate Action', IMF, 16 January 2023 – https://bit.ly/3XyzTkY

22 Martin Chorzempa and Adnan Mazarei, 'Improving China's Participation in Resolving Developing-Country Debt Problems', Peterson Institute for International Economics, May 2021 – https://bit.ly/3LW392d

15. ACHIEVING OUR GLOBAL GOALS

1 Paul Ehrlich, *The Population Bomb*, New York: Ballantine Books, 1968.

2 N.E. Borlaug, 'The Human Population Monster', *European Demographic Information Bulletin* 9 (1978), 108–11 – https://doi.org/10.1007/BF02917806

3 J.Y. Smith, 'William Gaud, Advocate of "Green Revolution" at AID, Dies', *Washington Post*, 8 December 1977 – https://wapo.st/3hhwhUE

4 William S. Gaud, 'The Green Revolution: Accomplishments and Apprehensions', Remarks before the Society for International Development, Washington, DC, 8 March 1968, AgBioWorld – https://bit.ly/3FPqMqp

5 Norman Borlaug, 'The Green Revolution, Peace, and Humanity', Nobel Lecture delivered 11 December 1970 – https://bit.ly/3E5wPpp

6 'Facilitating the flow of remittances', United Nations, accessed 22 November 2022 – https://bit.ly/3rufNxy

7 'Closing the SDG Financing Gap in the COVID-19 era', OECD and UNDP, 24 February 2021 – https://bit.ly/3i5uFO6

8 'World Energy Investment 2022: Overview and key findings', International Energy Agency, 2023 – https://bit.ly/3Obav2M

9 Kenza Bryan, 'COP27: Mark Carney clings to his dream of a greener finance industry', *Financial Times*, 8 November 2022 – https://bit.ly/474mZkr

10 'Tracking development assistance for health and for COVID-19: a review

of development assistance, government, out-of-pocket, and other private spending on health for 204 countries and territories, 1990–2050', *The Lancet* 398:10308 (2021), 1317–43 – https://doi.org/10.1016/S0140-6736(21)01258-7

11 Ibid.

12 Ibid.

13 Bill Gates, *How to Prevent the Next Pandemic*, New York: Knopf, 2022.

14 Alex Wooley, 'Belt and Road bailout lending reaches record levels, raising questions about the future of China's flagship global infrastructure program', AidData, 27 March 2023 – https://bit.ly/3PWB8cY

15 Aloysius Uche Ordu, ed., 'Foresight Africa: Top Priorities for the Continent in 2023', Brookings: Africa Growth Initiative, 2022 – https://bit.ly/3XrYeKt

16 Ibid.

17 'Free Trade Pact Could Help Lift Up to 50 Million Africans from Extreme Poverty', World Bank, 30 June 2022 – https://bit.ly/4oqIpEY

CONCLUSION

1 Dotan Leshem, 'Retrospectives: What Did the Ancient Greeks Mean by *Oikonomia?' Journal of Economic Perspectives* 30:1 (2016), 225–38.

INDEX

Page references in *italics* indicate images.

Index

323

Index